L

Women and Domestic Experience in Victorian Political Fiction

Women and Domestic Experience in Victorian Political Fiction

Susan Johnston

Contributions in Women's Studies, Number 186

GREENWOOD PRESS
Westport, Connecticut • London

Library of Congress Cataloging-in-Publication Data

Johnston, Susan.
   Women and domestic experience in Victorian political fiction / by Susan Johnston.
     p.   cm.—(Contributions in women's studies, ISSN 0147–104X ; no. 186)
   Includes bibliographical references and index.
   ISBN 0–313–31634–1 (alk. paper)
     1. English fiction—19th century—History and criticism. 2. Domestic fiction,
English—History and criticism. 3. Political fiction, English—History and criticism. 4.
English fiction—Women authors—History and criticism. 5. Politics and literature—Great
Britain—History—19th century. 6. Women and literature—Great Britain—History—19th
century. 7. Women in literature. 8. Home in literature. I. Title. II. Series.
PR868.D65 J64   2001
823′.809358–dc21   00–034114

British Library Cataloguing in Publication Data is available.

Library of Congress Catalog Card Number: 00–034114
ISBN: 0–313–31634–1
ISSN: 0147–104X

First published in 2001

Greenwood Press, 88 Post Road West, Westport, CT 06881
An imprint of Greenwood Publishing Group, Inc.
www.greenwood.com

Printed in the United States of America

The paper used in this book complies with the
Permanent Paper Standard issued by the National
Information Standards Organization (Z39.48–1984).

10 9 8 7 6 5 4 3 2 1

Copyright Acknowledgment

The author and publisher gratefully acknowledge permission from Basic Books, a member of
Perseus Books, L.L.C., to reprint excerpts from *Emile; or, On Education*, by Jean-Jacques
Rousseau by Allan Bloom, translator, (c) 1979 by Basic Books, Inc.

Contents

For my parents,

Wayne and Kathy Johnston,

from whom I first learned that education is nothing

if it is not the call to and practice of freedom.

Preface

Some debts can never be paid, although I will try here to meet the interest. The questions that inform this study were first formulated in the early 1990s, at McGill University; I am indebted to the McGill Alma Mater Society, the Social Sciences and Humanities Research Council of Canada, and the Principal's Dissertation Fellowship for affording me the time to begin investigating those questions. The work was completed during my tenure as Visiting Assistant Professor at Concordia University in 1999–2000; a thousand thanks to Dean of Arts Martin Singer and to David Sheps and Terry Byrnes of the Department of English at Concordia University, who so welcomed me. It is also a pleasure to thank the librarians and staff of McLennan Library at McGill, and the Folger Shakespeare Library, who were generous with time and suggestions.

Greater even than these debts, however, are those to the friends and colleagues who showed me what an academic community can and should be: Brian Trehearne, Mette Hjort, Leanore Lieblein, Maggie Kilgour (who taught me teaching), and Kerry McSweeney; William James Booth discussed this project with me at a critical time, and it would not be what it is without both his generosity and his seminal work; my colleagues Bill Howard, Martin Bergbusch, Nick Ruddick, Cameron Louis, Margaret Wigmore, Dean Knuttila, and Jeanne Shami, especially, at the University of Regina, for manning the barricades in an academy under seige: if this project is the past, I nonetheless look forward to building a freer, juster future with all of you; Nicola Nixon, Frederick C. DeCoste, Sally Mitchell, Marc Cooper, Stephen Ahern, Jessica Slights, Adam Muller, Catherine Graham, and Carla Norman all asked smart questions and I have tried to answer some of them here; my research assistants, Cornelia Ratt, Jennifer Woodard and Chiraz Agrebi — what is clean, clear, true, or just in this I owe to all of you. Christine van Moorsel and, again, Nicola Nixon, made it happen, as did Dr. George F. Butler and Bobbie Goettler of Greenwood Publishing Group.

The hardest to thank is Michael D. Bristol: Where do I begin? If I am a scholar today it is because of him; if I am a teacher it is because I learned from him that there is no more significant line of work; if I profess anything it is the passion for inquiry and justice he lives every day. He began it all, and saw me through to the end. He is now and will always be the teacher I hope to become. I cannot pay him back; I hope to pay him forward.

Finally — without whom, nothing — Damon Marcel DeCoste. Our Katy lies sleeping in the next room; the twins lie, sleepless, beneath my heart. You have given me my life, over and over again, not only by sharing it with me, but by sharing the work that defines us both. May we always share a long life, wine, and friends.

Susan Johnston,
Montreal

Abbreviations

"Conceptions"	Gilligan, "In a Different Voice: Women's Conceptions of Self and of Morality"
Contract	Rousseau, *On the Social Contract*
Correspondence	Locke, *The Correspondence of John Locke*
Critique	Kant, *The Critique of Judgement*
Discourses	Rousseau, *The First and Second Discourses*
Education	Wollstonecraft, *Thoughts on the Education of Daughters*
Emile	Rousseau, *Emile, or On Education*
Essay	Locke, *An Essay Concerning Human Understanding*
Ethics	Aristotle, *Nicomachean Ethics*
Great	Dickens, *Great Expectations*
Hard	Dickens, *Hard Times*
"Impartiality"	Iris Marion Young, "Impartiality and the Civic Public"
Liberty	Mill, *On Liberty*
Mary	Wollstonecraft, *Mary, A Fiction*
"Materialism"	Sartre, "Materialism and Revolution"
Men	Wollstonecraft, *A Vindication of the Rights of Men*
North	Gaskell, *North and South*
Observations	Kant, *Observations on the Feeling of the Beautiful and the Sublime*
Papers	Taylor, *Philosophical Papers*
Politics	Aristotle, *The Politics*
Sources	Taylor, *Sources of the Self: The Making of the Modern Identity*
Subjection	Mill, *The Subjection of Women*
Thoughts	Locke, *Some Thoughts Concerning Education*
Truth	Sartre, *Truth and Existence*
Two Treatises	Locke, *Two Treatises on Government*

Util.	Mill, *Utilitarianism*
Vindication	Wollstonecraft, *A Vindication of the Rights of Woman*
Voice	Gilligan, *In A Different Voice: Psychological Theory and Women's Development*
Wives	Gaskell, *Wives and Daughters*
Wrongs	Wollstonecraft, *The Wrongs of Woman, or Maria; A Fragment*

Introduction:
Political Fictions, Domestic Plots

The "engaged" writer knows that words are action. He knows that to reveal is to change and that one can reveal only by planning to change.
— Jean-Paul Sartre, *What Is Literature*?

If Sartre is right in contending that words are actions, and I believe that he is, the question with which I once began this investigation was, what kind of words are *political* actions? But, in addressing myself to the possibility of fiction as a species of political action, I opened the Pandora's box of articulating and defining what it is I meant by politics, and thus encountered the problem of distinguishing between the public and political realm, and that of the private or domestic. And indeed it is this distinction that finally concerns me here. What is the relationship between the private and the public, the affective realm of intimacy and emotion, and the effective domain of politics, economics, and reason?

The transformation of society brought about by the industrial revolution has long been held·to have brought about a notion of society as split into "private" and "public" spheres. While this division was historically situated and constructed, a product of the emerging capitalist bourgeoisie, as Terry Lovell points out, it masked its own origins through an essentializing and universalizing discourse (36). This discourse was also gendered, it has been argued, locating women's place solely in the household, at the centre of the family, from which point they provided a kind of moral protection over public man in his competitive sphere, freeing him from the contaminating influences of the amoral marketplace. For Ruskin, then, "the true nature of home" is as "the place of Peace; the shelter, not only from all injury, but from all terror, doubt, and division. . . . so far as the anxieties of the outer life penetrate into it, and the inconsistently-minded, unknown, unloved, or hostile society of the outer world is allowed by either husband or wife to cross the threshold, it ceases to be home" (59). Moreover, this "sacred place," this "vestal temple, a temple of the hearth watched over by Household Gods" comes into being wherever — and only wherever — "a true wife comes" (60). Basch suggests that women's moral influence in this ideology was perceived both qualitatively and quantitatively in direct proportion to their passivity and subjection to masculine authority (6), and this seems to be confirmed both by Ruskin's insistence that women must be wise, "not for self-development, but for self-renunciation" (Ruskin 60), and by Coventry Patmore's angel, whose will is "indomitably bent / On mere submissiveness to him" (II.1.31–32). Man's sphere is action, woman's emotion, so that, as the poem's prologue reveals, art is his province, inspiration hers: "[I]n his heart, his thoughts were rife / How for her sake to earn a name" (I.1.11–12). Crucially, the masculine "public" sphere of action was also the exclusive domain of politics, which thereby were articulated as an exclusively male concern: "man's duty, as a member of a commonwealth, is to assist in the maintenance, in the advance, in the defence of the state. The woman's duty, as a member of the commonwealth, is to assist in the ordering, in the comforting, and in the beautiful adornment of the state" (Ruskin 72).[1]

Not surprisingly, perhaps, given the carceral dimension of separate spheres ideology, feminist accounts of the nineteenth century began in the 1970s and early 1980s to argue for its falsity, typically on two significant grounds. First, as Fox-Genovese shows, this ideology sought to naturalize women's economic dependence and confinement to the household ("Placing Women's History" 23–24) even as it masked its own class origins with the bourgeoisie. Second, and no less important, this ideology was subjected to critique because in creating a false distinction between work and the family, it distorted our understanding of women's labour and of their place in both society and politics (Greene and Kahn 16). Such analyses, while taking as axiomatic the interdependence of public and private domains, curiously assumed this interdependence to be a discovery of their own. I argue, by contrast, that such thinkers as Ruskin, Patmore, and Ellis were writing prescriptively, not descriptively; the interdependence of spheres that modern critics have uncovered, I contend, informed both nineteenth-century literature and political philosophy.

More recent revisions of the idea of separate spheres have sought to articulate this prescriptive dimension of separate spheres ideology, provoking a renewed interest in the domestic and political fiction of the Victorian period, as well as in the political dimensions of domestic life. Mary Poovey's *Uneven Developments*, for example, has gone a long way toward complicating the private/public opposition, seeing the middle-class ideology of the period as constantly in the process of making and remaking itself and therefore "open to revision, dispute, and the emergence of oppositional formulations" (3). Yet despite this recognition, Poovey reads sexual difference in terms of binary oppositions (6), both socially and institutionally realized in the separation of spheres (8). While she ably reveals these binaries as undermining themselves, even as they sought to consolidate middle-class power through the naturalization of separate spheres doctrine, she takes the persistence of the earlier image of women as "aggressive, carnal magdalen[s]" (11) as the primary site of opposition to the vocabulary of the domestic ideal (9–12). Nancy Armstrong, similarly, takes the privatization of virtue and the consolidation of middle-class power in the domestic ideal as underwritten by a rhetorical opposition of gendered spheres (21–24). Using both political philosophy and educational treatises to show the formation of identity in and through fiction, she concludes in *Desire and Domestic Fiction* that Victorian domestic fictions, unlike their eighteenth-century and Romantic counterparts, contain and control political dissidence by transforming political issues into domestic and psychological ones (252–53). Unlike Poovey and unlike Nina Auerbach's earlier work on *Woman and the Demon*, Armstrong sees the monstrous, carnalized woman as part of this containment of politics within the embrace of the domestic sphere (165); the monstrous feminine, then, becomes for Armstrong a means of resituating political resistance as "individual pathology" (252) and thus vitiating its subversive potential.[2] But neither Poovey's *Uneven Developments* nor Nancy Armstrong's widely cited *Desire and Domestic Fiction* consider the possibility that is central to my investigation here, that the very notion of separate spheres may be essentially contested even while it is being constructed. This is not so of Leonore Davidoff's *Worlds Between*, which concludes with a careful investigation of private and public, and their interrelationships, but which nevertheless takes sexuality both as increasingly privatized through the nineteenth century, and as increasingly central to "the hermeneutics of the self."[3] As a result even Davidoff's treatment suggests that the conceptual divorce of public and private is a necessary consequence of liberal notions of the self, including the female self.[4] Barbara Leah Harman, in 1998's *The Feminine Political Novel in England*, provides a superb analysis of women's participation in that "public universe" conventionally inhabited by men (9), but her treatment of female public appearance as a transgression of both class boundaries and sexual boundaries leads her to foreground sexual intimacy as a defining characteristic of the private realm (51). While this emphasis allows Harman to express important links between public and private, it obscures other aspects of domestic ideology, and other relations besides the sexual that inform the intimate domain.

Elizabeth Langland's *Nobody's Angels* valuably contests the dominant critical view of that "Victorian social myth" of the Angel in the House (8) to articulate an important link between the domestic and the public spheres. Yet for her this link is money management; she analyzes the economic and political functions of the Victorian wife to show that while "[p]revailing ideology held the house as haven, a private sphere opposed to the public, commercial sphere . . . [i]n fact, the house and its mistress served as a significant adjunct to a man's commercial endeavors" (8). Expanding her focus beyond the Victorian angel-wife to the Victorian Other, the domestic servant (11), Langland notes the importance of money and labour management to the genteel middle-class home and reads the "moral vocabulary" of domestic ideology as a naturalization, not simply of historically situated gender roles, but of class hierarchies (15). While Langland's recognition of the key role played by the discourse of domesticity in nineteenth-century social change is a welcome corrective to accounts that stress the withdrawal of women and the home from the public realm, she does not pursue the consequences of this linking of the spheres for our ideas of legal personhood, and it is these consequences in part which concern me here.   In this I am deeply indebted to the work of William James Booth, whose *Households: On the Moral Architecture of the Economy* investigates ancient and liberal households as communities of persons and examines at some length the norms and ends of such communities, "the purposes that bind individuals in their association and that define the moral location of their community in a wider array of goods" (1). It is through Booth's treatment of the shifting moral location of the economy, and its links to virtue and freedom, that I was able to rethink the concept of the liberal household and its relationship to "political praxis and excellence" (47), that is, to the concept of the citizen. Yet he, too, takes the liberal household as separate from the market space to which it is opposed[5]; I argue, quite differently, that the liberal household continues to exist as the site of ends rather than nonmarket means, and that as such the intimate space of that household is both end and origin of the liberal polity.

My project here is to challenge these arguments about the division of the political from other fictional genres and the private from the public sphere, reformulating the place of the household in the liberal polity. I want to uncover, in political and domestic fiction from Wollstonecraft to Dickens, a common concern with the preconditions of liberal selfhood with a view to showing that liberalism identifies the *household* as the primary space in which the political rights-bearer, defined by emotional interiority and mental qualities, comes into being. While political philosophers such as Booth and Jürgen Habermas have argued that this rights-bearer is defined by purely formal, abstract, procedural reason, such arguments depend on the exclusion of educational writings by thinkers whose idea of reason, misunderstood, Booth and Habermas call into question.[6] But I will be reading the educational writings of Locke and others as revealing an idea of reason that includes the capacity for emotion. Through works by Mary Wollstonecraft, Amelia Opie, Maria Edgeworth, Elizabeth Gaskell, and Charles Dickens, I will show that this fuller idea of reason is part of a concept of the liberal self in which the emotional relations of the household play a constitutive role. I will argue that because the intimate space of the household is constitutive in this sense, it does not exist separately from or in opposition to the public, political, and economic domains, but rather is the foundation on which liberalism conceives them. Here I hope to revise generic understandings of political fiction, which I take to include domestic plots as integral to the political plots. Far from containing or confining politics in the intimate sphere, I suggest that domestic plots point to the link between political and domestic fiction, that is, to their shared focus on the nature and implications of the liberal idea of the self. Even as political fiction often argues for the *extension* of citizenship in the liberal sense, domestic fiction takes as its focus the cultivation of the liberal self in the household and, as its project, the disclosure of that self in terms of its vision of the good. I conclude by contending for a new model of domestic space as the foundation of, rather than the occluded counterpart to, the liberal polity, arguing that an account of the household in which the liberal self is disclosed is at the centre of Victorian political fiction, as it is at the centre of its political philosophy.

And yet this last claim returns me to the question with which I began. If words

— if fiction — can be action, what kind of words are political action? Nancy Armstrong, after all, seems to suggest that, in retreating from political dissidence, Victorian domestic fiction retreats from the political itself.[7] And yet, perhaps unfortunately, we err when we assume that some sets of opinions on a subject are political, while other opposing opinions on the same subject are nonpolitical; surely the Progressive Conservative Party is as political as the Liberal Party or the Reform Party; Clinton's Democrats were as political as his Republican opponents. We must, I think, reject any notion of political fiction as fiction that simply opposes — resists, subverts, interrogates — the status quo, and to this end I treat both the emancipatory work of thinkers like Wollstonecraft, and the apparently confining, quietistic, even reactionary work of her near-contemporary Amelia Opie. Moreover, in situating the domestic sphere as the locus of this retreat from subversion, Armstrong confirms and extends the divorce between the household and the polity even as she narrows the domain of politics to opposition alone. Her view of the political, then, refuses the possibility both of reconciliation and negotiation proffered by a nonoppositional model of politics, and of a meaningful role for the feminized domestic sphere in politics of any kind. And both these difficulties derive, I suggest, from a conception of middle-class ideologies as both totalizing and seamless.

However, as Lovell remarks, the ideas of the dominant class may themselves be more diverse and more deeply contradictory than has previously been assumed. As an instance of such diversity, Lovell points out that nineteenth-century bourgeois culture involved the growth of both production and consumption; *Consuming Fiction* convincingly shows that this interdependency involved the coexistence of aesthetic education and the expansion of wants associated with consumer culture with that repression, utilitarian calculation, and deferral of gratification associated with producer culture (19–43). Lovell's argument suggests that a notion of political fiction that, like Armstrong's, encompasses only the subversive may finally be inadequate, when even the oppressors are a heterogeneous group whose needs, desires, and wants are often flatly contradictory. In this sense the private may indeed be political, even when it refuses outright dissent; in this sense the household, as a site of those contradictory needs, wants, and desires, may signal a shift in cultural conceptions of what it means to live the good or the just life. These concerns are indeed the domain of politics, broadly construed; moreover, in these concerns we see the conjoining of private and public, since the question of the good life is bound up both with what it means to be a citizen, in political space, and what it means to be an individual, in private life. In what follows I take these two projects of definition to be fundamentally interrelated.

It should be clear from the foregoing that I take the political to be the domain of those social arrangements through which groups of selves — the polity — draw their rights and privileges. While these social arrangements, and the rights and privileges they bring into being, are centrally bound up with our notions of the good, the just, the noble life, and indeed it is the province of the political to protect and extend these notions of the good life through such arrangements, it is the question of rights that concerns me here. The political is the domain of sanction, of the codification of conventions and rules as laws, and the domain of the distribution of resources, which is — crucially — a question of access to power. Under such a definition the question of the origin of these selves, these members of the polity, and the question of where their rights are drawn from, becomes crucial to a full understanding of the political domain. And it is in this question, in how we conceive the self both politically and privately, that this book intervenes.

I am taking the self not as prior to culture but as constituted in and by culture; culture in this sense provides the "horizon" within which the Victorian middle class — that is, *pace* Watt, the novel-reading and writing class — perceived the self-as-citizen. This notion of horizons of identity comes from Hans-Georg Gadamer, who argues in *Truth and Method* that our present horizon cannot be formed without the past (273). Charles Taylor adopts the idea of "horizons" to contend that, even as we come to selfhood inside a horizon that constitutes our identity, that horizon is itself continually being formed (*Papers* 1: 22–44). Crucially, however, both Gadamer and Taylor, like Habermas and Seyla Benhabib, refuse to take culture as inescapably *equivalent* to identity; all four argue for a concept of autonomy in which the constitutive culture can be subjected to the scrutiny of reason (Benhabib 203–41 esp. 229; Gadamer 31–34; Habermas 84–90; Taylor *Papers* 1: 22–28). This view I take to be fundamentally liberal; as I will show, liberalism's concept of the self claims for that self critical reflection and evaluation — that is, the ability to reflect on what is culturally given — as well as the constitution of that self *by* and *in* culture. What is more, liberalism asserts the rights of the citizen precisely on the grounds of such evaluation, reflection, and reason. And because, as I will show, these capacities are posited by liberalism as potential that must be realized in the community, it is to the first of these communities, the household, that such political philosophy looks for the ground of rights.

The self-as-citizen, construed by liberalism, both constitutes and is constituted by the cultural discourses that comprise the horizon of identity. As should by now be clear, I am arguing for the constitutive discourses of the household, the fictions and philosophies of the domestic sphere, as the significant foundation of political identity; I will thus be examining the ways in which political and domestic discourses become intertwined in fiction and philosophy in order to map the terrain of the Victorian liberal self. My method here owes something to Catherine Gallagher's excellent study of the industrial novel, which investigates social discourse, a term that embraces both what is said on a subject and the "largely unstated rules that govern what can and cannot be said" (xiii). Discourse, then, is "transideological," existing between and within ideologies and thereby creating "the coherence and legibility of ideological conflict" (xiii), and her project in *The Industrial Reformation of English Fiction* is to read these conflicts within literary forms. Industrial fiction, on Gallagher's account, is that which formalizes and reveals — which is not to resolve — the conflicts between social and political theory raised in the public debates over industrialism; her analyses uncover these conflicts in the novels at both textual and subtextual levels. Significantly, Gallagher rejects the idea that such conflicts or ideological ruptures are automatically subversive, or that discourse itself may serve a single and identifiable class interest (xiii–xiv). Rosemarie Bodenheimer builds on Gallagher's work to describe social problem fiction as defining (and thereby delimiting) imagined possibilities for social thought, action, and change: Such fiction evokes both social wishes and social fears, and then negotiates between them (3). For Bodenheimer, such novels confront and negotiate the rift between public languages that theorize social relations, and the temporal experience of individual histories.[8]

Such formulations are particularly valuable for a cultural-political study not simply because they foreground the analysis of discourse of all kinds, but because they offer a way of thinking about nineteenth-century middle-class society that need not depend on a conception of the private and the political as separate spheres. Ultimately, however, both Gallagher and Bodenheimer retreat from the implications of their own arguments in this regard, Gallagher to discover in the condition-of-England novel a consistent undermining and ironization of the official novelistic tropes that connect the private and the public spheres (178) and Bodenheimer to treat the political actions of the middle-class heroine as fantasies, alternatives to the utilitarian marketplace that neither attack its assumptions nor challenge its power (17–18). I take seriously, however, both those novelistic tropes of connection between the spheres Gallagher concludes do not stand, and the political alternatives posed by the middle-class heroine; I take seriously, in other words, that *connection* between the public language of social and political relations, and the domestic idiom of the private individual just as I take seriously the connection between political and domestic fiction. These connections matter because it is through them that the relationships between the different realms of the liberal polity may be discerned.

My notion of political fiction, in line with the insights of Gallagher and Bodenheimer, concerns just such negotiations between the public and the private, and between the individual and the collective. I see political fiction as fiction that addresses itself to the contemporary social arrangements from which rights are derived,[9] that takes as axiomatic the instability of those arrangements, and, because of this instability, argues for the defense, the alteration, or the abolition of certain of these arrangements. And it is in this argumentative dimension that political fiction differs from other types of fiction; while it would be difficult to imagine a novel, particularly an early novel, that did not in some way represent social arrangements, the project of political fiction does not stop with representation. Rather, representation — claims about what the world *is* — in political fiction becomes the basis for prescription — claims about what the world *ought to be*. Such prescription aligns political fiction, in intellectual intent, with the political philosophy by which it is informed; while in other ways these discourses differ even radically, not least in the amount of license that might be extended to novelistic rather than political representation, this shared intent suggests that it is worth taking seriously the prescriptive claims of political fiction. This is not to say that political fiction produces consistent or even, necessarily, coherent worldviews, or that these worldviews always aptly transcribe philosophical intent, but simply that these purposes and intentions deserve — after the "death of the author" and her subsequent rebirth in contemporary theory — analysis and elaboration.

I would add that the failure of the political text to resolve its political question, to offer a workable or plausible solution to the problem under examination, does not, by this definition, constitute sufficient reason for considering the text nonpolitical. Nor, importantly, does subsuming the political or public dimension into an individual or domestic or private resolution abrogate the politicality of the text. Indeed, a key part of my argument in this book is to show that such apparently private resolutions can extend and fulfill the politics of a fiction, rather than containing or subverting them.[10] I will argue that extending what Bodenheimer terms the boundaries of social possibility (3) requires the extension of our vocabularies, and that this linguistic and social contest is as much the province of domestic fiction as it is of political fiction because domestic fiction investigates the norms, goods, and values that inform everyday life, and thus the formation of the citizen-self.

This is not to conflate political and domestic fiction, although I see them as linked. Where political fiction is concerned with the social arrangements of the polity, in their public implications, domestic fiction involves the social arrangements of the household or of a set of households, and does so in terms of the intimate and affective relations to which these arrangements give rise. In the context of these arrangements, domestic fiction situates the household in relation to other significant spaces of the polity, such as the marketplace of the liberal state; in the same context, domestic fiction likewise situates the private self in relationship to the self-as-citizen, and indeed, as I will show, addresses the arrangement of the household as crucial to the development of the citizen-self. Here, too, I perceive a link between political philosophy and literary fiction: The political philosophy of liberalism casts education as a necessary precondition for the creation of the citizen, insofar as it considers the end of education as the cultivation, in the self, of that reflection, evaluation, and will that is central to the autonomy of the citizen. And if the household, in the late eighteenth and nineteenth centuries, is the space above all others in which this education for citizenship is figured, as Victorian attentiveness to the home attests, it is also within the household — within the domestic fictions that engage and constitute that household — that the claim of citizenship for women may be made.

It might be argued at this point that the ideology of domesticity, far from enabling the claim to juridical personhood, to selfhood and its attendant rights in the civic sense, instead simply cloaks the disenfranchisement of women in the soothing rhetoric of moral influence. After all, women in Britain remained, throughout the nineteenth century, profoundly alienated from access to some of the most fundamental rights of liberal citizenship; moreover, as scholars from Basch to Harman have shown over and over again, this refusal of access to public power went hand in hand with an elaboration of the private sphere as the pre-eminent site of some more abstract and intangible power. In this sense, my argument for the powerful role of the household in the liberal polity might be seen as buying into the same mystification that for years confined women to their private place. But if indeed the discursive intertwining of the spheres did maintain the status quo, did keep women in their place by masking their lack of access to real power, it could do so only through a self-defeating contradiction. I suggest that to whatever extent domestic ideology's mystification of women's role sought to shore up the status quo, it did finally fail to do so, and it did so because by its own account of the value of the household as a precondition for liberal selfhood, it ultimately laid the groundwork for access to that citizen-self. In figuring the household as the originary space of critically reflexive virtue, male and female, such ideologies ultimately undermined even their own impetus to deny the exercise of such reflexivity. As the early chapters of this book try to show, once the potential for critical inquiry is attributed to the self, whether in the service of 'rational motherhood' or women's rights, it cannot long sustain an external foreclosure on the exercise of reason; in later chapters, I show the refusal of such foreclosure through the claiming of civic space. After all, the intent of the framers of the American Declaration of Independence in claiming that all men are created equal was not to challenge institutionalized slavery, but nevertheless that central claim has fueled emancipatory movements from suffrage to civil rights. In my reading of the philosophy of the household, I try to show how intimate space figures such emancipatory possibilities.

It might be further objected, however, that such emancipation, if emancipation indeed it is, in taking middle-class space as its precondition, occurs for women of this class at the expense of the working classes and the poor, and indeed my emphasis throughout this project on the middle classes seems to lend some support to such a claim. Yet I see this as a necessary emphasis for two reasons; first, as such scholars of the novel as Ian Watt and, more recently, Terry Lovell, have shown, the nineteenth-century novel is predominantly a middle-class genre. As such, it is middle-class political philosophy that forms its discursive background; moreover, the growing influence of the middle class throughout the period marked by the first and second Reform Bills points to the increasing power of these political philosophies. The question of whether this increasing power enabled the middle classes by disabling those beneath them, however, is more fraught; I will argue that such political fictions as *North and South* and *Hard Times* assign affectivity and interiority to the working classes as part of a demand for recognition of the workers as *kindred* selves. If this occurs primarily through attributing to the workers and the poor a middle-class sensibility and access to the middle-class household in which that sensibility arises, it is not therefore disingenuous; indeed, although development of this point is not the primary function of this project, such movements as Christian Socialism's campaigns for working-class education arose out of the desire to extend to the children of the disenfranchised classes what the enfranchised took to be the preconditions for citizenship.[11] If the liberal political philosophy of the nineteenth century took the paradigmatic citizen-self to be the middle-class self, in other words, this need not point to the exclusion of the working classes from civic personhood, but to the possibilities of and for their inclusion. And it is conditions of possibility, possibilities of the citizen-self, which finally concern me here.

I begin in chapter 1 by investigating the role of education and domestic experience in late seventeenth- and eighteenth-century discussions of women's civic role, indicating which historical events and which developments in political philosophy led to the feminist claims of Mary Astell and Lady Mary Chudleigh, who argue the liberal case that women's submission to authority can only be grounded in the evidence of reason. Astell and Chudleigh differ strongly, as I show, from essayists Addison and Steele and, later, Rousseau, for whom the education of women is primarily sexual in its aims and ends. The chapter concludes with a discussion of Rousseau's *Emile* as political fiction that sought, in Nancy Armstrong's terms, to establish a vocabulary of identity that valued qualities of mind over external signs of rank and status. In chapter 2, I contend that qualities of mind play a key role in the construal of the liberal self as a juridical person, that is, as a bearer of rights. I show that when Mary Wollstonecraft set out to vindicate the rights of women in her political fictions, *Mary* and *The Wrongs of Woman*, she proceeded in precisely this way, calling for rights for women on the basis of common capacity, and likewise laying claim to the education of the reason. Reason, for Wollstonecraft, is the ground of private virtue and of citizenship; this is so for Wollstonecraft because only through the cultivation of interior qualities may we become capable of exercising full citizenship. My readings of Amelia Opie's *Adeline Mowbray* and Maria Edgeworth's *Belinda* in chapter 3 highlight the ways in which these novels negotiate the tension between the liberal self and the liberal polity. Here I elaborate the constitutive role played by the community in the cultivation of the liberal self, a role that both Opie and Edgeworth suggest confers obligations on the self-as-citzen. These obligations include commitment to the shared goods of the community and the practice and extension of individual virtue, through the cultivation and enculturation of that practical reason on which the social good depends.

In chapter 4, I investigate the nature of the liberal self as a bearer of rights. Arguing that rights are assigned to the self as self, that is, as a creature of interiority capable of both emotion and reason, I treat the household as the originary space in which the liberal self comes to be. In this sense the household is not private space; rather, it is "intimate space," a term of art I adopt to highlight the affective relations of the household. These affective relations are, I contend, crucial to the idea of the liberal self. I develop this notion of intimate space through a reading of Elizabeth Gaskell's *Wives and Daughters*, revealing the household as the space of ends rather than market means and thus as the foundation of the liberal state, figured as a polity that seeks to ensure the self's right to pursue and realize its own ends, its own vision of the good. Chapter 5 argues that, if the domestic sphere is indeed the foundation of the liberal polity, then domestic fiction and political fiction may be inextricable from each other. Here I show that the household, foundation of the polity, is neither withdrawn nor separate from that polity. The claim to rights, I suggest, is made through a revelation of the other as a self in the liberal sense; documenting this revelation in Gaskell's *North and South*, I contend that it is in the intimate space of the household that the political rights-bearer is disclosed. Finally, in chapter 6, I address the ways in which recent political philosophers, Alisdair MacIntyre in particular, have misunderstood the project of liberalism. In response to MacIntyre's famously posed choice for political philosophy "after virtue," Nietzsche or

Aristotle, I outline John Stuart Mill's contribution to the debate over rights and suggest his liberalism as the alternative to despotism that Dickens sought. I conclude with readings of *Great Expectations* and *Hard Times* that redress the difficulties of the "separate spheres" paradigm and that situate the intimate space of the household as the origin of liberal politics rather than its boundary.

NOTES

1.   But note that even Ruskin's highly relational view of women sees domestic virtue in the context of public virtue; thus, for example, his command to women to practice charity (72–74). Other notable nineteenth-century versions of the prescription for separate spheres include Ellis and Sandford.

2.   Harsh disagrees, arguing instead along Auerbach's lines that the figure of the demonic, victimized woman leads "beyond the orderly world of domesticity to a realm in which radical, dramatic transfiguration is imaginatively possible" (73).

3.   The term is Halperin's; he contends that the centrality of sexuality to self-interpretation is a product of the "modern, bourgeois West" and its obsession with sexuality (271). See Davidoff 263–64 for a discussion of this point.

4.   Davidoff and Hall's *Family Fortunes* takes a slightly different tack, treating masculine middle-class aspirations to status in terms of their underpinnings of familial and female support, and — significantly — dealing with domestic harmony "as the crown of the enterprise as well as the basis of public virtue" (18). The primary concern of this massive study, however, is the gendered nature of class identity, rather than the nature of juridical personhood or literary articulations of domestic and public domains.

5.   95–176. I return to Booth in detail in later chapters.

6.   Habermas, for example, espouses a teleological model of moral development, whose goal is "autonomous ego organization" (70); while his discourse ethic calls for the consensual resolution of conflicts, and thus would seem to stress a relational view of the citizen, his ideal speech situation calls for "competent agents" to agree "independently of accidental commonalities of social origin, tradition, basic attitude, and so on" (88). Agreement, then, arises from procedural reason, "the very structures of possible interaction" (88), rather than from any sense of the particularity or situatedness of the agent, much as it does with Rawls's "veil of ignorance" (Rawls 136–42). See Benhabib 68–120 and Taylor, *Sources* 85–88 for critiques of Habermas's notion of reason; Benhabib takes up the Rawlsian "veil" as well (160; 166–68).

7.   Nancy Armstrong is by no means alone in identifying "politics" as the politics of resistance. Edward J. Ahearn, in *Marx and Modern Fiction*, for example, following Frederic Jameson's assumption that the ideas of the ruling class are invariably the ruling ideas, looks to irony and ironic literary forms for that resistance to historical and material oppression which constitutes, for him, the domain of the political (24–26). Other unhelpfully narrow views of the political in fiction are advanced by Joseph Blotner in *The Modern American Political Novel* and Morris Speare in his massive *The Political Novel: Its Development in England and in America*; both Blotner and Speare are concerned with works that deal, in subject and in theme, with the institutions of party politics (Blotner 8; Speare ix). Both exclude those works that, like the social-problem novels of the early and mid-Victorian period, concentrate on the conditions that may give rise to political action rather than on institutionalized political processes themselves. Still other works, like Louis Cazamian's classic study of the social novel in England, locate the politicality of the fiction in authorial

intent. For Cazamian, the term "social novel" is a restricted term, referring to a novel with a social thesis (7), and his object domain is further delimited by his desire to describe the main threads of the idealist and interventionist reaction to the problems of industrialism. Thus for Cazamian the social novel is one that "aims at directly influencing human relations, either in general, or with reference to one particular set of circumstances. Of course, private manners and public affairs are too closely connected for the former to be altered independently of the latter. Every moral critique has its social repercussions. Nevertheless, those works which only examine the private failings of individuals in society have been ignored, together with any which do not directly assert their reformatory intention" (8). Patrick Brantlinger's study of the social-purpose novel similarly directs attention toward literature that strives toward social amelioration, a set that can encompass self-consciously improving fiction and didactic fiction as well as revolutionary fiction (1–9, 258); here, too, the intentions of the author are the most important criteria for determining the politicality of fiction. Helena Bergmann's description of the industrial novel as one "written to give the reading public insight into the social conditions of the country, with the specific aim of bringing about an improvement of these conditions" (13) has a similar emphasis, as does Arnold Kettle's discussion of the early Victorian social-problem novel as addressed to a middle-class audience by middle-class writers in order to engage their consciences and inform their ignorance (171).

8.   Bodenheimer 231–32. A similar, though less rigorous and considerably less useful, definition of political fiction is available in Victoria Middleton's *Elektra in Exile: Women Writers and Political Fiction*. Middleton considers such texts as Mary Shelley's *The Last Man*, Virginia Woolf's *The Years*, and Doris Lessing's *The Four-Gated City* as political because they dramatize power struggles between persons in which personal and public conflicts are interdependent, so that the political novel is the locus of intersection between two fictive worlds, the public one of political conflict and the private one of character development (4).

9.   Although historical novels such as Dickens's *Barnaby Rudge*, if they bear on contemporary issues in a significant way, might pose a borderline case.

10.   Josephine Guy suggests, most valuably, that much criticism of the social-problem novel suffers from a failure to recognize that definitions of "society" or "the social," and therefore of "social problems," are "historically unstable" (26); individualism and interventionism were not, in other words, opposing categories in nineteenth-century Britain, and therefore what strikes modern critics as a private solution is in fact in line with the social atomism which "underwrote" most responses to social problems (44). See *The Victorian Social-Problem Novel: The Market, the Individual and Communal Life* for a fuller development of this point. I differ from Guy primarily in my account of liberalism's concept of human nature, which she takes as changeless and essential (115), in contrast to what I take to be the importance of education in these texts.

11.   See Brantlinger's discussion of this point in chapter 6 of *The Spirit of Reform*, esp. 147–49.

1
Calling the Question

God created man in his image,
in the divine image he created him;
male and female he created them.
　　　　　— Genesis 1:27

So the LORD God cast a deep sleep on the man, and while he was asleep, he took
out one of his ribs and closed up its place with flesh. The LORD God then built up
into a woman the rib that he had taken from the man. When he brought her to the
man, the man said:
　　"This one, at last, is bone of my bones
　　　　and flesh of my flesh;
　　This one shall be called 'woman,'
　　　　for out of 'her man' this one has been taken."
　　　　　— Genesis 2:21–23.

There is a story about a University of Toronto professor of sociology who began the
semester by telling his class that anybody can get a Bachelor of Arts degree. "If you
show up," Lorne Tepperman is reputed to have said, "if you write the exams and
submit your work, you can get this degree. It might not be a good degree, but
anybody in this room can get a B.A. The important question," he said, "has nothing
to do with the people who are here. It is the question of those who are not here,
who never had a chance to be here."[1] This story is an interesting one for my
purposes because in raising the "important question . . . of those who are not here"
our professor in fact raised two questions, both central to my project here. First,
and perhaps most obviously, his question has to do with issues of social arrangements and access to power. Second, and I will return to this in due time, his
question concerns the issue of who is *not* there. And this who, as I hope to show,
has to do both with what kind of self we imagine the educated self to be, and with
a self's ability to project herself into the role of the educated.

This chapter investigates the intertwined roles of education and domestic experience in late seventeenth- and early eighteenth-century discussions of women's civic role. First, it details the significance of Enlightenment political philosophy to the early feminism of Mary Astell and Lady Mary Chudleigh, who argue that women's submission to authority can only be grounded in the evidence of reason. In this they oppose the views of essayists Addison and Steele, as well as the later claims of Rousseau, for whom the education of women is primarily sexual in its aims and ends. I conclude with a discussion of Rousseau's *Emile* as political fiction that sought, in Nancy Armstrong's terms, to establish a vocabulary of identity — of selfhood— that valued qualities of mind over external signs of rank and status. What this self is or ought to be, as I show here, is conceived for these thinkers in terms of the education that creates and furthers that self.

I argued in the Introduction that the political domain is the domain of social arrangements, from which groups of selves draw their rights and privileges; that it is the domain of sanction, of the codification of conventions, rules, and laws; and that it is the domain of distribution, and thus of access to power. So defined, this domain must contain questions about access to education, because this latter, in the modern West as in nineteenth-century Britain, involves access to political power, cultural influence, and economic resources. This is so, as that University of Toronto professor evidently knew, because even in states that subsidize education, access to educational resources is inextricably bound up with the delimitations of class, sex, and race, and thus with the distribution of political power, cultural influence, and economic resources. The question of education, in other words, is not simply one of the removal of barriers, but one of an imaginative ability to project ourselves forward, into our own educated future; access in this sense is both economic and cultural.

Pierre Bourdieu and Jean-Claude Passeron help to explain this double problem of access. They argue in *Reproduction* that the chances for social upgrading through education are institutionalized; these institutionalized, even codified chances themselves condition our attitudes *toward* education and, specifically, toward upgrading through education (156). These attitudes, in turn, determine how likely we are to embark on an educational project, to adhere to its highly codified norms, and to master those norms (156). Thus an educational system is *culturally* successful when, through these codified norms, it sanctions and transmits the dominant cultural worldview[2]; success in the case of individual students depends, they argue, on the affinities between a student's earliest upbringing and the dominant model, from which the dominant worldview is derived (49–50). This last claim is limited to social formations in which the dominant worldview subordinates practical or technical mastery to symbolic mastery or symbolic practices (49)[3]: The law, for example, or architecture over the police or bricklaying.

Even within these limits to their claim, however, Bourdieu and Passeron have articulated a theory of educational access and reproduction useful for our purposes. Certainly, they have carefully refused to include here those social formations that do *not* privilege symbolic mastery over practical mastery, but the debate over the kind of education suitable for women can be described in no other terms.

Programmes for female education that are based on the belief that women, less rational than men, are therefore less capable of abstract thought, clearly privilege symbolic mastery over feminine "accomplishment." Certainly, Bourdieu and Passeron have further limited this important claim to traditional modes of inculcation, and made much of the way in which such modes presuppose an already existing horizon of identity and meaning that matches the worldview they seek to impose. As I will show, many of the thinkers who articulated their stance on the education of women did so in terms of the degree to which the disposition of women could correspond with that of the ideal addressee posited by the thinkers themselves; we are dealing, in other words, with a positing of the female self. While it is not my project here to chart the degrees to which the education of women in the nineteenth century produced or attempted to reproduce the dominant habitus, I will observe that the demand by women for access to the ancient seats of Oxford and Cambridge in no way sought to challenge the position of those institutions as the final arbiter of what Bourdieu and Passeron term the dominant cultural arbitrary. Indeed, such demands, made not only by women but, in the earlier decades of the nineteenth century, by Roman Catholics and by other disenfranchised groups, far from interrogating the pedagogic authority of those institutions, in fact consecrated and reproduced that authority.[4]

Moreover, we may see from Bourdieu and Passeron's emphasis on *attitudes* that, for example, the limited number and range of professions open to women in the nineteenth century contributed to the form that many arguments in favour of women's education took.[5] Likewise, the relationship Bourdieu and Passeron identify between social upgrading and attitudes to education may explain the coincidence between social agitation for extended employment opportunities and agitation for increased access to education.[6] Moreover, since until very recently women's class affiliations were largely relational, even in societies with considerable class mobility, many women may have been attracted only to those forms of education that would increase their desirability to men of their own or a higher class, that is, the kind of education we shall see advocated by Addison and Steele. This is so because women's chances for social upgrading were institutionalized, not directly through education, but through marriage and kinship. I will return to this point, but for now let me suggest that one of the implications of Bourdieu and Passeron's claim is that major changes in cultural notions of female desirability were necessary for changes in the system of female education to occur. What intrigues me here is that Bourdieu and Passeron's radical politicization of education turns on their understanding of the ways in which the pedagogic project always posits a very specific self as its ideal addressee. By this I mean that the contest over education cannot, finally, be divorced from debates over the nature and political status of human selves, or from their capacity for critically reflexive agency. I am not contending — let me be clear — that human selves own a kind of transparent "essence" that education may allow them to fulfill; rather, my claim is that eighteenth- and nineteenth-century ideas about education point to contemporary ideas about what is valuable or worthwhile or (sometimes) necessary in a self, conceived as a citizen.

What does it mean to say that theories of education always take the nature of the self as their point of reference? A well-known example may help to illustrate this claim. Belenky, Clinchy, Goldberger, and Tarule argue in *Women's Ways of Knowing* that women's thought is more concrete, particular, and experience-based than that of men. From this, they follow Carol Gilligan in claiming that women's judgments are based on differential relational considerations, rather than on the rigid categorizations of men.[7] Contending that the female self is a radically different type of knower than the male self, "connected" rather than "separate," Belenky and colleagues argue for a new women's education, one that will emphasize connection, acceptance, collaboration, and process-oriented research over separation, assessment, debate, goal-driven evaluation methods, and that will allow time for learning based on experience rather than abstract reasoning (229). They argue this on the assumption that traditional modes of inculcation handicap women. This conclusion, it should be clear, is based on a series of claims about the nature and capabilities of the female self. Similarly, theories and manuals of education in the eighteenth and nineteenth centuries — most notoriously Rousseau's *Emile*, though as I will show his sex-based system is the rule rather than the exception — based their systems of education on sets of theories about the separate natures of women and men, girls and boys. Part of my project here is to unravel such claims about the nature of the female self, and to chart the ways in which these claims were themselves articulated in fiction.

At the close of the seventeenth century in England, large numbers of women, even those of the wealthy classes, had no education at all as we understand the term.[8] Those of the landed classes who did receive training received it largely in "accomplishments": Needlework, music, drawing, dancing, and modern languages such as French and, possibly, Italian.[9] Thus Chamberlayne's 1671 prospectus for a Ladies Academy on the model of Catholic convents promises "the best and ablest Teachers in *London* for Singing, Dancing, Musical Instruments, Writing, French Tongue, Fashionable Dresses, all sorts of Needle-Works; for Confectionary, Cookery, Pastery; for Distilling of Waters, making Perfumes, making of some sort of Physical and Chyrurgical Medecins and Salves for the Poor, &c" (6). Nor was Chamberlayne's proposal unusual, as we may conclude from the mid and late seventeenth-century explosion of attacks on just this kind of women's education as calculated "to give our sex a degenerate way of thinking, and to reduce them to as narrow a way of acting."[10] Such training tended toward the decorative and ornamental; more than that, as Blease and others have pointed out, it was sexual training, since its object was to develop qualities that would excite desire in men (Blease 28–29; Nancy Armstrong 19–20, 59–60; Browne 5–6). Nor is the sexual dimension of this training a discovery of twentieth-century critics; Chamberlayne's Academy self-consciously proposed to inculcate "that handsome Becoming Deportment, which usually sets off, and recommends young Ladies to good Husbands" (3–4). Reading and reflection were beyond doubt the privileges of men (Blease 29), and even those women who, like Hannah Woolley, believed it "wisdome in a woman to attain to what knowledge and learning she can" advised caution in the same breath: "[B]ut this we must be sure of, that we do not boast our selves above them, but rather subject our selves to be the inferiour of the two: for God hath given man the preheminence, and it must be so" (11).

Times, however, were changing. Part of this change can be attributed to a shift in beliefs about the nature of the self that arose from seventeenth- and eighteenth-century political thought. The significance of these philosophical claims for advances toward equality, not only for women but for other disenfranchised groups and classes, is now being rearticulated by feminists. Theoretical (post-structuralist) feminism has recently backed off from its often ahistorical claim that "two centuries of faith that the ideal of equality and fraternity included women has still not brought emancipation for women," and therefore that "ideals of liberalism and contract theory, such as formal equality and universal rationality, are deeply marred by masculine biases about what it means to be human and the nature of society."[11] A more tenable position is expressed by Elam and Wiegman in their Introduction to *Feminism Beside Itself*: "Although feminism offers some critique of Enlightenment liberation — insofar as feminism cancels the Enlightenment's project of realizing universal *man* by refusing the elision of the specificity of woman that this universality implies — nonetheless, feminism can be understood to perform such a critique because feminism itself is a coherent project in the Enlightenment sense."[12] Indeed, I suggest that feminism becomes possible only through the changes to both public and private life brought about by the liberal thought of the *Aufklärer* and their predecessors.

As Alice Browne points out, changes in intellectual and political life over the course of the seventeenth century had made it easier to argue seriously for the rationality of women (81–87). Descartes's (1596–1650) emphasis on independence of mind and body had contributed to a widespread discussion amongst intellectuals of the nature of rationality; the implications of mind-body dualism weakened the ancient argument from physiology against women's rationality, and furthered interest in the education of reason. In marked contrast to Judith Butler's assertion that "[i]n the philosophical tradition that begins with Plato and continues through Descartes, Husserl, and Sartre, the ontological distinction between soul (consciousness, mind) and body invariably supports relations of political and psychic subordination and hierarchy" (*Gender Trouble* 12), John Locke (1632–1704) was influenced by Cartesian reasoning to argue from common rationality that women and men should receive similar educations. This is the import of his letter to Mrs. Clarke on the subject: "Since therefore I acknowledge no difference of sex in your mind relating . . . to truth, virtue and obedience, I think well to have no thing altered in it from what is [writ for the son]."[13] I will return to Locke's notions of mind in due time, but for now let me only add that as a proponent of parliamentarianism in an age of civil unrest, he argued that political power was based on contract rather than on a divinely instituted patriarchal power, and in so doing removed one of the principal arguments for men's power over women.[14]

The repeated conflicts between monarch and parliament over the course of the seventeenth century had drawn attention to the arbitrary nature of patriarchally based power. The attempt of the Stuart kings to rule by virtue of divine right had ended in civil war and regicide in 1649, and despite the restoration of the Stuart monarchy in 1660, Parliament had again asserted its right to dissolve the social contract by instituting the so-called "Glorious Revolution" of 1688–89. Both the divine right of kings and the subordination of wives and daughters to husbands and fathers were symbolically based in the originary myth of Adamic authority, that is, on the account of creation in Genesis 2, which gave Adam sole dominion over the world and its creatures. It is to this second account of creation Woolley refers in her claim that "God hath given man the preheminence" (11). Since both the subjects of monarchy and the subjection of women were philosophically justified through notions of natural right and natural law, the undermining of the bases for one could not fail to draw attention to the capricious nature of the other. Political theory continued to evade the consequences of this relationship, and exclude women from public life as it continued to exclude them from the exercise of equitable power in private life. As Alice Browne points out, however, these same theories made it easier to question that exclusion (20). This is so despite Locke's unease with the familial consequences of his critique of patriarchalism. While he distinguishes between the power of the sovereign over a subject and the power of a husband over his wife (*Two Treatises* II.§2), his view of marriage as contractual renders a wife's subordination to her husband analogous to a subject's subordination to the monarch: "The *Power of the Husband* being so far from that of an absolute Monarch, that the *Wife* has, in many cases, a Liberty to *separate* from him; where natural Right, or their Contract allows it, whether that Contract be made by themselves in the state of Nature, or by the Customs or Laws of the Countrey they live in" (*Two Treatises* II.§82). Because it is a matter of contract, this subordination can, as Browne indicates, be varied or abolished altogether (20).

It is impossible to overestimate the crucial importance of a century of profound political unrest to the development of eighteenth- and nineteenth-century feminism. Because it is here that the naturalness of social arrangements based on Adamic myths is first questioned, the seventeenth-century interrogation of the right of kings, and its consequent calling into question of the rights of husbands and fathers, must be considered an important precondition of feminist assertions of injustice in male-female relations. Moreover, the development of social contract arguments in political theory is crucially related to philosophical claims for rationality. When Hobbes (1588–1679) had argued from his misanthropic view of man in the state of nature — "solitary, poore, nasty, brutish, and short" (186) — that peace, the goal of enlightened self-interest, could only be preserved through the concentration of power in the hands of an individual, that is, the sovereign (223–28), he had not challenged monarchy but the bases of its inheritance; there is nothing in Hobbes's contention that suggests a *given* monarch reigns by natural law, only that such laws require *a* monarch. John Locke, influenced by Descartes's assertion that "we should never allow ourselves to be convinced [of anything] except on the evidence of our reason" (Descartes 30), was able to refine Hobbes's argument to assert that the social contract, by which the government is licensed to govern, is possible only because of man's capacity, even in the state of nature, to govern and discipline himself. Not only does "[t]he *State of Nature* ha[ve] a Law of Nature to govern it, which obliges every one: [which is] Reason" (*Two Treatises* II.§6), but this same faculty of reason, "which God hath given to be the rule betwixt Man and Man" is "the common bond whereby humane kind is united into one fellowship and societie."[15] The sovereign, for Locke, is the state rather than a monarch, and the monarch rules by consent of the sovereign state.   This consent can only be legitimately achieved through an appeal to reason (*Two Treatises* II.§163–64).

It is Locke's notion of consent, rooted in Cartesian reason, that early feminists adopted in claiming the rationality of women, their duty to educate themselves, and their obligation to base all decisions, including submission to masculine authority, on rational understanding rather than on custom or Adamic law.   Thus Mary Astell argued this Cartesian point at the end of the seventeenth century in *A Serious Proposal to the Ladies* (1692), when she said that women must "Disengage our selves from all our former Prejudices, from our Opinion of Names, Authorities, Customs and the like, not give credit to any thing any longer because we have once believ'd it, but because it carries clear and uncontested Evidence along with it" (68).   If Astell challenges the prejudice of human authority here, Adamic or otherwise, she nevertheless roots her claim for rationality in a greater authority still. Since God "gives no Power or Faculty which he has not allotted to some proportionate use, if therefore he has given to Mankind a Rational Mind, every individual Understanding ought to be employ'd in somewhat worthy of it" (98). Women no less than men enjoy rationality, moreover, and therefore are equally obligated to develop that intelligence[16] to the ultimate end of God's glory:

For since GOD has given Women as well as Men intelligent Souls, why should they be forbidden to improve them? Since he has not denied us the faculty of Thinking, why shou'd we not (at least in gratitude to him) employ our Thoughts on himself their noblest Object, and not unworthily bestow them on Trifles and Gaities and secular Affairs? Being the Soul was created for the contemplation of Truth as well as for the fruition of Good, is it not as cruel and unjust to exclude Women from the knowledge of the one as from the enjoyment of the other? (18–19)

It is a key aspect of Astell's argument for improvements in the education of women that they possess souls, and that the soul is intelligent, a point that reappears a century later in Wollstonecraft's *Vindication of the Rights of Woman.* If, as Astell maintains, women have souls and are therefore rational beings capable of salvation, then they are capable of salvation only insofar as they possess rationality (62). Astell deduces from this a religious duty for women to develop their intelligence through the development of the mind. Piety founded on habit and affection is, for Astell, no piety at all, because it may readily be swayed; only reason and truth are immutable (13). Her proposal, then, is for the founding of a *"Religious Retirement"* (14) that will combine the functions of a monastery, a charitable order, and a college. While Astell describes religion as the main, even the only design of her institution, her conviction that true religion is only possible when accompanied by wisdom and discretion means that "one great end of this Institution shall be, to expel that cloud of Ignorance which Custom has involv'd us in, to furnish our minds with a stock of solid and useful Knowledge, that the Souls of Women may no longer be the only unadorn'd and neglected things" (17). Astell's proposed institution contrasts markedly with Chamberlayne's idea of a Ladies Academy, which, while promising instruction "in the true *Protestant Religion*, and in all Vertuous Qualities that may adorn that Sex" (tp), nevertheless, as we have seen, lists the worldly accomplishments first in its programme of lessons (6). The adornment of the body makes way in Astell's proposal for the adornment of the soul. Thus her "religious" will spend part of their day in worship, and the rest

imploy'd in innocent, charitable, and useful Business; either in study in learning themselves or instructing others, for it is design'd that part of their Employment be the Education of those of their own Sex; or else in spiritual and corporal Works of Mercy, relieving the Poor, healing the Sick, mingling Charity to the Soul with that they express to the Body, instructing the Ignorant, counselling the Doubtful, comforting the Afflicted, and correcting those that err and do amiss. (21)

The business of the ordinary day here seeks to inculcate not those qualities that might attract the good husbands promised by Chamberlayne (Astell 4), but qualities of the mind, conceived as immortal, which for Astell is the only permanent locus of beauty (1).

Despite her assertion in the second part of *A Serious Proposal*, published in 1697, that her institution would be "rather *Academical* than *Monastic*" (157), Astell's proposal had little hope of succeeding in the atmosphere of grave distrust surrounding Catholicism and monasticism at the turn of the century. Her adoption of the Catholic model may have made such objections inevitable. Certainly her careful and constant association of the education of women with right worship and religious practice, while it may have dispelled some objections to removing women from their "proper" sphere, did nothing to dissuade her critics from their conviction that her proposal smacked of the most pernicious forms of Popery.[17] Astell's secular monasticism was not, however, the first such proposal. Those convents that survived the Great Schism could not repeat the feat during the bloody years of the Protectorate, and they had not been replaced by other institutions providing homes and vocations for single women or adequate education for girls. Alice Browne's account of the origins of eighteenth-century feminism tells of Letice, Lady Falkland, who was prevented in the mid-seventeenth century by the outbreak of civil war from founding institutions dedicated to the retirement of widows and the education of girls; of a slightly later book called *The Ladies Calling*, attributed to Richard Allestree, which regretted the closing of the convents for similar reasons; and of Chamberlayne's 1671 pamphlet, which sought to raise funds for a college for single women and widows on the Germanic model, to which I have already referred (97). Despite these efforts, no like project was ever seriously undertaken.[18]

Charges of papist monasticism, however, were not the only ones levelled at Astell's *Serious Proposal*. In the Conclusion to the second part, Astell responds to "those who think so Contemptibly of such a considerable part of GOD's Creation, as to suppose that we were made for nothing else but to Admire and do them Service, and to make provision for the low concerns of an Animal Life" by charging them in turn with contempt for God (158). As "GOD's Workmanship," women are "endow'd by him with many excellent Qualities, and made capable of Knowing and Enjoying the Sovereign and Only Good" (159). Despite this assertion, however, Astell hastens to refute any allegation that she intends to abrogate male rights and privileges, or to assert those rights for women: "The Men therefore may still enjoy their Prerogatives for us, we mean not to intrench on any of their Lawful Privileges, our only Contention shall be that they may not out-do us in promoting his Glory who is Lord both of them and us" (159).

And yet Astell's concession here is ironic, even scornful; she makes it clear that those male "Prerogatives" are not desirable in and of themselves, because, she implies, they are worldly, and the qualities of the self such prerogatives posit are external rather than internal. She says,

[t]hey may busy their Heads with Affairs of State, and spend their Time and Strength in recommending themselves to an uncertain Master, or a more giddy Multitude, our only endeavour shall be to be absolute Monarchs in our own Bosoms. They shall still if they please dispute about Religion, let 'em only give us leave to Understand and Practise it. And whilst they have unrival'd the Glory of speaking as *many* Languages as *Babel* afforded, we only desire to express our selves Pertinently and Judiciously in *One*. We will not vie with them in thumbing over Authors, nor pretend to be walking Libraries, provided they'll but allow us a competent Knowledge of the Books of GOD, Nature I mean and the Holy Scriptures: And whilst they accomplish themselves with the Knowledge of the World, and experiment [sic] all the Pleasures and Follies of it, we'll aspire no further than to be intimately acquainted with our own Hearts. (159)

As Siskin argues, Astell's rhetoric both figures and configures a female self posited in terms of the capacity for inward improvement, rather than "the desire of and for men" (40). Crucially, such rhetoric proffers a model of female value predicated quite differently from that Astell seems to see governing masculine domains.

While Astell's program is not quite so limited as her promise not to vie with men might suggest — her reading for the ladies includes Locke's *Essay on Human Understanding* as well as Malebranche and Descartes, among other works of philosophy — she clearly wants to refute any notion that her proposal for educating women might in any way challenge either the established hierarchy between men and women or that among social orders and degrees. The religious duty to study truth is laid on everyone, "yet all are not equally enlarg'd nor able to comprehend so much" (84). Significantly, this difference in capacity arises, for Astell, from our place in society. Thus she says that "they whose Capacities and Circumstances of Living do not fit 'em for it, lie not under that obligation of extending their view which Persons of a larger reach and greater leisure do" (84–85). While Astell here appears to use larger mental reach as part of the natural province of the learned classes, her recognition of the importance of leisure means that her position is one of nurture — of education — rather than natural fitness or unfitness. In this Astell does not depart much from Locke, whose claim that the natural state is one of equality depends on his argument that "Creatures of the same species and rank promiscuously born to all the same advantages of Nature, and the use of the same faculties, should also be equal one amongst another without Subordination or

Subjection" (*Two Treatises* II.§4). Yet equality in the state of nature may be suspended by God; Locke qualifies the above by saying "unless the Lord and Master of them all, should by any manifest Declaration of his Will set one above another, and confer on him by an evident and clear appointment an undoubted Right to Dominion and Sovereignty" (*Two Treatises* II.§4). While Locke is here recognizing difference in capacity, as Astell does, his reasoning poses no radical challenge to class hierarchy, since, though "God gave the World to Men in Common . . . it cannot be supposed he meant it should always remain common and uncultivated. He gave it to the use of the Industrious and Rational, (and *Labour* was to be *his Title* to it)" (*Two Treatises* II.§34). Labour, then, and the property it creates, is the external sign of the inward play of reason; the improvement of the mind is signaled through the improvement of the estate. Yet despite the role of property in Locke's analysis of capacity, in which the subordination of one class to another appears to prove the inferior capacities of the first, and these inferiorities in turn justify their subordination, we can see the roots of nineteenth-century liberalism in his idea, and Astell's, that equality of rights should be based on internal capacity and not simply on external signs of status.

Similarly, Astell's friend and admirer, Mary, Lady Chudleigh, focused on mental autonomy alone in *The Ladies Defence* in 1701.[19] Like Astell, Chudleigh was interested in asserting woman's claim to reason and her consequent right to the education of the reason, and was likewise quick to deny that this education might intrude women into the provinces of men:

> "Your's be the Fame, the Profit, and the Praise;
> We'll neither Rob you of your Vines, nor Bays:
> Nor will we to Dominion once aspire;
> You shall be Chief, and still your selves admire.
> The Tyrant Man may still possess the Throne;
> 'Tis in our Minds that we wou'd Rule alone" (1.655–60)

But Chudleigh's agreement with Astell is, in this passage at least, shadowed by her satirical tone. *The Ladies Defence: Or, The Bride-Woman's Counsellor Answer'd* is a dialogue poem that mocks the characters of the mealy-mouthed parson from John Sprint's 1699 wedding sermon on wifely obedience, *The Bride-Woman's Counsellor*,[20] and the debauched husband, Sir John Brute, from Vanbrugh's 1697 play, *The Provoked Wife*. The speaker here, Melissa, willingly grants dominion over earthly empires to the men, but her description of masculine "'Vines and Bays,'" does suggest that women's "'unseen Empires'" (1.661) are both more valuable and less prone to decay than the ephemeral preoccupations of men:

> "Trace the first Heroes to their dark Abodes,
> And find the Origine of Men and Gods:
> See Empires rise, and Monarchies decay,
> And all the Changes of the World survey:
> The ancient and the modern Fate of Kings,
> From whence their Glory, or Misfortune springs" (1.645–50)

Empires of the mind do not, like those of men, decay; Chudleigh here not only posits the female self in terms of inner space, but in so doing inverts the values of internal and external "Dominion" she attributes to Brute and Sprint.

Both Astell and Chudleigh were formulating their notions of women's reason and rationality, and the type of education that ought to be consequent on that view, as Alice Browne points out, in contrast to an ornamentalism that sought to make women pleasing consorts for men (104). They called, instead, for a useful education that would improve women's performance in their apparently natural roles as wives and mothers. Astell did not so much seek to challenge that view of a divinely imposed moral order on which such an instrumental feminism depends as she sought to reinforce that order, through a Christian and feminine education, and to prepare women for their inescapable roles. She believed that the education of the reason would lead women to reasonable conclusions regarding their duty, and that these conclusions would necessarily be compatible with God's hierarchical plan (150–53). Similarly, Chudleigh's reply to John Sprint in *The Ladies Defence* adopts to some degree that instrumentalist position, when Melissa says that education will

> "Our struggling Passions within Bounds confine,
> And to our Thoughts their proper Tasks assign.
> This, is the Use we wou'd of Knowledge make,
> You quickly wou'd the good Effects partake.
> Our Conversations it wou'd soon refine,
> And in our Words, and in our Actions shine:
> And by a pow'rful Influence on our Lives,
> Make us good Friends, good Neighbours, and good Wives." (l.663–70)

But the implications of allowing women the autonomy of reason are drawn out by Lady Chudleigh in a way that Astell would not have permitted. Astell argues that submission to authority ought to be based on rational understanding, but goes on to suggest that a truly rational understanding, because it would involve insight into the providential order of hierarchies and degrees, would make obedience inevitable. Chudleigh makes a similar point, but is less sure of its results. Once educated, she says,

> "Unto the strictest Rules we should submit,
> And what we ought to do, think always fit.
> Never dispute, when Duty leads the way,
> But its Commands without a Sigh Obey.
> To Reason, not to Humour, give the Reins" (l.708–12)

The notion of giving the reins to "Reason" rather than "Humour" here might suggest self-control for women in matters of duty, but it might equally suggest a refusal to cede the conclusions of female reason to the power of male caprice. Reason matters, after all, partly because, as Descartes says, it frees us from our own capricious and insatiable appetites (3), but also because, as we have seen in Locke, it forms the social bond that prevents our being ruled by the caprice of others. Indeed, Melissa's long polemic against "'bloody Masters of the martial Trade,'" "'noisy Lawyers,'" "'[t]he envy'd Great. . . . / sway'd by Pride, and by Self-love betray'd,'" "'[t]he Courtier, who with every Wind can veer,'" and the Scholar, "'[t]ho' he perhaps is neither Wise, nor Good'" (Chudleigh l.722–91), indicates that this Lockean reading may be closer to Chudleigh's meaning. There are limits to rational obedience for Mary, Lady Chudleigh, as there are not for Mary Astell, and it is God's gift of sovereign reason that prescribes these limits:

> "[We'll] Be humble, mild, forgiving, just and true,
> Sincere to all, respectful unto you,
> While as becomes you, sacred Truths you teach,
> And live those Sermons you to others Preach.
> With want to Duty none shall us upbraid,
> Where-e'er 'tis due, it shall be nicely pay'd." (l.803–08)

I do not, however, wish to paint Chudleigh's work as a radical departure from Astell and other advocates for women in this period. As soon as her Melissa lays claim to women's right to refuse duty to man when it is unearned, she argues for final submission and resignation to fate in the interests of laying up a permanent reward in heaven (l.809ff). Despite her argument for the autonomy of female reason, then, Chudleigh, like Astell, finally presumes the inevitability of women's subordination to the claims of nature, and thus to men.

This discussion of education and the rationality it demands cannot, it seems, be divorced from a discussion of women's role in the social or moral order. I said that notions of the nature of the self form a crucial pre-text for educational theory; it now appears that what is at stake in such a debate is not merely the nature of female selfhood but where and when, and in what ways, that selfhood, perceived both as atomistic and in its relations to society and the state, may be asserted. To claim the independence of mind and will, the sovereignty of reason, as such thinkers clearly do, does not necessarily imply the evasion of social duty, although — as with Rousseau — it can lead to a potentially absurd isolationism. But atomism is rarely expressed as fully and as romantically as it is by the author of *Emile*, and for many writers, as for Astell and Chudleigh, the notion of the freedom of mind and will is put forward merely as a precondition for an exposition of the duties of mankind in all of the relationships of the social world. I am not arguing, as Françoise Basch has of the nineteenth century, that women far more than men were perceived at this time as "relative creatures," although there is substantial evidence for this view[21]; I am simply contending that men and women were perceived not merely in terms of their independent minds, of Cartesian rationality, but in terms of their established rights, duties, and roles. Both took their identities from their "Capacities and Circumstances of Living" (Astell 84), and both were implicated in a system of rights, duties, privileges, and prerogatives attendant on their circumstances. At the same time, growing interest in the historically determined nature of this system, and in the notion of reason as somehow prior to it[22] was leading to an unprecedented interest in the training of the mind to fulfill the duties of the body and its station.

It was these duties that most engaged Addison and Steele. Despite the importance of Astell and Chudleigh as early advocates for women's education, the essays
of Addison and Steele enjoyed far greater currency and had a greater influence on
its slow reformation. As Blease observes, *The Tatler, The Guardian,* and *The
Spectator* were primarily interested in the superficiae of society (39), but they
found in such superficialities ample evidence of the follies and frivolity of women.
Like both Astell and Chudleigh, Addison and Steele were prepared to assign
responsibility for all of these errors to want of education. Thus, the efforts of "the
beauteous Cleomira," at the age of fifty, to appear fifteen, whilst recommending
gravity and cirumspection to her daughter are for Steele a "great evil" proceeding
from "an unaccountable wild method in the education of the better half of the
world" (*Tatler* 61: 344). In a similar vein, Addison recommends the study of
astronomy as a curb to malicious gossip:

If the female tongue will be in motion, why should it not be set to go right? Could they
discourse about the spots in the sun, it might divert them from publishing the faults of their
neighbours. Could they talk of the different aspects and conjunctions of the planets, they
need not be at the pains to comment upon oglings and clandestine marriages. In short, were
they furnished with matters of fact, out of arts and sciences, it would now and then be a great
ease to their invention. (*Guardian* 155: 221–22)

Addison's discourse on feminine study shares with Mary, Lady Chudleigh's only
an attitude of ironic contempt for the pursuits of women.
    Addison and Steele are far more concerned with the reformation of manners than
with any systematic social reform, and indeed their essays counter the positing of
the female self in internal (mental) space rather than external, worldly space. If,
as Clifford Siskin argues of Mary Astell, "[s]patially, avoiding the gaze from
'without' entails . . . a turn 'within'" (40), for Addison and Steele the turn within is
but a means of satisfying the gaze from without. While it is fair to say that like
others of their time they saw reason and morality as closely linked, their notion of
immorality often seems a matter of taste. For Steele, for example, want of reflection
— intellectual idleness — is therefore a primary cause of vice: "Palestris . . . is
supported by spirits to keep off the return of spleen and melancholy, before she can
get over half of the day, for want of something to do, while the wench in the kitchen
sings and scowers from morning to night" (*Tatler* 248: 322). Steele's objection,
however, is that Palestris's habits are "disagreeable," and he is almost as disgusted
with "Lady Goodday," who, "at a very polite circle, entertained a great lady with
a recipe for a poultice. . . . in the harshest tone and coarsest language imaginable"
(323). Appropriate reading, Steele says, will mitigate both these evils, but his plan
for a Female Library that will furnish women "with reflections and sentiments
proper for the companions of reasonable men" (*Tatler* 248: 323) is clearly an
instrumental one. *The Ladies Library*, published by Steele in 1714 but "written by
a lady,"[23] interestingly enough, mitigates the instrumentalism of the original plan to
some degree. The Introduction pleads that it is "the business of ingenious
debauch'd Men, who regard us only as [made up of Affectation, Coquetry,
Falsehood, Disguise, Treachery, Wantonness, and Perfidiousness], to give us those

Ideas of our selves, that we may become their more easy Prey" (5). *The Ladies Library* promises to redress the errors of such pernicious rogues by introducing "more solid Authors" and in general inculcating "Constancy of Mind" (5). Indeed, Steele's compilation is, as Hilda Smith observes, "an unusual mixture" of materials directed at a female audience, including both conservative materials on the proper moral, domestic, and religious states for women and some that were highly critical of these traditional models (198). Moreover, substantial portions of the three-volume set are taken directly from Astell's *Serious Proposal to the Ladies*,[24] in particular the chapter on "Ignorance," and it is the self-reliant feminism of such material that most clearly points up the distinction between the inward and the outward-looking female self.

It is, as Alice Browne points out, difficult to disentangle conservative from progressive works on the education of women in the eighteenth century, in part because many opposing works in fact adopt similar arguments (3–4). Feminists like Chudleigh and instrumental feminists like Addison and Steele argue that improvements in women's education will improve both the companionable dimension of marriage and women's capacity as rational mothers. The essayists, however, tended to see this instrumental dimension as the sole end of women's education, while others had broader aims in mind. This said, it is also true that the wide circulation of papers by Addison and Steele meant the wide circulation of their view of women as capable of reason.

For example, Addison criticizes the employments ("amusements") of women, which "seem contrived for them, rather as they are women, than as they are reasonable creatures; and are more adapted to the sex than to the species" (*Spectator* 10: 49). Such an emphasis on women as reasonable beings, advanced by the arbiters of fashion and manners, was invaluable, despite its association with the limited and limiting aims of the instrumentalists. Certainly Addison argued, often satirically, that female virtue was a domestic virtue, and that the family, therefore, was the proper province for women to shine in. But just as certainly did he make a case for women and their claim to reason:

Learning and knowledge are perfections in us, not as we are men, but as we are reasonable creatures, in which order of beings the female world is upon the same level with the male. We ought to consider in this particular, not what is the sex, but what is the species to which they belong. At least I believe every one will allow me, that a female philosopher is not so absurd a character, and so opposite to the sex, as a female gamester; and that it is more irrational for a woman to pass away half a dozen hours at cards or dice, than in getting up stores of useful learning. This therefore is another reason why I would recommend the studies of knowledge to the female world, that they may not be at a loss how to employ those hours that lie upon their hands. (*Guardian* 155: 222–23)

While the final lines of this passage accentuate the superficial and instrumental dimension of Addison's concerns for women's education, by depicting female knowledge as a diversion similar to, although more appropriate than, gambling, the opening lines can be read as arguing for the province of learning and knowledge as an asexual one. The implications of such a claim, I suspect, would have been handily and hastily rejected by Addison himself; nevertheless, it is impossible to read his argument for reason as a property of the species rather than the sex without recognizing that the dissemination of such a notion prepared the ground for the later and more radical thinkers who would contrive to develop the notion of nongendered education more fully.

The notion that education was sex-driven rather than species-driven was not uncommon; indeed, it was far more prevalent than the reverse and overshadowed even claims that women, like men, were reasonable beings. Perhaps the most influential discussion of this notion came in Book V of Rousseau's *Emile*. Here Rousseau begins his description of the vapid Sophie by arguing that, but for sex, a woman is a man, that "everything man and woman have in common belongs to the species, and that everything which distinguishes them belongs to the sex" (*Emile* 358). But despite this promising beginning, it soon appears that the differences of sex are pervasive, and extend to the moral nature of men and women:

> In the union of the sexes each contributes equally to the common aim, but not in the same way. From this diversity arises the first assignable difference in the moral relations of the two sexes. One ought to be active and strong, the other passive and weak. One must necessarily will and be able; it suffices that the other put up little resistance.
>
> Once this principle is established, it follows that woman is made specially to please man. If man ought to please her in turn, it is due to a less direct necessity. His merit is in his power; he pleases by the sole fact of his strength. This is not the law of love, I agree. But it is that of nature, prior to love itself.
>
> If woman is made to please and to be subjugated, she ought to make herself agreeable to man instead of arousing him. Her own violence is in her charms. It is by these that she ought to constrain him to find his strength and make use of it. The surest art for animating that strength is to make it necessary by resistance. Then *amour-propre* unites with desire, and the one triumphs in the victory that the other has made him win. From this there arises attack and defense, the audacity of one sex and the timidity of the other, and finally the modesty and the shame with which nature armed the weak in order to enslave the strong. (*Emile* 358)

I have quoted this passage at length because Rousseau's notion of the moral natures of men and women was profoundly influential, and continued to affect ideas about women's education well into the nineteenth century, as we shall see in later chapters. Where Addison's instrumentalism nevertheless enabled him to argue that women possessed reason, insofar as they are human, for Rousseau reason is apparently a secondary sexual characteristic, given to man by God in order to control his "immoderate passions" (*Emile* 359). These thinkers are, I contend, instrumentalists; the key difference between them lies in their location of feminine attraction. For Addison and Steele, as we have seen, it is primarily external and aesthetic; for Rousseau, on the other hand, it is the qualities of mind, the internal and ethical, that alone render woman "agreeable to man."[25] Thus, where God "abandon[s] man to immoderate passions, He joins reason to these passions in order to govern them" (*Emile* 359); women, on the other hand, have modesty to control their "unlimited desires" (*Emile* 359).

While the only differences between men and women are sexual, only for women is the sexual difference completely defining. Rousseau says that "[t]he male is male only at certain moments. The female is female her whole life or at least during her whole youth" (*Emile* 361). Because the bearing and raising of children is the proper business of women whether they engage in it or not (*Emile* 362), all of a woman's life and education must, for Rousseau, be devoted to this single purpose. As sexual difference is all-important in Rousseau's scheme, so must the education of men and women be completely different (*Emile* 363).

The hermetic significance of sex not only requires a different education for women, but also alters the direction of that education. Autonomy of mind and will is not at all the end that Rousseau prescribes for women. While he preaches mutual interdependence between men and women, he nevertheless sees men as dependent on women only through their desires, while women are dependent on men through both their desires and their needs (*Emile* 364). Thus, because she cannot fulfill her "proper purpose" — for Rousseau, her only purpose — without masculine aid, goodwill, respect, and desire, then "[b]y the very law of nature women are at the mercy of men's judgments" (*Emile* 364):

It is not enough that they be estimable; they must be esteemed. It is not enough for them to be pretty; they must please. It is not enough for them to be temperate; they must be recognized as such. Their honor is not only in their conduct but in their reputation; and it is not possible that a woman who consents to be regarded as disreputable can ever be decent. When a man acts well, he depends only on himself and can brave public judgment; but when a woman acts well, she has accomplished only half of her task, and what is thought of her is no less important to her than what she actually is. From this it follows that the system of woman's education ought to be contrary in this respect to the system of our education. Opinion is the grave of virtue among men and its throne among women. (*Emile* 364–65)

This is a far cry from the education prescribed for Emile, who is to be taught dependence only on things, which is natural and amoral, and thus "is in no way detrimental to freedom and engenders no vices" (*Emile* 85). This is because Sophie's education should not merely be different from a man's, but ought, *instrumentally*, to relate to men: "To please men, to be useful to them, to make herself loved and honored by them, to raise them when young, to care for them when grown, to counsel them, to console them, to make their lives agreeable and sweet — these are the duties of women at all times, and they ought to be taught from childhood" (*Emile* 365). Thus girls must not only be taught to be attentive and industrious, but made accustomed to restraint[26]:

From this habitual restraint comes a docility which women need all their lives, since they never cease to be subjected either to a man or to the judgments of men and they are never permitted to put themselves above these judgments. The first and most important quality of a woman is gentleness. As she is made to obey a being who is so imperfect, often so full of vices, and always so full of defects as man, she ought to learn early to endure even injustice and to bear a husband's wrongs without complaining. It is not for his sake, it is for her own, that she ought to be gentle. The bitterness and the stubbornness of women never do anything but increase their ills and the bad behavior of their husbands. Men feel that it is not with these weapons that women ought to conquer them. (*Emile* 370)

Rousseau claims to preach mutual interdependence and a notion of the sexes as different but equal, but his plan suggests otherwise. Men need women to fulfill their desires, while women need men not only for their desires but for the fulfilment of their special purpose; the pleasing arts, therefore, are for Rousseau the province of women. It is women's task both to amuse and to obey their husbands, that this special purpose may be fulfilled. The social relation of the sexes may, for Rousseau, produce "a moral person of which the woman is the eye and the man is the arm" (*Emile* 377), but since the woman can never be above man's judgment, the man is also the mind. He may describe this hybrid as a kind of moral symbiote, whose interdependence means that "the woman learns from the man what must be seen and the man learns from the woman what must be done" (*Emile* 377), but since her conduct is "enslaved by public opinion" and her beliefs "enslaved by authority" (*Emile* 377) this power of necessary action seems minimal at best. Both female conduct and female religion are, finally, controlled by external authority, the first prescribed by public opinion and the second by husbands and fathers: "Since women are not in a position to be judges themselves, they ought to receive the decision of husbands and fathers like that of the Church" (*Emile* 377). Thus where, in the (male) child, dependence only on things is prescribed, so that he may know only the constraint of nature (*Emile* 85–86), and thus grow into perfect freedom, women must depend on men. But Rousseau says earlier that "[d]ependence on men, since it is without order, engenders all the vices, and by it, master and slave are mutually corrupted" (*Emile* 85). This is not so, of course, for Rousseau's women.

It should be clear from the foregoing that Rousseau distinguishes between kinds of freedom for men and women, as he distinguishes between kinds of reason. Women, where they have reason, have for Rousseau practical reason only; men have symbolic reason. Where women can develop an experimental morality, men can reduce it to a system. Because of this distinction, women are always dependent on the symbolic mastery of men for notions of right conduct, right action, and right worship. Rousseau argues that since a woman "depends on both her own conscience and the opinions of others, she has to learn to compare these two rules, to reconcile them, and to prefer the former only when the two are in contradiction" (*Emile* 383). This erection of female conscience as an autonomous arbiter may appear to mitigate or even contradict his edict that women are "subject to the judgment of men" (*Emile* 383), but this gesture toward moral autonomy occurs only in the context of the obedience and fidelity to a husband, which, for Rousseau, is the first law of the female conscience. Certainly, reason and morality remain closely linked, but for Emile, an action is considered moral only when it is the clear outcome of reason, while for Sophie, actions are finally moral only if they do not counter the rules of obedience and fidelity. Under Rousseau's notion of female practical reason, it is conceptually incoherent for female reason to discern right action in opposition to male judgment, since practical reason begins with this judgment.[27]

The same is true of freedom. An adult man is, finally, the only judge of his own conduct; his freedom is a positive freedom, involving, as Charles Taylor describes it, the belief that freedom resides in the exercise of control over one's own life. Taylor calls this an exercise-concept; positive freedom involves self-realization, so that in order to be free in this sense an agent must exercise his freedom (*Papers* 2: 213). Emile is thus free to the extent that he has, in Taylor's terms, effectively determined his own identity and the shape of his own life (Taylor, *Papers* 2: 213). The adult man is, for Rousseau, always free in this way because he is always free to resign from the social contract that subjects him to rule by the state; thus the state cannot be seen as altering his essential freedom. Sophie's freedom, by contrast, is negative freedom, which means that it relies on what Taylor calls an opportunity-concept; in its strong form this means that it is a sufficient condition of negative freedom that nothing stand in the way.[28] Sophie's freedom, whether of belief or action, does not for Rousseau depend on the fulfilment of her most basic purposes; she is free only negatively, in the absence of obstacles to her purposes. The absence of obstacles, moreover, cannot be secured by Sophie herself, but only by male judgment and public opinion. Let me elaborate. Emile's freedom, properly understood, requires that, in order to be free, his desires not run counter to his basic purposes, which purposes, under Rousseau's analysis, are discoverable only in himself. By contrast, Sophie must subject her actions to a three-tiered test. Public opinion, "the grave of virtue among men and its throne among women" (*Emile* 365), is the first level; this may be overruled by conscience, which is the source of practical reason and the second level of evaluation. Because male judgment, however, the arbiter of the female conscience, is the third tier and the final source of right action and right conduct for women, female freedom must resort more often to the opportunity-concept implied by negative liberty than to the self-realization model of positive freedom.

It must, of course, be remembered at this point that Rousseau holds that women's "particular purpose" (*Emile* 364) is also their most basic and "proper" purpose (*Emile* 362). From this perspective, his notion of the female conscience as the mechanism for determining that female desires do not run counter to this purpose would mean that female freedom is positive rather than negative. Such an argument could be strengthened by pointing out that the self-realization view of freedom always allows for the possibility of second-guessing by external authority, since it implies that an agent can err in the classification of wants, needs, and desires.[29] Thus, both Emile and Sophie must be for Rousseau understood in terms of positive freedom, and any differences that arise in the exercise of this freedom can be explained in terms of differences in their basic purposes. Such an argument would match Rousseau's view of education, whose aim and end is the ability to correct self-interpretations and evaluate desires, bringing them in line with our basic purposes.

But it matters that Rousseau depicts Emile's basic purposes as essentially discoverable only in himself. Indeed, the goal of a man's education is to achieve this state[30]; Emile is fully free only when his needs, wants, and desires no longer *need* correction or refinement. The same is not true of Sophie's education. Despite the possible objection I have detailed, Sophie is not educated to achieve positive freedom in its ideal form, and must, as Rousseau makes clear, become habituated to restraint. If her freedom is of the positive kind, then it is so in a grossly lessened form. Where Emile is a romantically atomistic individual, Sophie is a highly relational one; this means that Rousseau's description of mutual interdependence is largely vitiated by the almost total moral autonomy and self-reliance of his creature, Emile. Nor can his argument in favour of separate but equal domains for women and men be taken at face value, as he privileges positive freedom over negative freedom and symbolic mastery over feminine "accomplishments" and "wit" (see esp. *Emile* 386–87). As a result, the apparent sovereignty of women in their own domain is wholly derived from the true sovereignty of men. The social relation of the sexes may make up one moral person, but that person is clearly the man, just as earlier political theory held the person of the sovereign to be the embodiment of the state.

I have treated *Emile* at such length because it represents an early fictional attempt to treat the nature of female selfhood in and through education. Mary, Lady Chudleigh's *The Ladies Defence* was of course published almost half a century earlier, but Rousseau's *roman à thèse* enjoyed far wider circulation and a more influential following than Chudleigh's work. Yet the political implications of *Emile* are vexed. Rousseau's adoption of a Lockean notion of the infant as *tabula rasa*, "capable of learning but able to do nothing, knowing nothing" (*Emile* 61), does suggest an acknowledgment of social arrangements as non-natural, a suggestion confirmed both by his idea of the social contract and by his insistence that Emile should be raised as a man and a citizen, rather than for a particular social station. Yet his discussion of the nature of the female self and the social arrangements between the sexes shows that he considered these arrangements to be governed by natural law. Thus Sophie's education is limited, as are the rights accorded to the female self, because both proceed from the duties imposed on her by nature, and indeed it is the goal of women's education to "[s]how them in their very duties the source of their pleasures and the foundation of their rights. Is it so hard to love in order to be loved, to make oneself lovable in order to be happy, to make oneself estimable in order to be obeyed, to honor oneself in order to be honored? How fine these rights are!" (*Emile* 390).

At the same time, however, we must not be too quick to dismiss Book V of *Emile* as simply another natural law argument in favour of female subordination. Its politics are more complicated than that. According to Nancy Armstrong's ambitious discussion of domestic fiction, educational treatises and other forms of domestic fiction actively sought to disentangle the language of sexual relations from the language of politics. These fictions thus introduced a new form of political power, which emerged with the rise of the domestic woman who profoundly influenced British culture through her dominance over all aspects of private life (3). Armstrong claims that writing about the domestic woman, a figure apart from the political world of men and thus one not accurately represented by birth, title, status, or fortune (4), offered a means to contest the dominant notion of sexuality that understood desirability in terms of fortune, status, and kinship webs (8). Thus, Rousseau's history of Sophie, and indeed the whole history of Emile's search for Sophie, which ultimately dismisses the claims of the women of the aristocracy to desirability, is for Armstrong a powerful political gesture, one that contested reigning ideas of kinship relations that attached power and privilege to certain families (5). If, as Armstrong argues of such fiction, neither birth nor status, but only behaviour, accurately reflects the worth of the individual, then such writing, in the very process of making this case, introduces a new and significant vocabulary for social relations, which attaches precise moral value to qualities of mind rather than to social orders and degrees (4). Even Rousseau, then, through his ideas of what is worthwhile and desirable in the female self, contributes significantly to that turn away from external worth we have seen at work in the feminist heirs of Descartes and Locke.

I observed above that one of the implications of Bourdieu and Passeron's theory is that a major change in the cultural apprehension of female desirability was a necessary condition for change in the system of female education. On their account, our chances of upgrading through education structure our attitudes toward education. Since class mobility was, for women, primarily a relational function, their chances of ascending the class hierarchy were dependent on their desirability to men of their own or a higher class. It is therefore no small matter that, as Armstrong says, domestic fiction began to attach that desirability to qualities of the mind rather than to social orders and degrees or to the signs and symbols of the "fashionable" life. If what is desirable is mental qualities, and it is in these qualities that feminine worth is located, then the education of the female mind for something more than watercolours and fancy needlework becomes imperative. And that education, once fairly begun, has wide-ranging significance for the position and condition of women, as we shall see in the next chapter. This is so because even the radical instrumentalism that informs Rousseau's view of women cannot abrogate the political implications of autonomy of mind, even when the potential for such autonomy remains unrealized.

While Nancy Armstrong argues that, in its inception, domestic fiction made this claim for interior qualities on behalf of women alone (4), Rousseau insists throughout *Emile* that this is the only vocabulary that can accurately assess his protégé. Armstrong argues that the development of the male character as less a political creature than a domestic one, the product of desire and of the domestic life, was a refinement introduced in the nineteenth-century novel. But it is as true of *Emile* as it is of her examples, *Wuthering Heights* and *Jane Eyre*, that while gender is the sign of the most important differences among individuals, this difference is, as is clear from Rousseau's description of female education, necessarily understood in terms of respective qualities of mind. On this account, if we go so far as to correct Armstrong by arguing that her description of domestic fiction in the nineteenth century is anticipated by the domestic romance that closes *Emile*, Rousseau's educational treatise must be seen as a profoundly political fiction. Moreover, it is so *because* it is domestic. A fuller discussion of this point must wait on our discussions of Gaskell, but for now I will remark that by his very insistence on the all-importance of gender in social relations, Rousseau makes a powerful political argument for the rising middle class by insisting that value for male and female selves alike was necessarily separate from considerations of rank and fortune. He does not, to be sure, question the so-called natural origins of female subordination, nor does he suggest that there can be anything in the essential female self that is not reducible to gender, but his location of human worth in mental qualities almost alone is a crucial step toward the nineteenth-century liberal understanding of the self.

Significantly for Nancy Armstrong, domestic fiction represents sexual relationships according to a notion of the social contract that empowered qualities of mind over membership in a particular group (30). Rousseau's description of the social relations between the sexes assumes the existence of such a contract; this is the implication of his assertion that natural law prevents coercion in sexual matters:

The freest and sweetest of all acts does not admit of real violence. Nature and reason oppose it: nature, in that it has provided the weaker with as much strength as is needed to resist when it pleases her; reason, in that real rape is not only the most brutal of all acts but the one most contrary to its end — either because the man thus declares war on his companion and authorizes her to defend her person and her liberty even at the expense of the agressor's life, or because the woman alone is the judge of the condition she is in, and a child would have no father if every man could usurp a father's rights. (*Emile* 359)

In Nancy Armstrong's articulation, the contract requires two different parties for the enactment of the mutually beneficial exchange, but these parties cannot be adversarial (31). The fiction of the contract requires both that the two parties be essentially the same prior to the contract, that is, able to enter into the contract, and that the exchange differentiate the two parties (31). The individuals are transformed by the contract, which creates the single moral person of husband and wife, but this transformation does not repress the individuality of the contracting parties. Rather, it extends and perfects their individuality (31) by consecrating their freedom to form the contract. The sexual contract in Rousseau thus fulfills individual freedom because in the contract desire coincides with reason, for men, and this is the nature of the free act. For women, likewise, the free resignation of individual freedom required by the contract itself fulfills that freedom. This is undoubtedly what Rousseau intended to suggest when Sophie's parents declare their willingness to allow their daughter free choice of her own husband.

This notion of consenting parties, however, both in the social contract and the sexual one, is itself fictive because it depends on education. The entire history of Emile's education shows the truth of Armstrong's observation that Rousseau recognizes the necessity for directing the desire of the people toward the right objects in the right way (N. Armstrong 32). In order for the contract to occur, therefore, Rousseau must install a social force prior to the contract, that of education and language, which force is intended to manipulate those desires that Rousseau wants to represent as wholly natural (N. Armstrong 33). In the sexual contract these manipulations are not immediately apparent, except in the relatively minor aspect of Rousseau's misrecognition, not to say misrepresentation, of certain forms of sexual desire as wholly natural after the fact of their historical manipulation. In fact, desire throughout *Emile* is explicitly manipulated through education; heterosexual desire, however, and in particular the desire between

Sophie and Emile, misleadingly played up as untutored, fulfills those tastes both have been taught to value. Neither the form of these desires, nor indeed any social force, can exist prior to the formation of society; Nancy Armstrong argues that it is this idea of a prior social force, necessary to the formation of the social contract, that renders it wholly untenable. It is untenable because in its very essence the social contract relies on an idea of positive freedom as the inalienable right of each individual; Rousseau remarks in Book II of *Emile* that "[t]he truly free man wants only what he can do and does what he pleases" (84). He distinguishes desires, which belong to men, from the caprices or whims of children, which can only be satisfied with the help of others (*Emile* 84). The child's freedom is negative only, where it exists; the adult's freedom is positive because he can do and does do what he truly desires. More accurately, because the adult "wants only what he can do," that is, seeks to fulfill his basic purposes only through those actions to which there is no obstacle, Rousseauean man achieves manhood when negative and positive liberty merge. Made free, then, man is able to form the compact that preserves and extends his freedom; it is this ordering of events that provokes Armstrong's dismissal of the contract as fictive.

However, Armstrong errs in her account of the order of events. The human child is born into society because he is born into a family, and thus it is inside the sexual compact, conceived rather vexedly in Rousseau both as a natural order (*Contract* I.ii.47) and as the paradigmatic civil order (*Emile* 448), that he first grows into liberty: "[C]hildren remain bound to the father only as long as they need him for self-preservation. As soon as this need ceases, the natural bond dissolves. The children, exempt from the obedience they owed the father, and the father, exempt from the care he owed the children, all return equally to independence. If they continue to remain united, it is no longer naturally but voluntarily, and the family itself is maintained only by convention" (*Contract* I.ii.47). It is inside civil society, therefore, that "all are born equal and free;" this freedom is not, crucially, in place in its fullest sense until the child reaches "the age of reason" and thus may become "his own master" (*Contract* I.ii.47), capable of renewing or arrogating the family compact. It is the compact itself, however, that is the guarantor and first instance of man's liberty. More than this, it is through the social contract that freedom comes into being, that freedom that secures all others: "[T]he social order is a sacred right that serves as a basis for all the others. However, this right does not come from nature; it is therefore based on conventions" (*Contract* I.ii.47). It is the conventional basis of right, I suggest, that provokes Armstrong's dismissal of the social contract, and by extension, the sexual contract that is its prototype, as fictive. Rousseau himself advances this view of it as conventional, but Armstrong misunderstands the point of his argument here: It is a *necessary* fiction because it is through the contract that real freedom (in which positive and negative freedom are merged) comes into being.

The idea of the sexual contract is, as I hinted above, more vexed. Because Rousseauean women are always subject to a three-tiered test in which finally even their own free will is formulated through male judgment, they cannot in this sense move beyond negative freedom to that positive freedom that negative liberty may secure. As I have said, this means that their desires are not free. They are incapable of entering freely into the social contract, and likewise incapable of forming a sexual contract; thus does Rousseau contradict himself. A still graver problem is Rousseau's notion that women achieve their freedom in the moment when that freedom is suspended, in the sexual contract. This cannot be so. If the sexual contract or family compact is, as he claims, the prototype of civil order and thus of the social contract, it is worth recalling that freedom cannot meaningfully be renounced. Thus in *On the Social Contract*, "[t]o renounce one's freedom is to renounce one's status as a man, the rights of humanity and even its duties. There is no possible compensation for anyone who renounces everything. Such a renunciation is incompatible with the nature of man, and taking away all his freedom of will is taking away all morality from his actions" (50). In other words, as we will see again and in more detail with John Stuart Mill, one cannot contract oneself into slavery, because in the moment that freedom is suspended, the contract must likewise be suspended, because the contract cannot exist without that freedom it creates, extends, and sustains. Moreover, Rousseau's notion of education, which involves manipulating desire so that it may fall on right objects, indicates that even for the fully atomistic individual who is the ideal addressee of this education, desire is always formed by others. I have already shown that for Nancy Armstrong this means that Rousseau is engaged in disguising political realities as psychological ones; in the present context, this means that the transformation of the child into the man involves the transformation of caprices and other-originating desires into desires that are mythically self-originating, but which in fact originate in a previously existing habitus, which here is the family contract.

The fiction of self-originating desire, however, need not mean that the notion of positive freedom is inherently contradictory, at least as it occurs in the metaphor of the social contract. Through the idea of consent, without which the social contract cannot come to be, the free self realizes his freedom and assumes responsibility for his desires, as though they originated with himself. Charles Taylor clarifies this by pointing out that through our capacity for reason, we may evaluate our desires, so that they are no longer simply given by the communities in which we come to be, but are endorsed by us, and thus engage our responsibility (*Papers* I.28–29). In this sense our desires do originate with us, because we assent to them, and through this assent may we fulfill our freedom in the positive sense by consenting to the social contract. And so, too, does the contract originate with us, because, although it originates elsewhere, and although we are born into it, it is rearticulated and endorsed by us when we reach that age of reason — the very ground of freedom — when we, too, may compact with others. Thus, indeed, is Bourdieu and Passeron's previously existing habitus *reproduced*, because it constitutes the individual, but so too is the individual constitutive of the community, although in a much more limited sense.

It should be clear from the foregoing that even the very contradictions inherent in Rousseau's treatment of the sexual contract have significant implications for the positing of the female self. If consent to the contract is, for women, conceptually incoherent, it is nonetheless crucial that he represented the basis of their subjugation as contractual; this is so because in so doing he made it possible to conceive of women as free. Nor is what Armstrong perceives as *Emile*'s masking of its own political gestures through a vocabulary of private psychology and individual moral qualities truly an erosion of its political import. It is only through such interior qualities, through reason, which alone permits morality and freedom, that the free self can be posited at all. My next chapter, which will examine the contributions of Mary Wollstonecraft to the contest of ideologies, will undertake to unpack this vocabulary, and its attendant political strategies, in more detail. I will show that what is at stake for Wollstonecraft is not simply the nature of female selfhood, but the nature of the juridical person; it is her project to ask — and answer — the question of what is necessary for a woman to become a bearer of rights.

NOTES

1.   I am indebted for this story to Damon Marcel DeCoste.

2.   See Proposition 2.3.2 (29–30), which indicates that the success of a system of education in a given society will always be a function of the relations among the education system, the dominant social worldview, and the worldview inculcated from infancy in that class from which the students come. Bourdieu and Passeron are talking about the success of "pedagogic action," by which they mean any work that is explicitly directed at inculcating a worldview or set of ideas, from the earliest stages of upbringing to the university classroom. I have substituted "worldview" for their term, "cultural arbitrary," as the more lucid choice; this is not intended to downplay the arbitrariness of the horizons that we inhabit, which would in my view misrepresent Bourdieu and Passeron's work, but to bring this discussion into accordance with the vocabulary I have already established.

3.   This proposition is further limited to dominant educational methods that adopt a traditional mode of inculcation, and traditionalism in this sense is measured two ways. First, Bourdieu and Passeron measure traditionalism in terms of the degree to which the success of a teaching model presupposes that students are already equipped with an adequate "habitus," that is, a horizon of identity and meaning that is adequate in the sense that it accords with the worldview the teacher seeks to inculcate and extend (45). Second, traditionalism is measured by the degree to which the instruments of teaching are reducible to the practices of the dominant habitus and tend, merely by repetition by sanctioned pedagogic authority, to reproduce a habitus that is defined precisely by its ease of repetition (48).

4.   Witness the following: "[T]he existing Women's Colleges in the United States are little more than high schools, whose status is undefined, whose degrees, when won, mean little or nothing to the public, and whose domestic economy is usually so narrow, and their discipline so onerous, that women *accustomed to refined and easy modes of life* are unwilling to enter them. Girton College, for the first time in the educational history of England or America, brings women into direct competition with men, under the auspices of an institution of high character and wide reputation, and thus attracts to itself *the best young Englishwomen*" (E.T.M. 277; emphases mine).

5.   Thus, Mary Carpenter's argument for the reform of workhouse training (1862) takes as axiomatic that "[e]very girl should be so learned as to be *able* to fill the duties of a *home*: whatever else may be superadded, this is essential" (51).

6.   Josephine Butler, for example, enumerates three "principal obstacles" to the expansion of women's employment opportunities (75), saying that "[t]he defective training of the women themselves is the most serious of all the hindrances which I have been considering" (79).

7.   Belenky et al. 7–9. See also Gilligan, *Voice*.

8.   Cressy, for example, indicates that 89% of the women in the diocese of Norwich from 1580–1700 were illiterate, more even than labourers (119). While this figure is marginally lower for the diocese of Exeter (1574–1688), at 84%, a sampling of 706 from Durham (1561–1631) revealed that 98% were unable to sign their names (Cressy 120). By the 1690s, however, in London itself, illiteracy among female deponents at the ecclesiastical courts had been reduced to 52% (129).

9.   Blease 28; Cahn 113–14; Hilda Smith 19–26. Cahn, however, draws our attention to the "short-lived" educational project of sixteenth-century humanists, such as Richard Mulcaster and Henry Smith, who held that "a rigorous education was of positive benefit to women and their families, because it taught women virtue, religion, and even commercial skills" (Cahn 111). Such ambitions soon gave way to attacks on learned women, at the turn of the century (Cahn 112).

10.   'Sophia' 69. See also *Essay in Defence*; Neville; Woolley.

11.   Young, "Impartiality" 58. Among those Young notes as contributing to her understanding of this issue are Susan Okin's *Women in Western Political Thought* (1978), Lynda Lange and Lorrenne Clark's *The Sexism of Social and Political Theory* (1979), Jean Bethke Elshtain's influential *Public Man, Private Woman* (1981), Alison Jaggar's *Human Nature and Feminist Politics* (1983), Linda Nicholson's *Gender and History* (1986), and Zillah Eisenstein's sympathetic *The Radical Future of Liberal Feminism* (1979).

12.   Elam and Weigman 5. For a fuller attempt to bring postmodern feminism and liberal political theory into alignment, see Yeatman.

13.   *Correspondence* II.809, p. 686. Browne also makes this point (20). See Locke's *Thoughts* (§6, 117, 117n) for similar claims.

14.   Browne 20. I cite Browne here and above because her work first highlighted for me the significance of Locke's thought for eighteenth-century feminism. For Locke's critique of patriarchalism, see *Two Treatises* I.

15.   *Two Treatises* II.§172; for related claims, see also II.§13–14 and §86–91.

16.   Astell uses "rationality" and "intelligence" synonymously.

17.   Blease tells us that Bishop Burnet discouraged Astell's plan "on the ground that it savoured of monasticism" (36; Perry, *The Celebrated Mary Astell* 502n35). Fraser says, however, that toward the end of his life the bishop's disenchantment with contemporary education taught him the value of Astell's proposal (330–31). A different kind of attack appeared in the *Tatler* 32 (June 23, 1709), where the author pilloried "Madonella, a lady who had writ a fine book concerning the recluse life" (190). Blease suggests that Swift authored the piece (36), although I have found no evidence to this effect.

18.   Blease does mention a small private institution, set up by Harriet Harcourt, where she and a small community of women divided their energies between religious observance and higher study, but gives no indication of its fate (36).

19.   Chudleigh's proposed curriculum in the 1710 *Essays Upon Several Subjects in Prose and Verse*, however, is much more wide-ranging than Astell's, and includes logic, geometry, physics, metaphysics, geography, moral philosophy, scripture, and poetry.

20.   Sprint, a Nonconformist minister, presented Chudleigh with a copy of his sermon, a circumstance she refers to in her "Preface to the Reader" (11; 11n). See Hilda Smith's discussion, 164–69.

21.   Basch's 1974 treatment of what she terms "the 'help-mate' theory of [Victorian] women, of equality through difference" (269) takes nineteenth-century separate sphere arguments as descriptive *of* society rather than, as I do, prescriptive *for* society, but nonetheless it provided an important early cultural materialist analysis of the condition of women in the Victorian era.

22.   Only reason was prior, not ideas themselves; Locke's metaphor of the mind as *tabula rasa*, developed in Book I of *An Essay Concerning Human Understanding*, had gained considerable favour. For Locke, "all the materials of Reason and Knowledge" derive from "*Experience*: In that, all our Knowledge is founded; and from that it ultimately derives it self" (*Essay* II.i.§2). Experience in this sense means both sensation and reflection, the perception of external objects and the perception of the internal operations of the mind (*Essay* II.i.§2).

23.   Hilda Smith says that probably no such lady existed, but that Steele adopted this persona in an attempt to make the conservative tenor of the compilation more acceptable to women (198–99).

24.   Hilda Smith 198, 209n15; Perry's discussion makes it clear that Astell was aware of Steele's "borrowings" (*The Celebrated Mary Astell* 230).

25.   "[N]ature wants [women] to think, to judge, to love, to know, to cultivate their minds as well as their looks. These are the weapons nature gives them to take the place of the strength they lack and to direct ours" (*Emile* 364).

26.   So important is restraint to the education of girls in Rousseau's scheme that he insists that "[i]f they always wanted to work, one would sometimes have to force them to do nothing" (*Emile* 369), simply for the sake of accustoming them to compulsion and restraint.

27.   Rousseau's treatment of women's moral judgment here bears an intriguing resemblance to Carol Gilligan's early work on women's conceptions of self and morality. She said in 1977 that "the very traits that have traditionally defined the 'goodness' of women, their care for and sensitivity to the needs of others, are those that mark them as deficient in moral judgment. The infusion of feeling into their judgments keeps them from developing a more independent and abstract ethical conception in which concern for others derives from principles of justice rather than compassion and care" ("Conceptions" 484). Like Rousseau, Gilligan sees this devaluation of women's moral development as a misreading; unlike him, she argues that the final developmental stage occurs when the female self becomes an independent arbiter capable of subsuming both social convention and individual needs under her highest moral principle, that of nonviolence ("Conceptions" 498).

28.   Taylor, *Papers* 2: 213, although as Taylor remarks, most theories of negative liberty incorporate some notion of self-realization and thus require that individuals exercise their freedom to some degree. Moreover, notions of positive freedom depend in fact and in principle on that absence of coercion that is sufficient for negative freedom, so that negative freedom is the necessary ground of positive freedom.

29.   Taylor, who asserts the value of positive freedom, makes it clear that our self-interpretations, and thus our evaluations, are always corrigible, by ourselves and others. See *Papers* I.37–40.

30.   Rousseau's idealist principles, however, seem to have been largely unworkable. Robert Edgeworth, father of the novelist Maria Edgeworth, apparently educated his eldest son according to the principles laid down in *Emile*. It was a notable disaster, as was his friend Thomas Day's effort to raise two orphan girls as potential wives — intending to choose between them — according to Rousseau's plans for Sophie. See Butler's *Maria Edgeworth* 23, 37–39, 43–44, 50–52, 59, 71, and 100–101. Edgeworth herself pilloried Rousseau's notions of female education in *Belinda*, a point I take up in more detail in my discussion of that novel.

2

Visions of the Daughters of Albion

"Does he who contemns poverty and he who turns with abhorrence
From usury feel the same passion, or are they moved alike?
How can the giver of gifts experience the delights of the merchant?
How the illustrious citizen the pains of the husbandman?
How different far the fat fed hireling with hollow drum,
Who buys whole corn fields into wastes, and sings upon the heath!
How different their eye and ear! how different the world to them!
With what sense does the parson claim the labour of the farmer?
What are his nets & gins & traps; & how does he surround him
With cold floods of abstraction, and with forests of solitude,
To build him castles and high spires, where kings & priests may dwell;
Till she who burns with youth, and knows no fixed lot, is bound
In spells of law to one she loathes? and must she drag the chain
Of life in weary lust? must chilling, murderous thoughts obscure
The clear heaven of her eternal spring; to bear the wintry rage
Of a harsh terror, driv'n to madness, bound to hold a rod
Over her shrinking shoulders all the day, & all the night
To turn the wheel of false desire, and longings that wake her womb
To the abhorred birth of cherubs in the human form,
That live a pestilence & die a meteor, & are no more;
Till the child dwell with one he hates, and do the deed he loaths,
And the impure scourge force his seed into its unripe birth
Ere yet his eyelids can behold the arrows of the day?"
      William Blake, "Visions of the Daughters of Albion."

Some believe Blake's Oothoon to be Mary Wollstonecraft herself,[1] and indeed parts
of my epigraph strongly recall the arguments of her *Vindication of the Rights of
Woman*. While Blake's engraved illustrations of *Original Stories from Real Life*
establish that the poet was at least familiar with a portion of Wollstonecraft's work,
and the two unquestionably inhabited similar circles in London, no hard evidence

of their acquaintance has been unearthed. More interesting than such biographical speculation, however, is Blake's recapitulation in "Visions of the Daughters of Albion" of the feminist argument in terms of a vocabulary of personhood. I mean that Blake condemns a social code that describes the set of persons so as to exclude women, children, and many men. For Blake, this point cannot be divorced from an economic analysis. He suggests that it is the denial of legal or juridical personhood that permits slavery of many kinds, and, indeed, that the reduction of people to possessions is essential, rather than incidental, to capitalist economic structures. "Economy is the bone, politics is the flesh"[2]; on Blake's account, however, if political philosophy is about who counts, political economy is about the ends to which they count.

Nancy Armstrong's *Desire and Domestic Fiction* suggests quite powerfully that the terms by which people counted were shifting throughout the eighteenth century, from a vocabulary based on wealth and kinship to one based on qualities of the mind and behavior; in this philosophical shift, there is a concomitant economic shift in notions of the ends to which they count. And as Armstrong makes clear, thinking through these shifts involves rethinking the relationship between the domestic and the political domains. Rousseau's *Emile* is a milestone in this process, as I have shown, but I want now to examine the works of Mary Wollstonecraft, both devotée and critic of Rousseau's educational philosophy, in order to sketch some of the ways in which a vocabulary of mind may contribute to the negotiation of women's place, as persons and bearers of rights, in the state.

In *Mary, a Fiction* (1788), her first novel, Wollstonecraft undertakes, as she says, "to develop a character different from those generally portrayed" (*Mary* i). She will, she says, portray a woman who has "thinking powers. . . . [w]ithout arguing physically about *possibilities*" (*Mary* iii–iv). At this point we may usefully recall Rosemarie Bodenheimer's argument that social problem fiction circumscribes imaginative possibility for social thought, action, and change (3). Such fictions, for Bodenheimer, share the task of confronting and negotiating between the public languages of social relations and the intimate vocabularies of individual histories (231–32). On this account, Wollstonecraft's thinking woman may, in a fiction, "be allowed to exist" (*Mary* iv) precisely because Wollstonecraft is concerned with establishing the imaginative possibility of such a figure. Moreover, the process of defining and delimiting the boundaries of social possibility can, in this instance, be described as an extension of the imaginative horizon for women beyond, for example, that "particular purpose" Rousseau gives Sophie (*Emile* 364).

Charles Taylor points out that "[a]s men we are self-defining beings, and we are partly what we are in virtue of the self-definitions which we have accepted" (*Papers* 2:54). These self-definitions, for Taylor, are also definitions of norms, goods, and values, and thus they are also the "essential enabling condition" of certain social and political practices (*Papers* 2:107). Now, we saw with Bourdieu and Passeron that education always involves norms, goods, and practices in that it takes as its end the reproduction of that worldview from which its practice arises. Because this is so, educational practices always project an ideal addressee at the same time as they work to create that addressee. Among the implications of this dimension of educational practice is the importance of a real addressee's ability to project herself into the projected role of the ideal. What this means is that in order for women to lay claim to an education that posits the development of reason, they must first posit themselves as rational beings. It is clear from Taylor's analysis, however, that our self-definitions cannot be understood apart from the vocabularies used to describe them. Our self-understandings, because they are also definitions of what we hold to be good, right, and valuable, always require that we employ an evaluative vocabulary, such that our different desires can be characterized in relation to each other (*Papers* 1:19). Even the most simple weighing of alternatives will require such evaluation. But, as Taylor argues, the strong evaluator can perceive alternatives through a richer language, so that the desirable is not merely defined in terms of what is desired, or the desirability plus consequences, but also by a *qualitative* characterization of desires as higher, lower, noble, base, and so on (*Papers* 1:23). What is at stake, then, in the political-domestic fictions of Wollstonecraft, Opie, Edgeworth, Gaskell, and Dickens are precisely such self-definitions. I suggest that the conflict over the education of women is conducted through a debate over norms, goods, and values, and that, as Taylor claims, this debate necessarily involves a contest of self-understandings. This contest in turn involves contesting vocabularies. That is to say that the extension of the boundaries of social possibility requires the extension of our vocabularies, and this linguistic and social contest is the province of domestic fiction precisely because domestic fiction is concerned with the norms, goods, and values that define and delimit everyday life. Wollstonecraft's *Mary*, for example, makes use of a vocabulary of sublimity in deliberate counterpoint to other idioms of living. Such countering of idiom recalls Mikhail Bakhtin's argument in *The Dialogic Imagination* that old and new worlds are characterized by their own peculiar languages, which quarrel with each other (82). Bakhtin sees novelistic discourse as "heteroglossic"; that is, he defines the novel as the artistic organization of a diversity of social speech types and individual voices (262). In his reading, language is always dialogical because it is a struggle between socio-linguistic points of view (273). This, for Bakhtin, is true of any utterance in the novel, but it is also true of the work as a whole: It can be imagined as "a rejoinder in a given dialogue, whose style is determined by its interrelationship with other rejoinders in the same dialogue (in the totality of the conversation)" (274).

Mary, then, is a novel about idioms, or even idiolects. In it, Wollstonecraft does not simply privilege qualities of the mind over the signs of fortune and status, but presents a prolonged struggle between different vocabularies of the mind that results, finally, in the imperfect victory of the idiom of the sublime over the baser vocabulary of wealth. She does this, indeed, in much the same terms as Blake's Oothoon does in the passage that begins this chapter: First, by showing different idioms as incommensurable, and by asserting the superiority of one over the other, and second by linking this argument to one for the rights of women. Finally, I argue *pace* Taylor that, by introducing new terms in order to refine the evaluative vocabulary of female selfhood, Mary Wollstonecraft succeeds in altering the sense of the existing terms (see *Papers* 1:19).

Wollstonecraft posits, in the eponymous heroine of *Mary*, a being "whose grandeur is derived from the operations of its own faculties" (*Mary* iv). She opposes sublime creations like Richardson's Clarissa and Rousseau's Sophie[3] to the tamer paradigms of beauty, through which their imitators walk, "measur[ing] their steps in a beaten track, solicitous to gather expected flowers, and bind them in a wreath, according to the prescribed rules of art" (*Mary* ii). While Wollstonecraft's Mary is neither a Clarissa nor a Sophie, she too is intended to belong to the sublime moment, since, as Wollstonecraft says, her "grandeur" is self-creating and as such participates in the divine: "[D]rawn by the individual from the original source" (*Mary* iv).

But what does it mean to say that Mary's mental sublimity participates in the divine? Kant points out that "we are inaccurate if we term an object of nature sublime. . . . all we can say is that the object lends itself to a sublimity discoverable in the mind" (*Critique* 300). Clearly, for Kant, the importance of the sublime object lies not in the object itself, but in the emotions it arouses in the experiencing subject; the object — a mountain, a sea, a passage of Milton — is valuable because it is the means by which mental sublimity may be discovered and revealed. So it is with Mary:

Sublime ideas filled her young mind — always connected with devotional sentiments[4]; extemporary effusions of gratitude, and rhapsodies of praise would burst often from her, when she listened to the birds, or pursued the deer. She would gaze on the moon, and ramble through the gloomy path, observing the various shapes the clouds assumed, and listen to the sea that was not far distant. The wandering spirits, which she imagined inhabited every part of nature, were her constant friends and confidants. She began to consider the Great First Cause, formed just notions of his attributes, and, in particular, dwelt on his wisdom and goodness. (*Mary* 12–13)

I am not arguing that this passage should be read in terms of the aesthetic of the sublime. Instead of providing an account of the sublime moment, Wollstonecraft claims that moment as a property of Mary's mind. Significantly, Wollstonecraft links the experience of sublimity with the experience of the divine; the quality of mind that is signaled in her heroine is one that cannot be divorced from religious experience.

Thomas Weiskel describes a close affinity between the sublime moment and the religious one. He argues that the habitual system of reading landscape assumes a natural order of signs that is predicated on the authority of the Word, or Logos. To confound this order — to move between orders of meaning, to violate the habitual — is to confound reality (19). In Weiskel's reading the sublime moment begins where this habitual system breaks down and the accustomed order is invaded (19). In this collapse, as Weiskel points out, the mind makes the founding gesture of the human ego, and thus signals the move to another order of meaning, this time based on the authority of the human subject rather than on a transcendent, ordering Logos. An object, Weiskel says, is sublime "if the attempt to represent it determines the mind to regard its inability to grasp wholly the object as a symbol of the mind's relation to a transcendent order" (23). The object arrests the mind and fills it with an understanding of infinity and terror; a discontinuity ensues that ends when the mind begins to comprehend its own power, through a metaphorical identification with infinity. According to Weiskel's model, then, Mary's mountain retreat, where "twilight always reigned — [so that] it seemed the Temple of Solitude; yet, paradoxical as the assertion may appear, when the foot sounded on the rock, it terrified the intruder, and inspired a strange feeling, as if the rightful sovereign was dislodged" (*Mary* 25) affords such a moment. The sound of her own footsteps on the rocks inspires a terror that interrupts habitual modes of perception; but it is this interruption, by implication, that allows Mary to comprehend the power of her own mind. In this she fulfills Wollstonecraft's idea of the poet of original genius, "conversing with himself, and marking the impression which nature had made on his own heart. . . . when . . . the world seems to contain only the mind that formed, and the mind that contemplates it!" ("On Poetry" 8). This link to poetic genius is furthered by Mary's reading in her solitary retreat — Thomson's *Seasons*, Young's *Night-Thoughts*, and, significantly, *Paradise Lost*, all typically identified as sublime.[5]

While the invocation of a text on epistemological disobedience — Milton's Eve, after all, does bring mortality by eating the fruit of the tree of knowledge — may appear to be a caution against just the kind of mental aggrandizement asserted in the sublime moment, Wollstonecraft's treatment of *Paradise Lost* in the *Vindication* suggests otherwise. As Stephen Blakemore points out, Wollstonecraft criticizes Milton by inverting the myth of the fall: She says that "if men eat of the tree of knowledge, women will come in for a taste; but, from the imperfect cultivation which their understandings now receive, they only attain a knowledge of evil."[6] The fall here is into ignorance, rather than knowledge, because it is incomplete. Moreover, Wollstonecraft's *Paradise Lost* is clearly the Romantic, Blakean one, rather than the sterner Miltonic one she ably criticizes; while Milton's "pleasing picture of paradisiacal happiness" excites tenderness, she says that "instead of envying the lovely pair, I have, with conscious dignity, or Satanic pride, turned to hell for sublimer objects" (*Vindication* 94n2). And like Satan, Wollstonecraft and her Mary assert the sublimity of the human mind, which is "its own place, and in itself / Can make a Heav'n of Hell, a Hell of Heav'n."[7]

Yet Mary's reflections are not divorced from the god-term that Weiskel and others erect as a crucial reference point in the sublime moment. Wollstonecraft says that Mary's "Creator was almost apparent to her senses in his works; but they were mostly the grand or solemn features of Nature which she delighted to contemplate. She would stand and behold the waves rolling, and think of the voice that could still the tumultous deep" (*Mary* 27). Her association of religious devotion with the "grand or solemn" suggests that in claiming Mary's ability to experience the sublime, Wollstonecraft is likewise claiming for her the authority that the experience of the sublime confers in Weiskel's model. He suggests that what is achieved in the sublime moment is the ego's metaphorical identification with the infinity of God; this is that aggrandizement mentioned above as the founding gesture of an order of meaning that takes the mind of the human subject as its authority (23). I do not contend that Wollstonecraft's descriptions of Mary carry the vocabulary of the sublime to this conclusion. In the passage quoted above, as elsewhere, the apprehension of the sublime is arrested at that moment when Mary achieves the contemplation of the infinite, the Creator. She stops short of that metaphorical identification with infinity that Weiskel maintains as the moment in which the human mind may be erected as itself infinite. This leap would be left to the English Romantic poets who succeeded her. At the same time, Weiskel's analysis provides a helpful background for my claim that, by adopting the vocabulary of sublimity, if not its full content, Wollstonecraft is asserting the superiority, indeed the desirability, of Mary's qualities of mind over those of her companions and relatives. Moreover, as her allusion to *Paradise Lost* may suggest, the assertion of these mental qualities is itself a revolutionary claim.

If Mary's qualities of mind are articulated in terms of their capacity for the great and the sublime, her friend Ann's province is clearly that of the beautiful: "In every thing it was not the great, but the beautiful, or the pretty, that caught [Ann's] attention. And in composition, the polish of style, and harmony of numbers, interested her much more than the flights of genius, or abstracted speculation. She often wondered at the books Mary chose" (*Mary* 35). Ann's domain is the one Edmund Burke associated with the tame, the nonthreatening, and the submissive, ideas that are in turn linked to the passion of society and turn on gratification and pleasure (Burke 40–42). While both the sublime and the beautiful can be read in terms of their ability to assert the value of the human ego[8] — the notion of submission suggests both the control of the beautiful object by the human perceiver and the use of that object for human gratification — Wollstonecraft deliberately privileges the sublime. In so doing, she regenders an aesthetic advanced by Burke in particular as a masculine one.[9] But she also claims for her heroine a moral and intellectual superiority over her companions that is attributed in all cases to the greatness of her passions and the strength and cultivation of her mind. Ann, quite differently, is "timid and irresolute, and rather fond of dissipation; grief only had power to make her reflect" (*Mary* 35).

But grief, however strong, is not one of the grand passions in this paradigm. Burke tells us it is the result of a total and permanent loss of pleasure: "It is the nature of grief to keep its object perpetually in its eye, to present it in its most pleasurable views, to repeat all the circumstances that attend it, even to the last minuteness; to go back to every particular enjoyment, to dwell upon each, and to find a thousand new perfections in all, that were not sufficiently understood before" (37). This account aptly captures Ann's habits of constantly recalling her lost lover, of playing over his favourite songs and sketching views in which they walked together. But while grief is a passion, it belongs, for Burke, neither to self-preservation nor to society, the domains of the most powerful ideas (39). These are Mary's provinces. While Ann may experience some of the passions of society, particularly those relating to generation — she is most often associated with the appreciation of beauty, which belongs to the passions of propagation in Burke's account (40) — her predominant passion is grief. Sympathy, imitation, and ambition, which Burke describes as the three principal forms of the passion of general society (44), are alike closed books to her.

Mary's passions, however, are on a grander scale. Bound to Ann by pity for her friend's misfortunes, Mary is reconciled to her marriage of convenience in order to save Ann. A set of melodramatic coincidences leads Mary's father to propose her marriage to a friend's son as a means of settling an inheritance dispute at the same time as her mother lies dying and Ann and her mother stand on the verge of eviction. Mary's first reaction is one of "extreme horror at taking — at being forced to take, such a hasty step," but her friend's "miserable situation" recalls her to herself: "She loved Ann better than any one in the world — to snatch her from the very jaws of destruction — she would have encountered a lion. To have this friend constantly with her; to make her mind easy with respect to her family, would it not be superlative bliss?" (*Mary* 39). Pity, according to Burke, arises from love and social affection (46), but such emotions are incomprehensible to the unfeeling creatures who surround Mary. For her father, arguments drawn from philanthropy and friendship are in "a language he did not understand, expressive of occult qualities he never thought of, as they could not be seen or felt" (*Mary* 42–43). If Wollstonecraft's heroine is unconventional, she is so in the precise sense of one whose vocabulary of living departs from that of those around her. If conventions are indeed a type of social norm, they also, as Jon Elster points out, provide social equilibrium, in that when all follow the convention, not only does nobody want to deviate, nobody wants anybody else to deviate either (32–33). This is so because conventions may be understood in part as we understand language, such that on them depends much of what is cooperative and communicative in human behaviour (see Hjort xii–xiii). In this way much of the conflict of *Mary, a Fiction* may be understood metaphorically as linguistic, in the sense that Wollstonecraft seeks to evict the vocabulary of rank, fortune, state, and status as the idiom of living and replace it with a vocabulary of the mind.[10] Moreover, Wollstonecraft does so because she understands that the idioms of living are evaluative vocabularies, indeed normative ones, and that those vocabularies that succeed do so by becoming new equilibria, in Elster's sense.

It is the fashionable ladies that Mary and Ann meet in Lisbon, however, who are the occasion for Wollstonecraft's most pronounced attack on the customs and manners prevalent among women of her day:

Their minds were shackled with a set of notions concerning propriety, the fitness of things for the world's eye, trammels which always hamper weak people. What will the world say? was the first thing that was thought of, when they intended doing any thing they had not done before. Or what would the Countess do on such an occasion? And when this question was answered, the right or wrong was discovered without the trouble of their having any idea of the matter in their own heads. This same Countess was a fine planet, and the satellites observed a most harmonic dance around her. (*Mary* 65)

Ann may be a flawed, weak woman, capable of self-reflection only in grief, but she does, at least, have that power; these three ladies are "brought out of their nursery" rather than brought up in it, "[w]ithout having any seeds sown in their understanding, or the affections of the heart set to work" (*Mary* 66). If Ann can be understood as ignoble, then these ladies are base: "It appears to me," says the narrator, "that every creature has some notion — or rather relish, of the sublime. Riches, and the consequent state, are the sublime of weak minds: — These images fill, nay, are too big for their narrow souls (*Mary* 67).

Here aesthetic categories are being used quite differently than they were for Addison and Steele, where, as we have seen, immorality and vice is largely a matter of bad taste. For Wollstonecraft, although the aesthetic, the moral, and the social are closely linked, this is not because vice is disagreeable or unattractive, although it is these things. Rather, the sublime is itself both a moral and an ethical (and therefore social) category. In this she does not so much depart from Burke as revise his notions: In her letter to him on the French Revolution, *A Vindication of the Rights of Men*, she begins by saying that "truth, in morals, has ever appeared to me the essence of the sublime; and, in taste, simplicity the only criterion of the beautiful" (*Men* 7). The baseness of the Lisbon ladies, then, is a moral one, revealed through their misapprehension of the sublime as an object, and their consequent failure to dispose themselves as capable of aesthetic judgement.[11]

It might well be objected at this point that the Lisbon ladies, like Ann, are represented not only as moral commoners, but social ones. This is so because, though for Wollstonecraft morality is not merely a matter of taste, it is also taste; as Cottom makes clear, it is precisely because they are not common, "a property of the common people," that aesthetic judgments matter (367). Paradoxically, even as aesthetic judgments, like moral ones, pretend to universality, they remain the province of the educated and therefore the exceptional. Indeed, for Cottom, the pretension to universality lies in the stance of impartiality assumed by the observer, and this is a stance available only to the aristocracy (371). This is so also of moral judgments, of course, and thus we may gather from Cottom's argument that both moral and aesthetic perceptions are "tool[s] of eighteenth-century social order" (371). Yet must the social privilege inherent in the concept of a privileged mode of cognition necessarily deploy this mode as a tool of oppression?[12] The key lies in the grounds of privilege here. While I have no wish to deny to socio-economic grounds of the aesthetic of the sublime, the location of this privilege in a mental quality, accessible through education (if only education were accessible) means that as a sign of the aristocratic mind it effaces its own origins in economic privilege. Moreover, this effacement in its turn promises that the democratization of both taste and the morals with which it is associated may, indeed, be someday open to all. From this we may see that Cottom's otherwise fine analysis neglects the link between the education necessary for the aesthetic observer and the increasing eighteenth-century philosophical interest in the expansion of educational opportunity.

While Mary's passions are represented as more noble than Ann's or the fashionable ladies', however, passion alone does not suffice as an indicator of a noble mind in Wollstonecraft's analysis. In *Thoughts on the Education of Daughters* (1787), she returns again and again to the idea that passion, uncontrolled by reason, cannot lead to happiness (8; 79; 99–101; 116). Happiness in this usage is inextricably bound up with the idea of the moral life. We are happiest, she suggests, when we fulfill our moral duties, which are laid down for us by religious principles, and fulfill them rightly and well. The duties of women are those of the loving wife and the rational mother (*Education* 58), and so it is in these duties that passion and reason meet. The aim of education is to enable us to fulfill these duties — that is, to join reason to passion — in which we are sustained by faith (*Education* 58; 102; 126–27; 129). This, Wollstonecraft argues, is only possible because right education is not confined to instilling the necessary modesty in girls, but also involves teaching them the ability to combine ideas, which is reason. Only reason, so trained, enables us to fulfill our duties and find happiness in them: Only in working out our domestic duties in this way can we fulfill the duties of religion, which lead us to true and lasting happiness.[13] This may seem at first glance like a return to the conventional idioms of living, and indeed Wollstonecraft does not occupy in *Thoughts on the Education of Daughters* that more radical position she would come to in her *Vindication of the Rights of Woman*. But even here we may see the seeds of her later argument in her reliance on reason not simply to suppress the passions but to combine with them so that our desires may truly fulfill our basic purposes and not the caprices of the moment.

Right reason, in other words, is central to Wollstonecraft's political philosophy as it is central to *Mary, A Fiction*. Without right reason, Ann must be unhappy because she is ruled only by her grief, and such a passion, uncontrolled, must always be ignoble. Cut off from the great passions, both Ann and the fashionable ladies are also cut off from all that sets Mary apart. She is capable of great passion because she is great in mind and heart. Incapable of affection, the fashionable ladies must be incapable likewise of that sympathy that arises from it. In this sense the noble ladies must always remain base because they can lay claim to kinship only with the aristocracy of blood and not the aristocracy of mind. To be sure, they practice both imitation and ambition, which Burke includes with sympathy among the passions of general society (44). But where Mary's "taste and judgement were both improved by contracting a habit of observation" (*Mary* 43), the ladies substitute imitation for thought, as their "servile cop[ying] of the Countess's airs" (*Mary* 65) shows. They do not observe the world, forming their own manners, opinions, and lives in response to it, but are governed by it.[14] We saw in the last chapter that such government by public opinion is, for Rousseau, the "throne" of a woman's virtue (*Emile* 365); for Wollstonecraft, however, as we see in the born ladies, the abandonment of reason in favour of opinion is the abandonment of virtue as well. Indeed, her Mary is not Sophie, but Emile himself; the ladies in Lisbon, on the other hand, have the purposes and desires of Rousseau's women without their endorsement or responsibility for either. While they are not without ambition, their ambitions are confined to "riches, and the consequent state" (*Mary* 67); they have little in common with that satisfaction in excelling that Burke claims was given to man by God to prevent us remaining as brutes (Burke 50). Indeed, they are as incapable of experiencing the sublime as brutes, and as such must be understood almost as creatures without souls, an image that recalls Wollstonecraft's summary assertion in *Thoughts on the Education of Daughters* that fine ladies lack moral qualities (157). Exterior accomplishments, she argues, "[i]f the understanding is not employed" (*Education* 25), are "at best but trifles" (*Education* 26). Without the ability to think, which only right education can grant, even faith and religious principles must remain empty, and the moral domain closed off.

It is worth recalling at this point that Mary is, for the most part, self-taught, as she is self-governed. I have already remarked the importance of "observation" in Wollstonecraft's Mary; habits of observation are treated here as both self-determining and conducive to self-reflection. Wollstonecraft appears to attribute both Mary's failings and her virtues to this autodidacticism. More precisely, Mary's self-government falters in part *because* she is self-taught. Mary's reading affords an awareness of the sublime lacking in the other characters, but at the same time, because Wollstonecraft discredits the idea of a native genius (a point I will return to), the absence of a real teacher renders her "too much the creature of impulse" (*Mary* 17). In this Wollstonecraft's ideas resemble those of Rousseau, not for Sophie but for Emile. Jean-Jacques's teaching is incomplete when it depends only on the simplicity of nature (*Emile* 444), because, while "nature delivers us from the ills it imposes on us, or it teaches us to bear them . . . nature says nothing to us about those which come from ourselves. It abandons us to ourselves" (*Emile* 445). In abandoning us to ourselves, moreover, it abandons us to our passions, and the untrammelled rule of the passions is slavery. Jean-Jacques tells Emile, "[a]ll passions are good when one remains their master; all are bad when one lets oneself be subjected to them" (*Emile* 445); only reason, which permits us to conquer our passions and to do our duty, enables us to be virtuous by enabling us to be really free (*Emile* 444–45). Mary cannot be really free in this sense, as she cannot be really virtuous, because even apparently virtuous passions must be governed, and not govern, the moral self. But insofar as her impulses are never corrected, and thus come to govern her, self-teaching cannot fully become self-government.[15] Mary then is not fully virtuous because her impulses render her "the slave of compassion" (*Mary* 17), but even her imperfect education is sufficient to render Mary morally superior to her fellows. With the possible exception of her lover, Henry, Mary remains the only character capable of truly sublime passions, and thus the only one able to comprehend the divine. This is clearest, I think, in the shipwreck incident.

I remarked earlier that Wollstonecraft, on many occasions, does not so much provide an account of the sublime moment as she adopts its signs to claim that capacity for Mary; the shipwreck incident remains an important exception. Mary is on her way back to England when she witnesses the last-minute rescue of several victims of a storm. She takes charge of one of the victims, and after putting her to bed, returns to "view the angry deep": "[W]hen she gazed on its perturbed state, she thought of the Being who rode on the wings of the wind, and stilled the noise of the sea, and the madness of the people — He only could speak peace to her troubled spirit! she grew more calm; the late transaction had gratified her benevolence, and stole her out of herself" (*Mary* 123–24). Here, the "angry deep" recalls God for Mary, and in the moment of that recollection, she is "stole[n] out of herself"; that is, her thoughts are arrested and she turns to the contemplation of infinity in "the great day of judgement" (*Mary* 125). Her meditations on "this awful day" (*Mary* 125) begin with submission to the transcendent god-term — "The Lord God Omnipotent reigned, and would reign for ever, and ever!" (*Mary* 124) — but in that submission, Mary obtains a kind of self-transcendence that recalls Weiskel's model of the sublime. Weiskel points out that the "proud flight" of the soul in the sublime moment appears, simultaneously, to acknowledge the authority of God and to fulfill the identity of the experiencing subject (10). Mary internalizes the infinity on which she meditates, and in that internalization achieves her own transcendence by asserting the power of her own mind: "'I try to pierce the gloom, and find a resting-place, where my thirst of knowledge will be gratified, and my ardent affections find an object to fix them. Every thing material must change; happiness and this fluctating [sic] principle is not compatible. Eternity, immateriality, and happiness, — what are ye? How shall I grasp the mighty and fleeting conceptions ye create?'" (*Mary* 127). Even in this moment of religious submission, Mary claims a mental authority that sanctions her claims to knowledge; while she does not restructure the god-term with herself at its centre through a moment of metaphorical identification, as later practitioners of the sublime would do, she invokes the transcendent as a means of establishing her own right, in religious terms, to achieve understanding through knowledge. Her inquiry into the nature of "[e]ternity, immateriality, and happiness," in Cartesian terms, is a subjection of all things, even transcendent authority, to interrogation by her own reason. Such interrogation is, for Wollstonecraft as it was for Descartes, a precondition of knowledge. Only right reason, derived from the ability to combine ideas and thus to think (*Education* 22), can lead to fixed principles, religious or otherwise, and only in the achievement of these principles can we achieve happiness, understood as a moral state.

I said in my introduction to this chapter that Wollstonecraft adopts the structure of the sublime moment as a political gesture that authorizes certain of her feminist claims. It is my claim that Wollstonecraft's effort to establish and to authorize a vocabulary of the mind culminates in this passage, where she, in effect, authorizes Mary's attempts to author a new idiom of female selfhood through reference to the divine. Here Wollstonecraft hearkens back to the same religious obligations that authorized Astell and Chudleigh's assertions of the proto-autonomy of women's reason. This is so despite those passages early in *Mary, a Fiction* in which Mary's overflowing passions are roundly criticized. It may be so that "she was too much the creature of impulse, and the slave of compassion" (*Mary* 17), she may indeed have been "in love with misery" (*Mary* 91), but these qualities are redeemed by their origin in love and affection, tamed by reason and knowledge, and so lead to the divine. Moreover, responsibility for Mary's faults is attributed to failures in her education, as are the faults of the fashionable ladies and the "vicious poor" (*Mary* 135); with the new authority acquired from an identification with God in the sublime moment, the "thirst of knowledge" is finally justified. More, the female self, posited in terms of qualities of the mind rather than station, becomes in the sublime moment the addressee of education, and thus potentially free as Emile is free.

The heroine of *The Wrongs of Woman, or Maria; A Fragment*, which remained incomplete at the time of Wollstonecraft's death in 1797,[16] resembles that of *Mary* in that she, too, is represented as a woman of noble sensibility. This characterization is deliberate; as in *Mary*, it is the extraordinary woman with whom

Wollstonecraft is concerned. Despite her declared intention to show the oppressions that are "peculiar to women," so that "the history ought rather to be considered, as of woman, than of an individual" (*Wrongs* I.viii), she clearly believes that this account will be more effective (and affecting) if the wronged woman possesses the kind of emotional and psychological depth signaled by a vocabulary of the sublime:

I cannot suppose any situation more distressing, than for a woman of sensibility, with an improving mind, to be bound to such a man as I have described for life; obliged to renounce all the humanizing affections, and to avoid cultivating her taste, lest her perception of grace and refinement of sentiment, should sharpen to agony the pangs of disappointment. Love, in which the imagination mingles its bewitching colouring, must be fostered by delicacy. I should despise, or rather call her an ordinary woman, who could endure such a husband as I have sketched.[17]

In *The Wrongs of Woman*, however, this vocabulary is part of a complex argument devoted less immediately to the "false system of education" (*Vindication* 73) than to erecting female selfhood as personhood in the civic and legal sense. Wollstonecraft addressed her novel to "the partial laws and customs of society" (*Wrongs* I.viii) that by refusing to grant women the rights and responsibilities of legal personhood, permitted the kinds of abuses she describes.

Crucially, Wollstonecraft concerns herself in *The Wrongs of Woman* largely with the status of married women, who were not properly persons at all in the legal sense. The eighteenth-century jurist Sir William Blackstone tells us that "By marriage, the husband and wife are one person in law: that is, the very being or legal existence of the woman is suspended during the marriage, or at least is incorporated and consolidated into that of the husband: under whose wing, protection, and *cover*, she performs every thing" (I.441; Blackstone's emphasis). Prior to the reforms of the nineteenth century, this was the condition of women during marriage, called *coverture*, because a wife (*feme-covert*, as opposed to *feme-sole*, a single woman past the age of consent) is said to be "under the protection and influence of her husband, her *baron*, or lord."[18] Indeed, English law enshrined Rousseau's fiction of the single moral person formed in marriage as a legal fact. Thus, by English common law, a man could not form covenants with his wife, and marriage itself voided any prior compacts between the two; while he was obligated to provide his wife with the necessaries of life, no charge could legally be made upon him for anything besides these necessaries. By civil law, a husband became master of his wife's "real property" (that is, freehold land), and any income from it, but could not dispose of it without her consent during her lifetime; a married woman could not will real property away from her children or other legal heirs. Any "personal property" — chattels and anything other than land — passed into absolute possession of her husband. The gentry by and large adopted the practice of marriage settlements, under the laws of equity, so that the wife's property, with some restrictions, was held for her by a trustee, thus giving married women protected property rights analogous to those of a *feme-sole*. It was not, however, until 1870 that the first Married Woman's Property Act guaranteed wives personal enjoyment of their own earnings, investments, inheritances, rents, revenues, and larger gifts of money.[19]   Blackstone points out that the disabilities of the wife, through coverture, "are for the most part intended for her protection and benefit. So great a favourite is the female sex of the laws of England" (I.445), but argues that the distinctions between men and women in both criminal law and civil rights — including rights of property — give him "little reason to pay a compliment to our laws for their respect and favour to the female sex" (I.445n23). Once married, moreover — once "the very being or legal existence of the woman [was] suspended" (I.441) — the newly created nonentity had little recourse, since prior to the controversial Matrimonial Causes Act in 1857, no civil procedure existed for the granting of divorce.[20] It is too strong to assign to Wollstonecraft or her predecessors direct responsibility for such reforms, and indeed Lawrence Stone asserts that the feminists of the late seventeenth and eighteenth century, like Astell and Wollstonecraft, apparently "had no practical effect at all except to alienate many men" (14). For Stone it is only in the 1830s, 1840s, and 1850s, when "well-born, well-connected, and intelligent but carefully unthreatening women like Caroline Norton and Barbara Leigh Smith Bodichon" begin to lobby the lords of the earth that significant changes to male attitudes and statute law occur (14). Yet even the "unthreatening" activities of Norton and Bodichon were, I suggest, enabled by the discourse of female selfhood, even *personhood*, created by those early feminists Stone dismisses.

As Wollstonecraft makes clear, it is in the first instance precisely such "matrimonial despotism of heart and conduct" that appears to her "the peculiar Wrongs of Woman" (*Wrongs* I.x), a despotism made possible through the denial of women's civil rights. As I will show, Wollstonecraft's argument is conducted first through an elaboration of that female self of exalted sensibility already described in *Mary, a Fiction*. In *The Wrongs of Woman*, however, Wollstonecraft goes on to link this argument explicitly to one that rejects the view of women as brute creation, to advocate for their personhood.

Like Mary, Maria's qualities of mind are articulated through her ability to appreciate the great and the sublime. Here, however, it is neither terrifying nature nor the creations of original genius that afford the experience of the sublime in the first instance, but the more solemn sight of fallen humanity. Imprisoned in a madhouse, Maria looks out on "the poor wretches who strayed along the walks":

What is the view of the fallen column, the mouldering arch, of the most exquisite workmanship, when compared with this living memento of the fragility, the instability, of reason, and the wild luxuriancy of noxious passions? . . . . Thus thought Maria — These are the ravages over which humanity must ever mournfully ponder, with a degree of anguish not excited by crumbling marble, or cankering brass, unfaithful to the trust of monumental fame. It is not over the decaying productions of the mind, embodied with the happiest art, we grieve most bitterly. The view of what has been done by man, produces a melancholy, yet aggrandizing, sense of what remains to be achieved by human intellect; but a mental convulsion, which, like the devastation of an earthquake, throws all the elements of thought and imagination into confusion, makes contemplation giddy, and we fearfully ask on what ground we ourselves stand. (*Wrongs* I.25–27)

I have quoted this passage at length because I think a number of rhetorical moves important for Wollstonecraft's purposes are being made here. First, as an experiencing subject capable of mental sublimity, Maria is erected as a noble figure, an extraordinary and great-souled woman in lucid counterpoint to those her lover Darnford later describes as frivolous, ignorant, and wanting both taste and ease (*Wrongs* I.60–61). Second, Maria's mental superiority is further underlined by the structure of the sublime moment. As in the shipwreck incident of *Mary* described above, the sublime moment is the occasion for the aggrandizement of the human subject, a moment in which the focus of contemplation turns inward, to the authority and potentiality of the human intellect.

More is going on in this passage, however, than the self-transcendence of Maria or of the human ego generally. It is not insignificant that the sublime moment is here afforded not by "crumbling marble, or cankering brass" (*Wrongs* I.26) but by "the most terrific of ruins — that of a human soul" (*Wrongs* I.25). By associating madness with overflowing passion (enthusiasm) and the failure of reason, Wollstonecraft returns to the point she made in *Thoughts on the Education of Daughters* on the dangers of passion uncontrolled by right reason. At the same time, the failure of reason is attributed less to "[e]nthusiasm turned adrift, like some rich stream overflowing its banks" (*Wrongs* I.25–26) than to wilful human error. It is this that terrifies,[21] that "throws all the elements of thought and imagination into confusion," because what man has done to these "poor wretches" he may do to anyone, and the speaker herself may be in danger. But it is also here that Wollstonecraft is clearly leaving room for the possibility of reform. Her view of the "poor wretches" excites more anguish than "the fallen column, the mouldering arch" because it is not an inevitable result, like those wrought by time, but a view of "what has been done by man."[22] The same phrase, I suggest, that asserts the transcendence of the human mind in the sublime moment, "what remains to be achieved by human intellect," also implies that what has been done can be undone. My reading here is borne out by Wollstonecraft's assertions, in *Thoughts on the Education of Daughters* as well as in her *Vindication of the Rights of Woman*, that it is the education of reason that alone can control the passions.[23]

The notion of right reason in Wollstonecraft's works is closely involved with her idea of what it is to be human. She argues in the *Vindication* that if women have souls, there is but one path to virtue: Through the education of reason. True virtue cannot, she says, be acquired without strength of mind, and without this ability to reason, women can only be the "gentle, domestic brutes" described by Milton in his Eve (*Vindication* 89). Wollstonecraft's claim that there can be no virtuous being "whose virtues do not result from the exercise of its own reason" (*Vindication* 90) can be understood as a successor theory to Descartes's idea of the sovereignty of reason in all deliberations. The Cartesian point, picked up by Astell and Chudleigh among others to feminist or proto-feminist ends, involved an important conceptual shift in that it placed responsibility for ideas and conduct squarely in the hands of the (female) individual. For Wollstonecraft, as for Astell and Chudleigh, this assumption of responsibility becomes a religious principle. If virtue lies only in the right use of reason, and without reason we are "a swarm of ephemeron triflers"

(*Vindication* 88), then as women are moral beings (*Vindication* 94) — as they are human — their obligation to God is the obligation, first, to think. Moreover, this obligation takes explicit precedence even over duties for Wollstonecraft, as it did not for Chudleigh or Astell: "Connected with man as daughters, wives, and mothers, their moral character may be estimated by their manner of fulfilling those simple duties; but the end, the grand end of their exertions should be to unfold their own faculties and acquire the dignity of conscious virtue" (*Vindication* 95).

The author of the *Vindication of the Rights of Men* makes explicit in her *Vindication of the Rights of Woman* what has been theoretically possible in political philosophy since the days of Locke and the parliamentarians: That the authority of husbands and fathers, like the authority of kings, is arbitrary and contingent.[24] This is, perhaps, clearest in her Dedication:

Consider . . . whether, when men contend for their freedom, and to be allowed to judge for themselves respecting their own happiness, it be not inconsistent and unjust to subjugate women, even though you firmly believe that you are acting in the manner best calculated to promote their happiness? Who made man the exclusive judge, if woman partake with him the gift of reason?

In this style, argue tyrants of every denomination, from the weak king to the weak father of a family; they are all eager to crush reason; yet always assert that they usurp its throne only to be useful. Do you not act a similar part, when you *force* all women, by denying them civil and political rights, to remain immured in their families groping in the dark? for surely, Sir, you will not assert, that a duty can be binding which is not founded on reason? (*Vindication* 67)

What is at issue here? The myth of Adamic authority, the originary myth of patriarchical power, has long been dismissed; in explicitly linking her dismissal of patriarchal male dominance[25] to the philosophies of Locke as well as to the American and French Revolutions,[26] Wollstonecraft does no more than recast the claims of Astell and Chudleigh in the form of a call to arms. Nor is her claim that women have souls, that they are indeed moral beings, particularly new. Significantly, however, she is also arguing that, granted these premises, women ought to be free "in a physical, moral, and civil sense" (*Vindication* 266), and in this she goes far beyond both Astell and Chudleigh.

This contention on behalf of women for legal personhood, for full humanity, cannot be considered apart from Wollstonecraft's claim that virtue stems only from reason. Right reason is no more an innate idea than the love of dress[27]; it can only be achieved through an education whose goal is "to enable the individual to attain such habits of virtue as will render it independent" (*Vindication* 90). But without an extension of moral and civic freedoms to women, this education cannot occur and the reason must lie fallow; in such a case women remain no more than brutes or slaves, with virtue forever closed to them:

Let woman share the rights and she will emulate the virtues of man, for she must grow more perfect when emancipated, or justify the authority that chains such a weak being to her duty. — If the latter, it will be expedient to open a fresh trade with Russia for whips; a present which a father should always make to his son-in-law on his wedding day, that a husband may keep his whole family in order by the same means; and without any violation of justice reign, wielding this sceptre, sole master of his house, because he is the only being in it who has reason: — the divine, indefeasible earthly sovereignty breathed into man by the Master of the universe. Allowing this position, women have not any inherent rights to claim; and, by the same rule, their duties vanish, for rights and duties are inseparable. (*Vindication* 266)

Wollstonecraft's concern in the *Vindication* is with what it means to be a person, in the legal and civic sense, as this passage clearly shows. This is also her concern in *The Wrongs of Woman*, where it is articulated in terms of a vocabulary of the noble and the base. The same may be said of *Mary, a Fiction*, but in *The Wrongs of Woman* Wollstonecraft takes the implications of this idiom one step further, so that this vocabulary of worth, expressed in terms of qualities of the mind rather than outward signs and symbols, is directed away from the focus on grand sensibilities that is the province of Wollstonecraft's first novel in order to emphasize what it *means* to be fully or properly human. This impulse is clearest in Wollstonecraft's treatment of Jemima.[28] When the madhouse attendant is first introduced, she is described in terms that suggest she is herself only a little better than a brute, with "little of the divinity of virtue" (*Wrongs* I.13). For Wollstonecraft, as I have shown, we are human only insofar as we partake of the divine. Divine virtue is dependent on right reason, as we know from Wollstonecraft's other writings, but it is also inspired by right feeling, and thus the humanization of Jemima cannot be divorced from the growth of her sensibilities. Her sympathy for Maria is the yardstick by which this process is measured; it is first awoken when she hears that Maria's child has been stolen from her (*Wrongs* I.15). Crucially, this awakening of sympathy is part of the awakening of reason: "A sense of right seems to result from the simplest act of reason, and to preside over the faculties of the mind, *like the master-sense of feeling*, to rectify the rest" (*Wrongs* I.16; emphasis mine).

Jemima's sympathy is, like Ann's grief, an awakened passion, but a more noble one. Although grief "had the power to make [Ann] reflect" (*Mary* 35), her reflections are barren and solipsistic, as we have seen. Jemima's sympathy, on the other hand, as one of the three principal forms of the passions of general society in Burke's model, is linked to love and social affection (Burke 46). Through sympathy, Jemima enters into the concerns of another, and ceases to be an indifferent spectator (see Burke 44); even more significantly, it is Jemima's compassion for Maria that turns this outcast toward society again, by reawakening right feeling "in a bosom long estranged from feminine emotions" (*Wrongs* I.15). I have already observed that Wollstonecraft attributes the failure of reason, not to internal causes, but to external ones; madness, in effect, is wrought by man. The failure of right feeling has a similar cause. Jemima has been "hunted from hole to hole, as if she had been a beast of prey, or infected with a moral plague" (*Wrongs* I.16); treated as a creature, she responds like one. Called upon for sympathy, however, she responds as a woman. Indeed, it is through Jemima that we may most readily understand the ways in which Wollstonecraft links the noble sentiments, that vocabulary of the noble mind that characterizes *Mary, a Fiction*, to her argument in *Thoughts* and in the *Vindication* for women's reason and consequent virtue.

"The culture of the heart," as Maria believes, "ever keeps pace with that of the mind" (*Wrongs* I.115). Both, like right feeling, depend on humanity in its fullest sense, even as it is these properties that determine our humanity. Brought to tears for the first time in her life by social enjoyment, Jemima "seemed indeed to breathe more freely; the cloud of suspicion cleared away from her brow; she felt herself, for once in her life, treated like a fellow-creature" (*Wrongs* I.76). It is sympathy that brings Jemima to this humanity, both her own initial compassion for Maria, and that affinity of fellowship she shares with Maria and Darnford. Even as these passions render Jemima more human, they do so in part because such qualities are finally about entering into the community, into society; this is why it is these qualities that determine our humanity. Insofar as we are human, we cannot be so outside of a community, however small it might be; Jemima's potential for humanity is therefore realized in her sympathy with and for Maria and Darnford.

I have said that *The Wrongs of Woman* delineates the struggles of extraordinary women, rather than of women in general. I was speaking there of Maria, but I suggest that this is likewise true of Jemima, at least in Wollstonecraft's account. Jemima is "no fool, that is, she was superior to her class; nor had misery quite petrified the life's-blood of humanity" (*Wrongs* I.11). Yet why, if Wollstonecraft wants to show that brutish treatment can create only brutes, even if those brutes are of the gentle and domestic sort, does she then render characters who are manifestly more than creatures? I will return to this point when I deal with Gaskell and the political dimensions of domestic fiction. I will show in detail there what I remark in passing here, that the extension of rights in the liberal polity depends on a conception of the bearer of rights as a being of inner depth and complexity. Insofar as political philosophy is about who counts, it describes the set of those who count as characterized by certain properties, and in the liberal state, these properties are internal ones. In this sense, Jemima counts. She counts because, even if she is poorly educated, even if she has descended almost to brutishness, she still possesses these qualities in principle and in potential, and in her these qualities may be brought forward. Thus she can in principle advance the political claims these properties enable. While in recent years the conception of the liberal individual as autonomous, rational, and capable of free action has been criticized for the way in which it circumscribes, constrains, and indeed misrepresents the human self as constituted in society, such accounts neglect the emphasis on education in liberal thought, an emphasis that means we achieve autonomy through our constitution as selves in society and not otherwise.[29] Such accounts ably point out the perils of atomistic conceptions of human life, but obscure those ways in which liberal notions of individual autonomy afforded rights for many who had for centuries been left out of the circle of those who count on external grounds. Wollstonecraft is part of the movement of liberalism in this sense; she emphasizes qualities of mind in order to redraw the circle of those who count on newly interiorized grounds.

Marilyn Butler has argued that the genre of the novel was progressive because it emphasized the individual hero or heroine and the inner life of the protagonist (*Jane Austen* 10–11). The sentimental novel in particular, she points out, was innovative in harnessing the sympathy of the reader (*Jane Austen* 17). While Butler also suggests, I believe wrongly, that Wollstonecraft, like the other "jacobinical novelists" of the 1790s, was unable or unwilling to adopt this technique (*Jane Austen* 32), she does pinpoint two of the ways in which the novel can gesture toward its characters as potential bearers of rights. I will return to this point in more depth in my next chapter, but for now let me observe that Jemima, however misshapen by her treatment, must be represented as more than a brute so that she can be shown to deserve nonbrutish treatment. At the same time, if it is part of Wollstonecraft's argument that the laws and customs of the land deprive women of their virtue by depriving them of humanity, her heroines must be extraordinary ones who have escaped the full weight of this system. Moreover, they must be extraordinary women for whom the line between the human and the nonhuman is easily blurred, so that "we fearfully ask on what ground we ourselves stand" (*Wrongs* I.27).

Jemima's story in particular demonstrates the ways in which the distinction between the human and the brute is readily lost: "'treated like a creature of another species . . . I began to envy, and at length to hate'" (*Wrongs* I.83). She has been, she says, "'described as a wretch,'" an "'obstinate mule,'" kicked about "'like the dog or cat'" (*Wrongs* I.87) — all terms that underscore her claim that she is a creature of another species. Described and treated as completely other, Jemima is inevitably completely estranged: "'[W]hat should induce me to be the champion for suffering humanity? — Who ever risked any thing for me? — Who ever acknowledged me to be a fellow-creature?'" (*Wrongs* I.127) And yet it is no part of Wollstonecraft's project to show Jemima's estrangement, her brutishness, as total; knit in with the terminology of the creature are the signs and signals of proper feeling. Jemima desires "'the caresses, and kind expressions'" of her step-mother (*Wrongs* I.83); finding herself pregnant, she feels "'a mixed sensation of despair and tenderness'" (*Wrongs* I.92), and when she finds a temporary harbour, she acquires a "'taste for the rational, nay . . . the virtuous enjoyments of life'" (*Wrongs* I.116–17). Her estrangement is thus mediated by a vocabulary not wholly base. This, I think, is necessary to Wollstonecraft's argument. If Jemima is capable of right feeling, then she is to some degree like us, and therefore to that same degree she is human; if human, she is like us a bearer of rights, or potentially so.

There is a serious tension in Wollstonecraft's vocabulary between the extraordinary and the ordinary, just as there is a tension between the idea of the creature and the idea of the human self. Wollstonecraft's difficulty with this last is that she wants to claim both that virtue (which makes us human) is a result of a proper education, which instills right feeling and right reason, and that it is brutal treatment that creates brutes. Implicit in this last is the idea that we are not born creatures, but become them through ill-treatment; this suggests an innate humanity, and thus an innate virtue, which in fact Wollstonecraft disavows. I want to argue, however, that while the tension between these two impulses creates problems for Wollstonecraft's vocabularies of selfhood in *The Wrongs of Woman*, it does not, finally, hamper her argument. This is so because our notion of personhood, in the legal and moral sense, rests philosophically as much on potential capacities as it does on actual ones. When, for example, we argue that newborn human infants, as well as adults, are legal persons and thus bearers of certain rights under the law, we are arguing for the rights of the infant based on future capacity. It is important to note in this respect that the law extends rights to children only in a limited sense. Thus they have the right to life (the murder of a child is equal under the law to the murder of an adult), but they do not have the right to vote, or to form contracts.[30] This distinction is made by drawing a line between legal persons and legal adults, which last refers to a kind of agency, understood in law by the term "competence."

As humans, then, we are bearers of rights in a way that animals and things are not. We cannot, for example, be bought, or sold, or killed with impunity; we have these rights at minimum, because as humans we have, as Charles Taylor says, certain capacities that are the condition of this moral status: We have a sense of self, a notion of the future and of the past, we can hold values, make choices, adopt life-plans. Philosophically, and legally, a person is the kind of being who is in principle capable of these things, and thus is a being with her own point of view on things, whose choices and actions are in some sense attributable to her as their point of origin.[31] I suggest that the vocabulary of personhood introduced by Wollstonecraft in *The Wrongs of Woman*, and carried out in terms that contrast the creature and the thing with the human self, is making an argument for liberal personhood in this legal sense. The *OED* says that "to wrong" is to do harm or injury *to a person*; only if we are bearers of rights can we be wronged. Wollstonecraft's difficulty, then, between the idea of the creature and the idea of the self is logically and philosophically no difficulty at all. She need not claim an innate virtue, or innate reason, in order to contend for the humanity of women; she need only claim the in-principle capacity for these things. Moreover, emphasizing reason and virtue as capacities rather than essences enables Wollstonecraft to suggest in her fiction what she argues in her prose: That it is education alone that enables the individual to become independent, to fulfill these capacities, as a full person or a competent adult.

I have so far been focusing attention on the ways in which Wollstonecraft makes private virtue dependent on education. My discussion of the ways in which the notion of virtue is linked to a complex vocabulary of personhood, however, should make it clear that this issue of private virtue and personal education cannot, for Wollstonecraft, be divorced from wider questions about the nature of the polity. Like Rousseau, she believes that the purpose of education is to form citizens (*Vindication* 233–34); again like Rousseau, she understands citizenship in terms of qualities of the mind — and these qualities are affective as well as rational. She says in the *Vindication* that "if you wish to make good citizens, you must first exercise the affections of a son and a brother. This is the only way to expand the heart; for public affections, as well as public virtues, must ever grow out of the private character" (234). This means that for Wollstonecraft there is no such thing as a private sphere, not, at least, in the way twentieth-century critics have understood the term; rather, public virtue is characterized as an aggregate of that private virtue on which it is founded. With this understood, we see that in Wollstonecraft's analysis, the "false system of education . . . considering females rather as women than human creatures" (*Vindication* 73), because it renders them incapable of virtue, destroys virtue in the state:

[T]he more understanding women acquire, the more they will be attached to their duty — comprehending it — for unless they comprehend it, unless their morals be fixed on the same immutable principle as those of man, no authority can make them discharge it in a virtuous manner. They may be convenient slaves, but slavery will have its constant effect, degrading the master and the abject dependent. . . . The box of mischief thus opened in society, what is to preserve private virtue, the only security of public freedom and universal happiness? (*Vindication* 67–68)

This is a significant claim. Wollstonecraft contends that public virtue — that is, the virtue of the polity — depends on the private virtue of its citizens. I maintain that this claim is central to nineteenth-century conceptions of the state, so much so that the household, in which we first achieve private virtue, is the cornerstone *of* the state. This is so for Wollstonecraft because she posits the legal person as capable of right feeling and reason, and thus a self; this self needs education in private virtue in order to become a proper citizen, exercising public virtue. Moreover, because the capacity for such virtue is internal rather than external, Wollstonecraft posits the female self as potentially a citizen in this sense. I will return to this point at length in chapter 4; in what follows, however, I will highlight the ways in which two revisions of Wollstonecraft's ideas nevertheless adopt her view of the significance of private virtue.

NOTES

1.   Nelson Hilton, reading "Visions of the Daughters of Albion" as Blake's reflections on the author of the *Vindication*, says "[t]hough circumstantial, the evidence that Blake was personally acquainted with Wollstonecraft is compelling" (70). Mary Lynn Johnson and John E. Grant assume acquaintance between the two and generate their reading of Oothoon as Wollstonecraft on these grounds (69). Raymond Lister, similarly, says Blake's "Visions of the Daughters of Albion" was at least partly inspired by the *Vindication of the Rights of Woman*, written by "his friend Mary Wollstonecraft" (47). James King dissents from this view, positing no acquaintance and questioning the depth of Blake's sympathy with Wollstonecraft (76).

2.   This phrase is Marge Piercy's. See "In the men's room(s)," *Circles on the Water* 80.

3.   Wollstonecraft is explicit about her character's difference from Clarissa and Sophie, and implicit about the sublimity of all of these: "These chosen few, wish to speak for themselves, and not to be an echo — even of the sweetest sounds — or the reflector of the most sublime beams" (*Mary* iii).

4.   Wollstonecraft may have included this clause in an effort to forestall criticisms of her work as "atheistical." Hannah More, whose *Strictures on the Education of Women* was published in 1799, attacked Wollstonecraft as a "professed admirer and imitator of the German suicide Werter" (I:45) as part of a general and vitriolic condemnation of the "blasphemy and unbelief" of contemporary educators (1–54).

5.   See Burke, 59, 61–62, 80, 174–75, and Kant, *Observations* 47.

6.   *Vindication* 89; qtd. Blakemore 454.   I am indebted to Blakemore for my understanding of the significance of this allusion in *Mary*, although I am uncomfortable with his conclusion that Wollstonecraft's use of the canon necessarily implicates her in Milton's value system, "restor[ing] the ideological configurations of a reactive, reactionary text" (478).

7.   Milton I.254–55. Gary Kelly notes in his discussion of *The Wrongs of Woman, or Maria* that Wollstonecraft shared this Miltonic belief with William Godwin and others of his circle (*English Fiction* 41).

8.   I have investigated eighteenth- and nineteenth-century landscape aesthetics in terms of human control and use elsewhere. See Johnston 29–42.

9.   For treatments of gender and aesthetic categories in Wollstonecraft's countering of Burke, see Myers; Paulson 81–84; Sapiro.

10.   I take the phrase "idiom of living" from the opening paragraph of Jane Rule's *Desert of the Heart*:

Conventions, like clichés, have a way of surviving their own usefulness. They are then excused or defended as the idioms of living. For everyone, foreign by birth or by nature, convention is a mark of fluency. That is why, for any woman, marriage is the idiom of life. And she does not give it up out of scorn or indifference but only when she is forced to admit that she has never been able to pronounce it properly and has committed continually its grossest grammatical errors. For such a woman marriage remains a foreign tongue, an alien landscape, and, since she cannot become naturalized, she finally chooses voluntary exile. (5)

11.   Meg Armstrong argues that this dual usage of the sublime, as "both an effect of an *object* which inspired terror *and* the disposition of a subject capable of aesthetic judgement" was an eighteenth-century effect of the work of Burke and Kant (214).

12.   Huet, whose essay on "The Revolutionary Sublime" has informed my thinking on this issue, concludes, with regret, that it must:

In a Revolutionary ideology that meant to channel the "sublime enthusiasm" of the people toward a sublime religion, that of a Supreme Being, and to make the people favor public over private interests, the "sublime project" suffered from a double threat: the moral law it proclaimed defied all representation, and the political structure it relied upon, by virtue of its representative principle, could only betray the sublime principles it meant to translate. The democratic intent of political representation was bound to be betrayed by the very system on which it relied. (63)

13.   Wollstonecraft anticipates here John Stuart Mill's revision of Bentham's greatest happiness principle. Mill writes in *Utilitarianism* (1861) that "[i]t is quite compatible with the principle of utility to recognise the fact, that some *kinds* of pleasure are more desirable and more valuable than others" (211). It is better, for Mill as for Wollstonecraft, "to be a human being dissatisfied than a pig satisfied; better to be Socrates dissatisfied than a fool satisfied. And if the fool, or the pig, is of a different opinion, it is because they only know their own side of the question. The other party to the comparison knows both sides" (*Util*. 212). See Chapter II of *Utilitarianism* for Mill's discussion of qualitative and quantitative measures of pleasure and happiness.

14.   See Burke's discussion of imitation, 49.

15.   This is despite Wollstonecraft's own sense, throughout *A Vindication of the Rights of Woman*, that, counter Rousseau's idea of education, nature itself, combined with reflection, is the best teacher (see esp. 180–81), since she is clear that knowledge of others teaches what the right object of the passions might be, to which imagination is at best a lying guide (*Vindication* 180).

16. *The Wrongs of Woman, or Maria; A Fragment* was first published in 1798 by William Godwin, who collated and revised the various drafts.

17. *Wrongs* I.ix–x. Godwin includes this passage, from a letter by Wollstonecraft to George Dyson (ca. May 15, 1797), in the Author's Preface to *The Wrongs of Woman*, and later editors follow his lead. For the full text of the letter, see No. 317 in Wardle's *Collected Letters of Mary Wollstonecraft* (391–92).

18. Blackstone I.441. See Harman for an excellent discussion of the ontological implications of this legal nullity ("In Promiscuous Company" 353–57).

19. The Married Woman's Property Act of 1870 essentially extended the principles of equity to all married women's property, but it wasn't until the reform of the Act in 1882 that married women were able to hold as their separate property both that owned at the time of marriage and any acquired thereafter. See Holcombe for a treatment of property law reform.

20. Prior to 1857 divorces could be granted only through the actions of the ecclesiastical courts, or through an Act of Parliament. Dickens touches on this problem through his treatment of Stephen Blackpool and his wife in *Hard Times*. See Stone's mammoth *Road to Divorce: England 1530–1987* for a history of the making and breaking of marriage.

21. Terror, of course, is productive of the sublime. According to Burke, "[w]hatever is fitted in any sort to excite the ideas of pain, and danger, that is to say, whatever is in any sort terrible, or is conversant about terrible objects, or operates in a manner analogous to terror, is a source of the *sublime*. . . . When pain or danger press too nearly, they are incapable of giving any delight, and are simply terrible; but at certain distances, and with certain modifications, they may be, and they are delightful, as we every day experience" (39–40).

22. In the chamber adjoining Maria's, for example, is a "lovely maniac" (*Wrongs* I.38) who, according to Jemima, "'had been married, against her inclination, to a rich old man, extremely jealous . . . and that, in consequence of his treatment, or something which hung on her mind, she had, during her first lying-in, lost her senses'" (*Wrongs* I.39).

23. And note that for Gary Kelly, Maria's "incorrect education" leads to "excessive sensibility, a culture of emotional excess" that is then exploited by her villainous husband, Venables (*English Fiction* 38).

24. Note that Wollstonecraft here anticipates John Stuart Mill's condemnation of domestic tyranny: "Not a word can be said for despotism in the family which cannot be said for political despotism. Every absolute king does not sit at his window to enjoy the groans of his tortured subjects, nor strips [sic] them of their last rag and turns them out to shiver in the road" (*Subjection* 286).

25. Patriarchy and patriarchicalism refer to a specific form of male dominance based by analogy on the Adamic myth, as is Sir Robert Filmer's 1680 *Patriarcha*, which Locke refutes in his *First Treatise*, in which "*the False Principles and Foundation of* Sir *Robert Filmer*, and His Followers, are Detected and Overthrown" (tp, rpt. *Two Treatises* 153). To refer to conditions of male dominance prevalent in North America in the late twentieth century as patriarchy tends to obscure the fact that conditions of dominance take many concrete forms.

26. Her title is a deliberate echo, both of her own work defending the French Revolution, and of Paine's seminal book.

27. *Vindication* 110–13; Wollstonecraft here attacks Rousseau's claim that the female role as ornament is natural to them, from their innate vanity and love of dress.

28. "[S]he had only a claim to a Christian name, which had not procured her any Christian privileges" (*Wrongs* I.15). Nor, I might add, did it entail much in the way of Christian virtue, as delineated by Wollstonecraft.

29.   Judith Butler, for example, argues in "Contingent Foundations" that the idea of autonomy "cover[s] over" the constitution of the subject through exclusion and differentiation (45–46). Thus, she says, "the autonomous subject can maintain the illusion of its autonomy insofar as it covers over the break out of which it is constituted" (46). Since "the constituted character of the subject is the very precondition of its agency" (46), to conceal its constitution represents for Butler a grave abandonment of the possibility of radical politics. Yet here she misconstrues the liberal use of autonomy, even as she challenges liberal misconstructions of her idea of the postmodern subject. This is so because, as we see in Wollstonecraft's treatment of Jemima, we achieve autonomy and rationality in the liberal sense through that education that constitutes us, and not otherwise; what exists prior to our constitution is not autonomy, not reason, but its possibility.

30.   In the Canadian case of the Crown v. Robert Latimer (November, 1994), in which Latimer was convicted of second-degree murder in the death of his twelve-year-old, severely disabled daughter, the moral and legal discourse surrounding the case turned on the question of to what degree quality of life may be considered a sufficient condition for abrogating these rights. The defense, significantly, in no way disputed the facts of the matter. Instead, they based their case on the notion that Latimer acted morally by putting an end to the suffering of his daughter. This case brings to the forefront of public debate the legal and moral question of at what point mental and physical handicaps constitute sufficient grounds for considering a human being to be entirely outside the domain of rights. The laws of Canada consider the severely mentally handicapped to be persons in a limited sense, as children are; that is, they are legal persons but not legal adults. If, as those opposed to the verdict in the Latimer case have argued, Latimer's actions do not constitute murder, then their argument must be based, at least implicitly, on the idea that Tracy Latimer was not a person, a claim I find repugnant.

31.   See Charles Taylor's "The Concept of a Person," *Papers* 2: 97–114, esp. 97.

3
Revisions

What, then, is the rightful limit to the sovereignty of the individual over himself? Where does the authority of society begin? How much of human life should be assigned to individuality, and how much to society?
— John Stuart Mill, *On Liberty*

Wollstonecraft's work is part of the revolutionary oeuvre of the 1780s and 1790s. The French Revolution had a powerful impact on the liberal intellectual avant-garde of late eighteenth-century Britain (Cazamian 36; Kelly, *English Fiction* 12, 24–42); it seemed to promise a real victory for individualism and the doctrine of free choice. But this movement, as Cazamian and others have pointed out, was abruptly foreclosed by the Terror and Britain's subsequent wars with France.[1] The effect of these events was to extend the conservative response to the French Revolution from the aristocracy, who genuinely feared that what happened in France could easily happen in Britain, to the middle classes. By 1800 intellectual Britain was firmly in the grip of an anti-Jacobin reaction, and the radical *roman-à-thèse* that had flourished under the Jacobins had become a thing of the past.

This is not to say, however, that the novel as a genre abandoned the revolutionary debate. Indeed, the debate continued in the novel long after Jacobin issues had all but vanished from political circles. Gary Kelly has shown that political anxieties in Britain, both domestic and foreign, led to renewed attempts to uncover "a 'national' consensus in transcendental values or 'national' culture," not in the now-outmoded novel of ideas but in domestic fiction or village tales.[2] These domestic and community realisms, however, are in fact a continuation of Wollstonecraft's project. I want to argue that the contest of vocabularies that so clearly marks Wollstonecraft's fiction continued throughout the Napoleonic period, and that this contest, and the debate over the nature and status of the self it marked, had effectively become the province of fiction. I claimed that Wollstonecraft's political philosophy depended on a belief in the innate perfectibility of mankind, and that this belief, for Wollstonecraft, betokens a belief that all human beings ought, in a just state, to stand as bearers of rights. To this end she introduced a vocabulary of qualities of the mind, which highlighted a kind of inner complexity, right feeling, and capacity for virtuous action that she saw as philosophically necessary to the liberal polity's conception of the free citizen. Significantly, this vocabulary does not vanish with the rise of more conciliatory fictions; instead, as I will show, thinkers like Maria Edgeworth and Amelia Opie had to contend with the vocabularies of selfhood introduced by the revolutionaries in order to defeat what they perceived as a dangerously atomistic individualism.

Maria Edgeworth's version of freedom, as it occurs in *Belinda* (1801), differs from the more extreme individualism advanced by Wollstonecraft and Rousseau. Like her father, Richard Lovell Edgeworth, Maria Edgeworth found Rousseau's notions of education, and the kinds of freedom to which such education led, profoundly distasteful. While Edgeworth's discomfort with the atomistic version of freedom Rousseau advocated for men can be attributed to her awareness of the ways in which this education had failed her brother Richard,[3] *Belinda* is equally uneasy with the profoundly relational freedom Rousseau accorded to Sophie. This novel, then, advances an idea of female education and a consequent notion of the nature and status of the female self in the polity that is at odds with the ideas of both Wollstonecraft and Rousseau. At the same time, *Belinda* can be seen as a kind of conciliatory move; Edgeworth's purpose here, I suggest, is to mitigate the kind of atomism advanced by Wollstonecraft and the romantic revolutionaries, without abandoning either their idea of the female self-as-citizen *or* the idea of interior qualities as the foundation of public virtue.

Edgeworth's heroine, Belinda Portman, is, as any heroine of the ingenue novel must be, "handsome, graceful, sprightly, and highly accomplished" (11: 5). For all that, however, her aunt's upbringing has failed in its object: "[H]er aunt had endeavoured to teach her that a young lady's chief business is to please in society, that all her charms and accomplishments should be invariably subservient to one grand object — the establishing herself in the world" (11: 5). This recalls Rousseau's conviction that "woman is made to please and to be subjugated" (*Emile* 358), and his related idea that all of a woman's education ought to be devoted toward this end. In this respect Belinda's aunt's teaching has failed; Mrs. Stanhope "did not find Belinda such a docile pupil as her other nieces" (11: 5). This failure is attributed to a conflict with the earliest stages of her education: Belinda "had been educated chiefly in the country; she had early been inspired with a taste for domestic pleasures; she was fond of reading, and disposed to conduct herself with prudence and integrity" (11: 5). Here, then, the education of reason not only conflicts with the sexual instrumentalism Mrs. Stanhope tries to inculcate, but *resists* that instrumentalism. Edgeworth's attempt in *Belinda* to negotiate between distrust of Wollstonecraft's idea of freedom and support for the education of women's reason is represented from the outset in terms of a conflict between different kinds of education. Mrs. Stanhope trains Belinda in the spirit of Rousseau's principles for Sophie, although to be fair it is unlikely that Rousseau imagined women acquiring the pleasing arts to such Machiavellian ends as Mrs.

Stanhope intends. Mrs. Stanhope's one concern is Belinda's "establishment," and "the course of documenting" (11: 8) she puts the girl through tends entirely toward this purpose. While Belinda escapes the ill effects of this training to some degree, becoming "more insensible to the praises of her personal charms and accomplishments than young women of her age usually are, because she had been so much flattered and *shown off*" (11: 8), she is a Rousseauean exemplar of docility and gentleness, acting "in general . . . but as a puppet in the hands of others" (11: 8).

Mrs. Stanhope wants Belinda to *appear* ingenuous; her machinations, however, do little but create a real ingenue, and it is on this tension between appearance and reality that much of *Belinda* turns. The character of Lady Delacour first signals this conflict: "Abroad she appeared all life, spirit, and good-humour — at home listless, fretful, and melancholy; she seemed like a spoiled actress off the stage, over-stimulated by applause, and exhausted by the exertions of supporting a fictitious character" (11: 9). Heather MacFadyen has linked Lady Delacour's fictions of the self to the educational conflicts of the novel through what she calls Edgeworth's "trope of fashionable reading" (426). The self-indulgent, even sensual, reading of Lady Delacour supports her "fictitious character," indeed supports a series of "nondomestic" appearances; Belinda's domestic reading, on the other hand, supports both her self-regulation and her ultimate ability to regulate Lady Delacour's desires.[4] And the contrast between these two modes of reading marks the imperfections of a world more than willing to take the appearance for the reality. When Belinda writes from Lady Delacour's house to Mrs. Stanhope, in a burst of moral indignation at the domestic misery of the Delacour house and what she reads — correctly — as Lady Delacour's moral equivocation, Mrs. Stanhope dismisses her objections. It is enough, for Mrs. Stanhope as for the world, that Lady Delacour continue to be visited "by the first people in town. . . . as long as the lady continued under the protection of her husband, the world might whisper, but would not speak out" (11: 14). This is the ugly and hypocritical side of the concern for reputation advocated by Rousseau for his Sophie; in a moral climate in which, as Rousseau says, "even appearances [are] among the duties of women" (*Emile* 361), it is the Lady Delacours whose qualities are prized by the world. This is so despite Rousseau's use of a vocabulary of selfhood that erects qualities of the mind over and above the external signs of rank, order, and fortune that had previously marked the desirable woman. The valuation of mental qualities cannot, for Rousseau's women, be divorced from the behaviour that signals those qualities, because, in his account, women are able to fulfill their basic purpose only in so far as they are *perceived* to be able to fulfill it. Such an understanding of selfhood, in fact, holds reputation (the interpretation of behaviour) to be unequivocally and unproblematically coincident with mental qualities, or indeed more notable than true or private character.

Belinda can be described as part of a backlash against Rousseau's notions of education, and the freedom that stems from it, in two ways. First, the gap between appearance and reality, which is a constant feature in Edgeworth's account of Belinda's social career, suggests that she intends to criticize roundly the weight

Rousseau gave to public opinion. Belinda is worthy, noble, and valuable because these are her qualities of mind and because her behaviour accords with the prudence and integrity of her character. She is seen, however, by Clarence Hervey and the fashionable men who surround him as yet another man-trap niece of Mrs. Stanhope, the "*catch-match-maker*" (11: 13). That the incident in which Belinda is exposed to these unflattering opinions occurs at a masquerade, and, moreover, at a masquerade at which Belinda and Lady Delacour appear each in the guise of the other (they trade their respective costumes secretly, at the last minute), merely underscores the folly of taking appearances for reality in Edgeworth's world. Even the cynical Lady Delacour recognizes this problem. It may be that she is cynical because she recognizes that "'it is so difficult to get at facts, even about the merest trifles. . . . Actions we see, but their causes we seldom see — an aphorism worthy of Confucius himself'" (11: 164).

At the same time, I think, Edgeworth's reluctance to endow public opinion with any kind of unusual clairvoyance does not mean that she is endorsing a notion of the individual as somehow metaphysically independent of society and its opinions. If she is repulsed by Sophie's education, and the wholly relational female self it implies, she likewise opposes the Aemilean independence Wollstonecraft tried to claim for women.[5] We see this in the value that Edgeworth does, after all, accord public opinion. Certainly Hervey and his fellows err in assuming that "'one of the Stanhope school'" is by this alone proven "'a composition of art and affectation'" (11: 23), but it is through this exposure to the world's views that Belinda becomes aware of the dangers of Mrs. Stanhope's training. Lady Delacour, trying to comfort Belinda's tears after the girl's encounter with public opinion, tells her: "'[D]ry up your tears, keep on your mask, and take my advice; you'll find it as good as your aunt Stanhope's'" (11:26). Belinda is revolted: "'My aunt Stanhope's! O,' cried Belinda, 'never, never more will I take such advice; never more will I expose myself to be insulted as a female adventurer. Little did I know in what a light I appeared; little did I know what *gentlemen* thought of my aunt Stanhope, of my cousins, of myself'" (11: 26). Edgeworth here criticizes that romantic individualism that takes its own self-understanding as incorrigible. There is a gap, certainly, between the light in which Belinda appears and her real self; public opinion is dangerous because it is unable to distinguish between the two. But it is also true in the fiction that the opinion the fashionable men hold of Mrs. Stanhope and Belinda's cousins is, on whole, seen as correct.

My notion here that Edgeworth is condemning both Wollstonecraft's regendering of romantic individualism and Rousseau's purely relational view of women raises, of course, the question of how, in fact, she sees the nature and role of women in the polity, and to what ends their education ought to be directed. Belinda debuts as an ingenue, but comes of age when she becomes capable of relying on her own conscience rather than on the dubious advice of either Lady Delacour or Mrs. Stanhope.[6] Living in Lady Delacour's house, Belinda is "really placed in a difficult and dangerous situation" (11: 137). The house is frequented by "[a]ll the fashionable dissipated young men in London" who "considered a niece of Mrs. Stanhope's as their lawful prize" (11:137). Nor are the ladies of London society any help to Belinda on her entry into the world; "while they affected to scorn, they sincerely feared, her charms" (11: 137). Thus abandoned, Belinda is

left entirely to her own discretion . . . exposed at once to the malignant eye of envy and the insidious voice of flattery; she had no friend, no guide, and scarcely a protector. Her aunt Stanhope's letters, indeed, continually supplied her with advice, but with advice which she could not follow consistently with her own feelings and principles. Lady Delacour, even if she had been well, was not a person on whose counsels she could rely. Our heroine was not one of those daring spirits who are ambitious of acting for themselves; she felt the utmost diffidence of her own powers, yet at the same time a firm resolution not to be led even by timidity into follies which the example of Lady Delacour had taught her to despise. Belinda's prudence seemed to increase with the necessity for its exertion. It was not the mercenary wily prudence of a young lady who has been taught to think it virtue to sacrifice the affections of her heart to the interests of her fortune — it was not the prudence of a cold and selfish, but of a modest and generous woman. (11: 137)

It is Edgeworth's idea of "prudence," as we see it here, that most accurately captures the ways in which her thought mitigates Wollstonecraft's romantic-revolutionary argument for the rights of women without ever fully adopting that counter-revolutionary emphasis on community goods over and against individual goods we will see in Amelia Opie. While Edgeworth delineates in lucid detail the ways in which the gaps between appearance and reality mean that reputation is always and inevitably a fallible — and fallacious — indicator of mental quality, she is not by any means ready to abandon the notion of community goods she sees as reflected partly in judgments from reputation. Certainly such judgments are not infallible, but, as Lady Delacour says, "'we must take the world as it goes — dirt and precious stones mixed together'" (11: 136). The world may be wrong in painting Belinda with her aunt's brush, just as it is wrong in advancing the rumour that Belinda will marry Lord Delacour if his lady should die (11: 186–87), but it is the role of prudence, which Edgeworth associates with moral courage and candour, to address such wrongs. This, indeed, is Clarence Hervey's argument on speaking to Belinda about these rumours. He says, "'I believe that half the miseries of the world arise from foolish mysteries, — from the want of courage to speak the truth. Now that you are upon your guard, your own prudence will defend you sufficiently'" (11: 187). Lady Anne Percival, Edgeworth's ideal type of the rationally moral woman, shares Hervey's opinion[7]:

"As we cannot alter the common law of custom, and as we cannot render the world less gossiping, or less censorious, we must not expect always to avoid censure; all we can do is, never to deserve it — and it would be absurd to enslave ourselves to the opinion of the idle and the ignorant. To a certain point, respect for the opinion of the world is prudence; beyond that point, it is weakness." (12: 17)

Now, "prudence," according to the *OED*, refers to an ability to "discern the most suitable, politic, or profitable course of action," a definition that seems to capture that kind of prudence Edgeworth describes as "mercenary" and "wily" (11: 137). The *OED*, however, goes on to describe prudence as referring especially to conduct.

It is "practical wisdom," "discretion," and stems either from the Latin *prudens*, meaning foreseeing and sagacious, or from *providens* by way of "provident," with some weakening of the notion of foreseeing. To be prudent is thus to be "sagacious in adapting means to ends"; it is "having sound judgement in practical affairs."[8] This emphasis on prudence as a kind of practical judgment, I think, captures Edgeworth's sense of the term, and the ways in which she sees it as a necessary quality for combating the calumny that, we are assured, "[n]o one can escape" (11: 187).

It is prudence, rather than Wollstonecraftian right reason, that Edgeworth sees as necessary to a happy and moral life, and this idea of prudence is one, I think, that suggests mental self-reliance. After all, it is Belinda's prudence that is exercised when she is unable to rely on the advice of her friends, first Mrs. Stanhope and Lady Delacour, and then even Lady Anne Percival, who desired Belinda to marry Mr. Vincent against her better judgement. It is an idea that, in Edgeworth's estimation, includes both reason and experience; Belinda is prudent not merely because she subjects her notions, her instincts, her desires to sober second thought, but because she is also willing to learn from the world. This is the trait above all others that Lady Anne Percival admires in Belinda; "'[h]appy are those,'" she exclaims beatifically, "'who can turn all the experience of others to their own advantage!'" (12: 16). Belinda comes to mental self-reliance not through any romantic notion of herself as independent from, and superior to, society and its claims, but through the operation of both reason and experience. Crucially, in Edgeworth's analysis, right reason is not merely the compound of rational reflection and proper feeling that it is for Wollstonecraft, but practical reason; it is reason in the world, "practical wisdom," and not philosophy outside of it.

Against this idea of prudence Edgeworth counterposes two important minor characters. The first is Virginia, Clarence Hervey's protégée, whom he has raised *à la* Rousseau, "secluded from all intercourse with the world" (12: 135). He plans, romantically, to educate a wife by taking a beautiful, innocent girl and keeping her from the contaminants of the fashionable world, as Rousseau's Sophie is kept. But Hervey fails to understand what is clear to Edgeworth, which is that, as Colin and Jo Atkinson point out, "the Rousseauian argument for preserving the 'natural' innocence and ignorance of women is absurd in a practical world."[9] Hervey's project, for Edgeworth, is predicated on the assumption that innocence and ignorance are identical (M. Butler, *Jane Austen* 142); it thus runs counter to even Addison and Steele's highly instrumentalist arguments for female virtue, which took a minimalist version of education to be necessary for the preservation of virtue. Without knowledge, as we have seen in thinkers from Chudleigh to Wollstonecraft, innocence cannot be virtue, because the wholly ignorant self is not properly a self at all. This assumption becomes clear when Virginia[10] rejects Hervey's gift of diamonds. Hervey wants to "prove the simplicity of [Virginia's] taste, and the purity of her mind" (12: 136); to this end, he presents her with a pair of diamond earrings and a moss rosebud, asking her to choose between them. She chooses the rose over the diamonds because it reminds her of her grandmother's cottage; the diamonds she rejects, saying "'[t]hey are pretty sparkling things — what are they?

of what use are they?'" (12: 136). Hervey is, of course, charmed by his "child of nature," seeing her indifference as "an indisputable proof of her magnanimity, and of the superiority of her unprejudiced mind" (12: 136) But his own prejudices have led him into error, in this case:

[T]here was more of ignorance and timidity, perhaps, than of sound sense or philosophy in Virginia's indifference to diamonds; she did not consider them as ornaments that would confer distinction upon their possessor, because she was ignorant of the value affixed to them by society. Isolated in the world, she had no excitements to the love of finery — no competition, no means of comparison, or opportunities of display; diamonds were consequently as useless to her as guineas were to Robinson Crusoe on his desert island. . . . These reflections could not possibly have escaped a man of Clarence Hervey's abilities, had he not been engaged in defence of a favourite system of education, or if his pupil had not been quite so handsome. (12: 136–37)

Innocence, in Edgeworth's vision, is not a valuable moral category; Hervey's creature, Virginia, is innocent when she is a child, but remains so only in so far as she remains ignorant. Innocence thus guarantees neither delicacy nor prudence; Belinda, discursing with Harriot Freke on the rights of women, blushes, as Mrs. Freke says, because she understands. Mr. Percival recognizes that Freke "'would have them understand without blushing'" (11: 221) but argues that the moral choice in educating women is not merely between knowledge and ignorance. Edgeworth is playing in this novel with different notions of innocence: One that counterposes innocence to knowledge, as Hervey does, and that is better understood as ignorance, and another that understands innocence solely in relationship to guilt. Knowledge need not be guilty knowledge, in Edgeworth's understanding, and prudence is a more likely guarantor of innocence than ignorance. Hervey learns his mistake by observing Belinda's conduct. Virginia is a child, "insipid, though innocent" (12: 143), Belinda his equal:

Belinda had cultivated taste, an active understanding, a knowledge of literature, the power and habit of conducting herself: Virginia was ignorant and indolent; she had few ideas, and no wish to extend her knowledge: she was so entirely unacquainted with the world that it was absolutely impossible she could conduct herself *with that discretion which must be the combined result of reasoning and experience.* Mr. Hervey had felt gratuitous confidence in Virginia's innocence; but on Belinda's *prudence*, which he had opportunities of seeing tried, he gradually learned to feel a different and a higher species of reliance, which it is neither in our power to bestow nor to refuse. The virtues of Virginia sprang from sentiment; those of Belinda from reason. (12: 144, emphases mine)

It is clear from this passage that ignorance, in Edgeworth's estimation, is anything but bliss. It is, rather, a defect, and not a particularly amiable one (see 11: 225), and if Edgeworth opposes Wollstonecraft's radical feminism she is no friend to those who would keep women ignorant under the pretense of preserving their innocence.

Significantly, Edgeworth concludes her chapter on the "Rights of Women" with a discussion among the Percivals, Mr. Vincent, and Belinda in which Vincent defends the ignorance and indolence of the Creole ladies he admires, and the

Percivals respond with an answer that anticipates that of John Stuart Mill to the narrow vision of human goods attributed by some to the utilitarians.[11]

> "And in general," said Lady Anne Percival, "does Mr. Vincent wish to confine our sex to the bliss of ignorance?"
> "If it be bliss," said Mr. Vincent, "what reason would they have for complaint?". . . .
> "You leave reason quite out of the question, then," said Mr. Percival, "and refer the whole to taste and feeling? So that if the most ignorant person in the world assert that he is happier than you are, you are bound to believe him."
> "Why should not I?" said Mr. Vincent.
> "Because," said Mr. Percival, "though he can judge of his own pleasures, he cannot judge of yours; his are common to both, but yours are unknown to him. Would you, at this instant, change places with that ploughman yonder, who is whistling as he goes for want of thought? or would you choose to go a step higher in the bliss of ignorance, and turn savage?" (11: 225–26)

If experience, like feeling, is a necessary part of prudence, it is clear from the foregoing that it is not a sufficient one. Reason, too, must come into play, and it is through the character of the aptly named Harriot Freke that Edgeworth draws this lesson. Freke, or "freak," as Atkinson and Atkinson point out, does not in *Belinda* denote a monstrosity or abnormality, but a whim or a caper.[12] This idea of Harriot as a creature ruled by her humours, her whims, is an important one. She is an irrational, capricious, and self-indulgent woman who is ruled not by principles or reason, but by her own momentary and fleeting passions. And Harriot's freaks have appalling consequences: She causes Lady Delacour to be compromised with Captain Lawless, who dies in the consequent duel with Lord Delacour; she instigates the ladies' duel in which Lady Delacour and her opponent, Mrs. Luttridge, narrowly escape a ducking at the hands of the outraged villagers, and Lady Delacour incurs the ulcerated wound in her breast; she terrifies a young black servant almost to death by playing on his superstitions; and the list goes on. Mrs. Freke, indeed, can be understood as a wanton in the philosophical sense; while she sets herself up as a defender of individual goods against the custom and usage of society, she in fact is represented as having no other notion of the good than what gives immediate pleasure. And here I disagree with Kowaleski-Wallace's claim that Lady Delacour's cure installs a new form of patriarchal domesticity by repressing important female desires, represented even as they are expelled through the figure of Harriot Freke. The repression of these desires is, for Kowaleski-Wallace, necessary to the "new-style patriarchy" that had gradually replaced the paternalism and hierarchy of old-school patriarchal despotism with an "appeal to reason, cooperation between the sexes, and noncoercive exercise of authority" (110). Kowaleski-Wallace sees the "home economics" of *Belinda* as advocating this new form of male dominance, which she calls patriarchy and not liberalism, because it involves the denial of female desires and the entrenchment of separate spheres.[13] But she errs in assuming that the desires Freke represents are, in fact, desirable — and that the freedom to act on them is a worthwhile freedom. As Marilyn Butler points out, for Edgeworth Belinda is more and not less free than Harriot Freke, who is ruled, in fact, by her passions (*Jane Austen* 142), and is therefore enslaved to them. Moreover, the private immorality provoked by Freke's self-indulgent passion inevitably has public consequences:

"It is difficult in society," said Mr. Percival, "especially for women, to do harm to themselves without doing harm to others. They may begin in frolic, but they must end in malice. They defy the world — the world in return excommunicates them — the female outlaws become desperate, and make it the business and pride of their lives to disturb the peace of their sober neighbours. Women who have lowered themselves in the public opinion cannot rest without attempting to bring others to their own level." (12: 23)

Self-indulgence, then, for Edgeworth as somewhat differently for Wollstonecraft, is a great evil that can only be combated by the right use of reason; but it is not a private evil. I will return to this point in greater depth in my next chapter, but for now let me remark that even for the domestic novelists, such as Edgeworth, the domestic sphere is *not* a separate one. There are crucial continuities between it and the public sphere in the domain of ethics and morals, which suggest that there can be no such thing as a private morality just as there can be no such thing as a private language. Moreover, I contend here that Edgeworth's emphasis on private virtue as the ground of public virtue is not, as Elizabeth Kowaleski-Wallace and Mary Jean Corbett have found it, a reinstallation of patriarchal values in terms of consent rather than coercion, but a substantial, and substantially liberal, shift away from ideas of dominance in this sense.[14] Consent is, after all, no small matter; it involves mental self-reliance and independence of the kind, for example, we have seen operating through the idea of prudence. And prudence, as defined by Edgeworth through the character of Belinda and in contrast to Harriot Freke and Virginia, consists, in fact, partly in determining what the public consequences of private actions will be, whether virtuous or vile.

Belinda, then, attempts to reconcile both Wollstonecraft's radical individualism and Rousseau's equally strong view of women as purely relational, and does so by examining the gap between appearance and reality, public "appearance" and private "reality." Only right reason — practical wisdom or "prudence" — can close this gap; only right reason, achieved through right education, can bring about the exemplary female self-as-citizen whose private morality stands as the foundation of public virtue. And Edgeworth's concern with the bridging of this gap, between appearance and reality, private character and public virtue, is part of a fundamental shift since Wollstonecraft in what I have termed the idioms of living, as we can see in Amelia Opie's rearticulation of these concerns in her 1804 novel, *Adeline Mowbray, or, The Mother and Daughter*. While far more conservative, Opie shared with Wollstonecraft and Edgeworth a profound concern with education and private virtue, just as she shared with them a belief that private virtue was the necessary ground of public virtue. If Edgeworth and Opie finally disagreed on the form and manner of this virtue, they shared with Wollstonecraft, Godwin, and their circle a belief in the control of the passions as a precondition for both public and private morality. Indeed, the reaction of anti-Jacobinical writers such as Jane West and Amelia Opie to what they perceived as the sexual immorality of the women revolutionary novelists can be attributed to their conviction that the intimate sphere is the originary space of the public domain, and thus that nothing less than the future of Britain rested on the virtue of its women.

Adeline Mowbray; or, The Mother and Daughter makes such a case. It is not, perhaps, surprising that Opie's work should betray some sympathy for and some continuity with the position of the Jacobin writers. She had once been, after all, a friend of both William Godwin and Mary Wollstonecraft, and her marriage with John Opie, Wollstonecraft's portraitist, enshrined her for a time firmly in the intellectual circles that surrounded the publisher Joseph Johnson in London in the 1790s.[15] Nor should it be surprising that *Adeline Mowbray*, finally, reveals more hostility to Wollstonecraft's position than sympathy for it; by the time of its publication in 1804, the anti-Jacobin reaction was firmly entrenched both politically and philosophically. But *Adeline Mowbray* can be a useful yardstick for measuring something besides the extent of the anti-Jacobin reaction in Britain. It also reveals the degree to which the vocabulary of moral personhood forwarded by Mary Wollstonecraft had finally and permanently altered the terms on which the debate over women's education took place.

Mary Wollstonecraft had argued from a belief in women's capacity for moral autonomy, based on assertions of right reason and right feeling, for the abolition of those laws and customs that kept women in a kind of permanent nonage. Amelia Opie addresses *Adeline Mowbray* not to abolition, but to the preservation of these customs. So radically had Wollstonecraft altered the terms of the debate, however, that Opie conducted her argument, as Edgeworth did, on grounds established by Wollstonecraft. Thus Opie's eponymous heroine, like those of Wollstonecraft, is an extraordinary woman; she is remarkable for her sensibility, her right feeling, and for an ability to reason. Her flaws, again like those of Mary and Maria, are attributed in all cases to a faulty system of education, and it is in the identification of those areas in which education fails Adeline that Opie's disagreements with Wollstonecraft are clearest.

The plot of the novel turns on Adeline's fall into sin. Her fall is a sexual one, but it is also epistemological; Adeline sins as much because of what she knows as because she knows no better. Indeed, as Eberle notes, Adeline is first seduced, not by dangerous masculine sexuality, but by male language: By Glenmurray's philosophy, not his person.[16] This is not, as Marilyn Butler says, because her education is "indulgent" (*Jane Austen* 121), but because it is not properly an education at all. Mrs. Mowbray's considerable ambitions are focused on educational theory, so that "she turned over innumerable volumes in search of rules on the subject, on which she might improve, anticipating with great satisfaction the moment when she should be held up as a pattern of imitation to mothers, and be prevailed upon, though with graceful reluctance, to publish her system without a name, for the benefit of society" (112). Meanwhile, however, as Mrs. Mowbray gives her attention to methods of clothing children, Adeline wears out her shoes and goes without (112–13); while Mrs. Mowbray devotes herself to inventing an "easy method of learning arithmetic," Adeline's grandmother teaches her to keep accounts (114). In short, Editha Mowbray's studies are "[f]atal and unproductive" (111), devoted as they are to some ever-receding future moment rather than to practical and immediate concerns:

> While, wrapt in philosophical abstraction, she was trying to understand a meta-physical question on the mechanism of the human mind, or what constituted the true nature of virtue, she suffered day after day to pass in the culpable neglect of positive duties; and while imagining systems for the good of society, and the furtherance of general philanthropy, she allowed individual suffering in her neighbourhood to pass unobserved and unrelieved. While professing her unbounded love for the great family of the world, she suffered her own family to pine under the consciousness of her neglect; and viciously devoted those hours to the vanity of abstruse and solitary study, which might have been better spent in amusing the declining age of her venerable parents, whom affection had led to take up their abode with her. (111–12)

Significantly, Editha Mowbray does not simply choose a vain future over the present moment on which alone such a future can be founded; she neglects the originary space of the home in favour of an imaginary public sphere. Without the private virtues, however, Editha's imagined goods cannot come to be. Thus Opie's diatribe here is devoted less to the utter uselessness of education for women in general, than it is to the misguided project of theoretical speculation. Where Wollstonecraft argued in favour of metaphysics and ethics as fields of study for women, Opie claims that "a little experience is better than a great deal of theory" (113). Where Wollstonecraft argued in favour of the Cartesian principle that refers everything to the evidence of reason, Opie saw this thesis as a dangerous one, because it insisted on the importance of individual reason over social convention. Indeed it is on this point that the plot of *Adeline Mowbray* turns.

Adeline acquires an enthusiasm for speculative philosophy from her mother, but what "only served to amuse Mrs. Mowbray's fancy, her more enthusiastic daughter resolved to make conscientiously the rules of her practice" (116). Among the thinkers whose doctrines the Mowbrays affect is Glenmurray, who, "by a train of reasoning captivating though sophistical, and plausible though absurd" (116), attacks the idea and institution of marriage. When, in London, the Mowbrays meet Glenmurray, Adeline and the philosopher fall in love. Mrs. Mowbray, meanwhile, is pursued by Sir Patrick O'Carrol, who "though much pleased with the wealth and appearance of the mother . . . soon became enamoured of the daughter's person" (121). It is before Glenmurray, Mrs. Mowbray, and Sir Patrick that Adeline first declares her approval of Glenmurray's doctrine on marriage. Sir Patrick sees this avowal as an opportunity to seduce Adeline, and the conversation that ensues among Adeline, Glenmurray, and Sir Patrick suggests Opie's position on the dangers of adopting principles, however sincere, which are at odds with the prevalent idioms of living. Indeed, while Glenmurray well understands that Adeline's innocence and moral purity lead her into an open disavowal of marriage, Sir Patrick sees it as a sign that his sexual overtures to the girl will be welcomed. The conflict turns on the notion of the "life of honour," which, for Adeline, refers to a "'pure and honourable union'" (122):

"Sir," cried Glenmurray, "this is a mistake; your life of honour and Miss Mowbray's are as different as possible; you are talking of what you are grossly ignorant of."

"Ignorant! I ignorant! Look you, Mr. Glenmurray, do you pretend to tell me I know not what the life of honour is, when I have led it so many times with so many different women?" [Sir Patrick replied]

"How, Sir!" replied Adeline; "many times? and with many different women? My life of honour can be led with one only."

"Well, my dear soul, I only led it with one at a time." (122)

The vocabularies of Adeline and Sir Patrick are incommensurable, it appears, and where Wollstonecraft's heroines behave rightly in asserting the superiority of their vocabularies, which reflect qualities of the mind over those of others, Opie places Adeline, however sympathetically, in the wrong. She is wrong because she follows the dictates of her own reason against those of society, and, by doing so, exposes herself to insults from those who, like Sir Patrick, speak a more worldly idiom.

When Sir Patrick arrives the next day to find Adeline alone, and takes her in his arms, she desires him to leave the room. His response emphasizes again the incommensurability of their vocabularies. Sir Patrick says, "you do not suppose, my dear creature, that you and I do not understand one another! Telling a young fellow to leave the house on such occasions, means, in the pretty no-meaning of your sex, 'Stay and offend again,' to be sure" (123). Adeline can only think Sir Patrick mad. Aware only of the insult, and not of the incommensurability of their vocabularies, she remains "unconscious how much her avowed opinions had exposed her to insult, [and so] continued to believe Sir Patrick insane" (124). It is worth remembering that when Belinda is misunderstood and insulted, even though Clarence Hervey is wrong about her, she nevertheless resolves to amend her life. Adeline makes no such resolution, even though the narrator makes it clear that she has exposed herself to, indeed invited, insult, however unwittingly.

Opie, to do her justice, never suggests that Adeline is anything but an innocent; between her and her mother, indeed, it is no contest as to whose qualities of mind are superior. The problem is, as Wittgenstein would later show of our vocabularies generally, that there are no private languages[17]; Adeline Mowbray, by herself, cannot reform the idioms of living in the world, and must thus consider herself bound to them. With this issue Opie most clearly takes on the work of Mary Wollstonecraft. Wollstonecraft believed that real moral virtue consisted in behaving only as the evidence of reason convinced one to behave, regardless of the opinions of the world and the consequences of the act. Opie responded to Wollstonecraft by showing those consequences in some detail. She recognized, far more than was apparently possible for Wollstonecraft, the ways in which, if we are moral selves, we are such in a community. Seeing this, she also saw that the community is only behaving in accordance with its own nature if it withdraws its support from those who do not affirm its values. The tragedy of Adeline Mowbray is that Adeline does not see that disregarding the community allows the community to disregard her.[18] She is, in other words, *imprudent*. For Opie, this is the real danger inherent in individualism, and Glenmurray's conversation with Adeline, subsequent to his duel with Sir Patrick, highlights the ways in which we, as selves in a community, can never fully divorce ourselves from the language of the community. Glenmurray says,

> "I should have been called a coward had I declined the challenge; and though I can bear the world's hatred, I could not its contempt; I could not endure the loss of what the world calls honour."
>
> "Is it possible," rejoined Adeline, "that I hear the philosophical Glenmurray talking thus, in the silly jargon of a man of the world?"
>
> "Alas! I am a man, not a philosopher, Adeline!" (125)

Opie's point is, I think, clear; insofar as Glenmurray is a man, and not a philosopher, he belongs to a community and takes his notion of himself and his goods from that community. Perhaps, were he wholly a philosopher, Glenmurray would be able to inhabit some Archimedean point from which he could truly adhere to the distinction between real honour — "the testimony of an approving conscience" (125) — laid out in his book, and the apparent honour that stems from worldly considerations. If his idiom is that of a "man of the world," it is because he is of the world.

Note that this discussion turns, as does the one among Adeline, Sir Patrick, and Glenmurray, on different notions of honour. Adeline's idea of honour may be most readily understood as closely related to Mary Wollstonecraft's notion of virtue, stemming from right reason as it operates on right feeling. The problem with this individualist paradigm of honour, for Opie, is that its atomism renders it incorrigible, despite Wollstonecraft's own emphasis on human corrigibility through education. For Opie, this perceived incorrigibility means that the atomistic individual is opposed to society rather than part of it, because she does not accept the validity of any assumptions but her own. Here we seem to be returned to Rousseau's idea that a woman's worth *is* her reputation.[19] Certainly Opie's *Adeline Mowbray*, like Rousseau's *Emile*, enshrines the value of public appearances, and extends this evaluative criterion to men through the characters of Sir Patrick and Glenmurray. This is so for Amelia Opie because she refuses to accept an atomistic view of the individual that disguises the ways in which even our self-interpretations are what they are against a background given by the community. Opie's disgust for atomism leads her to show Adeline and Glenmurray's philosophically independent self-understanding as incoherent and destructive. It is incoherent in the sense that, in so far as they place different meanings on actions and terms such as "honour," they are finally unable to speak the idiom of society, and therefore commit its grossest errors. The idea of reputation is important in Opie because reputation signifies the community's attempt to understand behaviour, and, through behaviour, the interior quality of an individual. But this attempt, too, is compromised. If Adeline's "honour" is unintelligible, Sir Patrick's is an empty signifier because it is wholly worldly; that is, it takes the appearance of honour as sufficient evidence of its existence. Such a version allows him to maintain the semblance of respectability, even while his behaviour is that of a rake, a "[b]ase, unmanly villain" (124). Thus it is that, when the story of the duel is repeated throughout the city, it is said to have originated in "Mr. Glenmurray's scoffing at religion, king, and constitution, before the pious and loyal baronet" (125). The community, no more than the individual, is not incorrigible in Opie's philosophy, and while she gives considerable weight to reputation as a sign of worth, there are, in a fallen and imperfect world, inevitable gaps between appearance and reality. These gaps create the tension I identified earlier[20] between Opie's anti-Jacobinical project and her adoption of Wollstonecraft's vocabulary of moral personhood, but they are also what links *Adeline Mowbray* to Edgeworth's anti-Rousseauean thesis in *Belinda*. If Opie is unable to reconcile the extremes of atomism and conventionalism, she nevertheless perceived the problem; in this way Wollstonecraft's idiom of feminist individualism indeed had succeeded the conventionalism for which Opie's narrator appears to long.

The conflict, as the exchange between Sir Patrick and Glenmurray just before their duel makes clear, is one between practice and principle. The baronet tells Glenmurray, "'men of your principles can have but few friends'" (124). Glenmurray responds, "'men of your practice ought to have none, Sir Patrick'" (125). Sir Patrick is a hypocrite because he espouses principles to which he does not adhere, and allows the semblance of honour to suffice for the reality. But Glenmurray is no less hypocritical; his speculative philosophies, which advance that strongly atomistic view of Cartesian reason upheld by Adeline, are ideas he soon finds untenable. He is, after all, a man of the world and in the world, not a philosopher somehow outside it.

It is the idea that we are inescapably part of a community that underlies *Adeline Mowbray*. Adeline's tragic flaw, the reason for her fall, is that despite her sensibility, despite her right feeling, in fact, she does not recognize the extent to which her de facto membership in this community confers on her significant obligations. And this flaw is one that Opie attributes to her faulty education. Where Wollstonecraft argued that the purpose of education was to train the reason, and thus to render the individual citizen free in a positive sense, Opie seems to suggest that the purpose of education is to train members of society in the duties society confers on them. Both might argue that their notions of education are directed toward the creation of citizens, but their notions of the citizen are again far removed from each other. For Opie, virtue must have an outward and social manifestation as well as an inner one, or it will ultimately fall. Sir Patrick's assessment of Adeline is, after all, the more realistic one: "Adeline appeared in his eyes not a deceived enthusiast, but a susceptible and forward girl, endeavouring to hide her frailty under fine sentiments and high-sounding theories. Nor was Sir Patrick's inference an unnatural one. Every man of the world would have thought the same; and on very plausible grounds" (129). For Opie, we do, finally, live in the world, and although it is imperfect — her depiction of Sir Patrick, I think, assures us that this is so — the point for her is not to change the world, but to live in it.[21]

With this understanding, Adeline's "fall" is a necessary one. It is not, however, unproblematic, even for Opie. While Adeline is willing, at first, to disregard society and its conventions entirely, she is not prepared to disregard her mother. It is only after her mother's misguided marriage to Sir Patrick, and the baronet's violent attempt to seduce Adeline,[22] that she goes to Glenmurray. Indeed, it may almost be said that Adeline is driven to her fate by an imperfect world, rather than by her disregard for that world. Opie does not allow this conclusion, however; Adeline refuses to marry Glenmurray, as a matter of principle, saying, "'you are to be governed by no other law but your desire to promote general utility, and are not to think at all of the interest of an individual'" (138). Adeline thus refuses the redemption Glenmurray offers, by refusing to contemplate any reconciliation of the individual and the social good. Again her atomistic philosophy perceives the two as at odds, rather than constitutive of, each other.

It may be that Adeline's reading of this conflict poses a problem for my claim that Opie is asserting the importance of social claims over and above those of the individual, since Adeline evaluates the situation in similar terms but places the choice against marriage squarely in the court of the social good, rather than the individual good. It matters, however, that Adeline is led into this assertion by Glenmurray's authorial conceit, which prevents him from disavowing his earlier beliefs. Glenmurray himself casts the moral choice in terms of Adeline's good over the social good of exemplary action, as does Adeline. But while their conviction of the social utility of their actions functions as a sign of Adeline's mental nobility, the pair are nevertheless mistaken. Mrs. Pemberton's reading of the situation reveals their error: "'Thou art one of the enlightened, as they call themselves — Thou art one of those wise in their own conceit, who, disregarding the customs of ages, and the dictates of experience, set up their own opinions against the hallowed institutions of men and the will of the Most High'" (163). For Mrs. Pemberton, Glenmurray and Adeline have acted out of individualist motivations, rather than social ones. Their notion of honour, of enlightenment, and of custom is a private rather than a public understanding, as we have already seen. The point here is that the domains of the individual and society must not — and cannot — be wholly split. Opie does not, after all, simply invert these domains to value the social over the individual, retaining their incommensurability. Rather, her emphasis on knowledge here shows these spheres to constitute and nurture each other. Thus Opie does not so much insist that the individual must give way to the social as she emphasizes the social domain as one of *shared* goods. It is because these goods are shared that, despite their imperfections, they must take precedence.

It is not that Adeline's motivations, her inner qualities, are ever called into question; like Wollstonecraft, Opie portrays a heroine whose mental superiority is unquestioned. Finally, however, mental qualities are not enough. Adeline herself comes to recognize this, writing to a friend that

I did not act in defiance of the world's opinion, from any depraved feelings, or vicious inclinations; but the world could not be expected to believe this, since motives are known only to our own hearts, and the great Searcher of hearts; therefore, as far as example goes, I was as great a stumbling-block to others, as if the life I led had been owing to the influence of lawless desires; and society was right in making no distinction between me and other women living in an unsanctioned connexion. (215)

Indeed, Adeline finally comes to agree with the view expressed in Rousseau's assertion that women's honour "is not only in their conduct but in their reputation; and it is not possible that a woman who consents to be regarded as disreputable can ever be decent" (*Emile* 364). Like Pompeia, she must be beyond even the appearance of reproach.[23]

I argued above that Wollstonecraft illustrated the instability of social conventions by revealing them as idioms of living, and that in the contest of vocabularies lay much of the political impetus of her novels. I went on to claim that in so doing, Wollstonecraft fundamentally altered the terms in which the quarrel over the nature and status of women in society was discussed in fiction. In Opie's *Adeline Mowbray*, Wollstonecraft's idioms of living are readdressed, this time from the perspective of private versus public languages. Opie, I contend, does not ultimately challenge Wollstonecraft's conclusion that social conventions are but idioms, and as such are unstable and contingent, giving way over time to newer idioms. What Opie does do, and this is indeed the tenor of her intervention in *Adeline Mowbray*, is suggest the ways in which the enormous weight of social inertia operates against the reinscription of the vocabularies of living. This, certainly, is Glenmurray's conclusion on his death-bed: "'I will own that some of my opinions are changed; and that, though I believe those which are unchanged are right in theory, I think, as the mass of society could never at *once* adopt them, they had better remain unacted upon, than that a few lonely individuals should expose themselves to certain distress, by making them the rules of their conduct'" (175–76).

For Opie, what is at stake in the contest of vocabularies is, as it is for Wollstonecraft, social and institutional change. Both suggest that private virtue depends on education, but whereas for Wollstonecraft it is a sufficient guarantee of virtue that the individual reason rightly, and act according to reason, Opie is unable to concede that the individual should not be subject to second-guessing by external authorities. This is so for Opie because, as I have shown, she sees the individual as first and foremost an individual inside of a community, and is prepared thus to assert that individual goods are good only insofar as they are shared by that community. What this means is that for Opie there is positive freedom — but this "freedom" is purchased at the cost of negative liberty, so that we are free *only* when our goods coincide with those of the community. And this "communitarian freedom," as I will call it, like Sophie's freedom, is not substantively freedom at all. There is another side to this formulation, however, namely that, for Amelia Opie, just as the nature of individual goods depends on social goods, social good is dependent on individual virtue. This, I suggest, is the point of Opie's exposure of moral hypocrisy in many of the minor characters of *Adeline Mowbray*. Sir Patrick's practice is at odds with his expressed principles, but the world is willing to take the word for the deed; this is the social immorality that drives Adeline to her fall. There is, finally, a serious tension between the individual and society, which even Opie's commitment to shared goods cannot mitigate. However much she stresses social virtue as dependent on individual morality, Adeline's story establishes, rather, the impossibility of individual virtue in a vicious society.[24] This last idea is one she shares with Wollstonecraft and Edgeworth. All three take private and public as inextricably linked, and find the virtue of the citizen as the consequence of education. But they differ on the nature both of this virtue, and the virtuously free self.

What does freedom mean? We saw that for Rousseau men ought to be positively free, such that their desires not run counter to their basic purposes, which purposes are discoverable only in themselves. Emile becomes fully free (and in Rousseau's analysis, fully adult and a virtuous citizen) only when his needs, wants, and desires are no longer corrigible. Mary Wollstonecraft's argument for women's rights and freedoms is predicated on the assumption that Rousseau's positive freedom is a good in itself. She challenges Rousseau, to be sure, but she does not challenge his assertion of positive freedom as the great virtue of the citizen; rather, her argument centres on the claim that, with right education, women can achieve this same kind of freedom.

Amelia Opie's argument is quite different. She nowhere asserts that women can or ought to achieve the radically atomistic individual freedom that both Rousseau and Wollstonecraft erect as the cornerstone of the virtuous society. Indeed, as we have seen, Adeline Mowbray's attempt to act according to such notions of freedom are disastrous. But it is not insignificant that this disaster is shared by Glenmurray. I am claiming, in fact, that in *Adeline Mowbray* part of Opie's project is to call into question the notion that positive freedom, in its radically atomistic form, can indeed be considered a good, for either man or woman. If Adeline's education, which leads her into this individualist error, is at fault, so too is Glenmurray's; he, like Adeline, has set up his own authority over and above that of social custom, and such freedom — which accords with that desired by Rousseau and by Wollstonecraft — is useless. In fact, Opie's critique of individualist notions of freedom can be read as a sustained argument for a general, rather than gendered, return to the weaker version of freedom Rousseau advocated for his Sophie, which allows, first of all, for the in-principle possibility that any agent can err in the classification of their needs, wants, and desires, and in which the point of education is not to render one's basic purposes discoverable only in oneself, but to ensure that those purposes are not at odds with basic social goods. Opie thus imagines a self wholly constituted by, and compatible with, the community, even as she perceives the citizen-self as constitutive of the polity. Edgeworth showed, in *Belinda*, that the conflict between self and society on which Wollstonecraft foundered (as does Adeline) can be navigated through prudence; this is a virtue, indeed for Edgeworth *the* virtue, in which practice and principle both reside. Adeline does not achieve this virtue until too late, because the domestic sphere in which it only can be taught is corrupted. Belinda, however, does so acquire it, and in so doing enables a new type of private domain that reorders the social space.

NOTES

1.   Marilyn Butler, *Romantics, Rebels and Reactionaries* 36–38, 94–95; Cazamian 36; Kelly, *English Fiction* 59–70. This foreclosure of radical liberalism was in part a genuine

fear on the part of writers and publishers. Marilyn Butler tells us that in 1798–99 Joseph Johnson spent ten months in prison for publishing "sedition," a pamphlet criticizing the conservative Bishop of Llandaff (*Jane Austen* 121).

2. *English Fiction* 71. While Kelly argues that these political anxieties also led to renewed, although not open, criticism of the powerful classes and entrenched institutions, he argues that the emphasis on subjectivity, community harmony, affection, and factuality represented a marked departure from the "Jacobinical utopianism" of Wollstonecraft and her circle. See *English Fiction*, Ch. 3, "1800–1814: Beyond 'Tales of the Times'" 71–110 for his discussion of this period.

3. Richard Lovell Edgeworth had attempted to educate his eldest son, Richard, according to Rousseau's principles in *Emile* for the first few years of his life. Marilyn Butler follows Edgeworth family tradition in her biography of Maria Edgeworth in attributing young Richard's faults to this primitivist education (*Maria Edgeworth* 23, 37–38, 43–44, 50–52, 59, 71, and 100–101).

4. MacFadyen 426. She sees fashionable reading here as a threat to the sexual economy, and thus to the domestic ideology, because of its emphasis on the "displayed female body" (429); legitimate literary display, on the other hand, foregrounds domestic harmony (438).

5. Marilyn Butler takes a stronger view of Belinda's relationship to authority, seeing the theme of the novel as learning to escape from authority, rather than to submit to it (*Jane Austen* 141).

6. Kelly disagrees. For him, Belinda does not become a paragon, but is already, when the novel opens, "an ideal representation of the late eighteenth-century Enlightenment in female form" (*English Fiction* 79) who functions "almost [as] a *deus ex machina*, repairing and reconciling from a height of reason and inward perfection that is preternatural" (*English Fiction* 80). While I agree with Kelly's conclusion that *Belinda* shares with Wollstonecraft a sense that independent judgment and moral and intellectual equality are necessary if women "are to conduct the rational, intimate, 'egalitarian' domestic life that is supposed to be the foundation of the social order" (80), his idea that Belinda is already this rational, egalitarian woman distorts this conclusion by failing to address education as the root of ideal domestic space. Yet Kelly's idea of the already existing paragon does capture our sense that, as Caroline Gonda points out, Belinda "seems to come from absolutely nowhere," so that, despite the repeated emphasis on educational activity of various kinds, "Belinda's own education is bizarrely without agency, a matter of passive constructions" (211). But Belinda's constructions are active, not passive, because, as I hope to show, reason for Edgeworth is always active.

7. I disagree here with Hawthorne, who argues that *Belinda* exposes the faults in Lady Anne's principles while Lady Delacour learns to temper behaviour with prudence but continues to be both emotional and imaginative, so that, for Hawthorne, "[t]he passionate sphere thus completely eclipses the rational" (45). Hawthorne's mistake, I suggest, lies in his assumption that emotion and imagination are not properly part of the rational sphere.

8. Teresa Michals places considerably more emphasis on the commercial valences of prudence than I do here. For her, Edgeworth's idea of the family is "a kind of domestic corporation underwritten by the moral and financial credit of its living and dead members, by their collective character" (7).

9. Atkinson and Atkinson 115. Most critics, including Atkinson and Atkinson, believe that Edgeworth takes this incident from Thomas Day's experience. Day took two orphan girls to France, intending to raise them in seclusion after the example of Rousseau's Sophie, in the hopes that one of them would make the ideal wife. He returned to England with the one he preferred, Sabrina Sidney, but finally did not marry her; Butler says that Sidney

offended Day over a trivial matter in 1773 and was sent away into "genteel retirement" (*Maria Edgeworth* 39).

10. Hervey renames the girl Virginia, baptized Rachel, when he adopts her. This renaming captures part of Hervey's error, which lies in his limited notion of innocence as sexual ignorance.

11. "It is better to be a human being dissatisfied than a pig satisfied; better to be Socrates dissatisfied than a fool satisfied. And if the fool, or the pig, is of a different opinion, it is because they only know their own side of the question. The other party to the comparison knows both sides" (Mill, *Util.* 212).

12. The variant spelling for "freak" is obsolete. Atkinson and Atkinson point out that the use of "freak" for monster is a much later one, and that Edgeworth uses the term in its correct turn-of-the-century sense. See 100.

13. Gonda criticizes Kowaleski-Wallace, not on these grounds, but for assuming that the authority of women in domestic space is false, that this space is inimical to a genuine female authority (204–38, esp. 238).

14. Julie Shaffer provides a refreshing counterpoint to such arguments, treating the marriage plot in *Belinda* and elsewhere as a transition into female domestic and romantic moral expertise.

15. Louis Cazamian places Opie in company with Godwin, Thomas Holcroft, Elizabeth Inchbald, and Charlotte Smith as a practitioner of the *roman-à-thèse*, describing Opie's *Adeline Mowbray* and Godwin's *Fleetwood* (1805) as the last representatives of the genre before the general public embraced the Tory reaction against radicalism and "French ideas" (36-37). In my view, however, he errs in placing Opie intellectually as well as socially in the company of the British revolutionaries.

16. 127. Eberle's excellent article reads the novel as a satire of the masculinist assumptions that mar Jacobin political theory, particularly that of Godwin; she takes Adeline's acceptance of social condemnation as the novel's second, "most tragic" seduction (137). This, I think, is too strong; Eberle's emphasis on the creation of an ideal community of women, at the end of the novel, neglects the ways in which this resolution finally enshrines community obligation, rather than critiques it.

17. See, for example, *Philosophical Investigations* I.275: "Look at the blue of the sky and say to yourself, 'How blue the sky is!' — When you do it spontaneously — without philosophical intentions — the idea never crosses your mind that this impression of colour belongs only to *you*. And you have no hesitation in exclaiming that to someone else. And if you point at anything as you say the words you point at the sky. I am saying: you have not the feeling of pointing-into-yourself, which often accompanies 'naming the sensation' when one is thinking about 'private language'" (96).

18. Gary Kelly notes that Adeline's error lies in "allowing her public character to become detached from her 'true' moral character" ("Amelia Opie" 10) and that, for Opie, society and duty will always defeat the individual self and individual rights (10).

19. See also Kelly, "Amelia Opie" 10.

20. Kelly describes this tension as a conflict between "official" and "unofficial" ideology ("Amelia Opie").

21. With apologies to Karl Marx, who said, "[t]he philosophers have only *interpreted* the world in various ways: the point is to change it" (5).

22. Opie attempts to mitigate what is to all appearances an attempted rape by her assertion that Sir Patrick "believed that [Adeline] would be a willing victim" (136). I suggest, from this attempt at mitigation, that the purpose of the scene, for Opie, is to further elaborate the ways in which Adeline's declared principles are believed to indicate a mode of practice that would allow or even invite Sir Patrick's assault. At the same time, I believe

Opie falls just short of blaming the potential victim here by finally enabling her to escape from the baronet. She escapes because, "strong in innocence, aware of his intention, and presuming on his [intoxicated] situation" (136), she is able to disengage herself from his grasp.

23.   Julius Caesar divorced his wife because her name was involved in an accusation against P. Clodius.

24.   Gonda notes a similar strain, showing that the "ugliness" of Adeline's 'respectable' marriage to Berrendale and the "viciousness" of 'respectable' society outweigh the reader's sense of Adeline's error (198–99). Marilyn Butler, however, sees in the novel "the usual cautionary tale of the anti-jacobins," mitigated only by "the relative amiability [and] the real if wrong-headed idealism of the principals" (*Jane Austen* 121). For Gary Kelly, the issue is one of moral identity, and he briefly remarks the reflection in Opie's work of increasing contradictions and ambiguities in the female condition (*English Fiction* 84–86).

4

Intimate Space: The Household
and the Polity in Domestic Fiction

> Thus it was out of the association formed by men with these two, women and slaves, that a household was first formed; and the poet Hesiod was right when he wrote, "Get first a house and a wife and an ox to draw the plough." (The ox is the poor man's slave.) This association of persons, established according to nature for the satisfaction of daily needs, is the household, the members of which Charondas calls "bread-fellows", and Epimenides the Cretan "stable-companions". . . . The final association, formed of several villages, is the state. For all practical purposes the process is now complete; self-sufficiency has been reached, and while the state came about as a means of securing life itself, it continues in being to secure the *good* life. Therefore every state exists by nature, as the earlier associations too were natural. This association is the end of those others, and nature is itself an end; for whatever is the end-product of the coming into existence of any object, that is what we call its nature — of a man, for instance, or a horse or a household. Moreover the aim and the end is perfection; and self-sufficiency is both end and perfection.
> — Aristotle, *The Politics* I.ii.1252b9ff.

In the preceding chapters, I have taken seriously Nancy Armstrong's argument in *Desire and Domestic Fiction* that eighteenth-century narratives of female selfhood, and of courtship and marriage in particular, made a powerful political gesture through attaching moral value to qualities of the mind. Such narratives, says Armstrong, contested the dominant notion of sexuality that understood desirability in terms of wealth, status, and kinship webs, and they did so by establishing the domestic woman as a figure apart from the political world of men (8). In this account the politicality of these fictions rests on their attempt to establish a new "idiom of living," as I have been using the term, one that runs counter to conventional vocabularies of female selfhood. I have shown the ways in which a rhetorical analysis of Wollstonecraft, Opie, and Edgeworth can, indeed, illuminate the projects of those writers with regard to the nature and status of women, and I suggest that here Armstrong's analysis of eighteenth-century narratives is a valuable one. But Armstrong does not confine her analysis to the eighteenth century, and it is in her discussion of Victorian domestic fiction that her analysis fails. She claims that by the time of domestic fiction's reemergence in the 1840s, narratives of courtship and marriage could no longer constitute the form of political resistance they did in the time of Opie and Edgeworth. Instead, Armstrong argues, vocabularies of domesticity had, by this time, themselves become conventional, and therefore functioned to confine political disruption inside a private and therefore apolitical framework (178). While some aspects of the female self resisted this acculturation, they did so only as the "monstrous" or "fallen" woman in a discourse that redefined political resistance as a kind of pathology, a diagnosis that removed it from competing economic and social interests (252). This monstrous woman is, for Armstrong, both agent and product of an individuating process focusing on motives and behaviours, and thus translates the historical and economic factors of race, class, and gender into psychological terms. This translation Armstrong describes as effectively confining disorder to the household (183).

I do not, as should be clear from the preceding chapters, dispute Armstrong's claim for the development of a "universalizing" vocabulary of qualities of the mind. Indeed, I have endeavoured, through my discussion of Opie and Edgeworth's responses to Wollstonecraft, to show some of the ways in which contesting vocabularies can be read as sites of cultural debate over the nature and status of women as selves. I do, however, take issue with the univocality that Armstrong attributes to this vocabulary in the nineteenth century, and I want to show that there are cases in which the language of domestic femininity can pose a powerful challenge to our own notions of Victorian private and public domains. Indeed, Armstrong errs with regard to Victorian domestic fiction precisely because she sees the domestic sphere as separate from a public or political sphere, an analysis that fails to capture nineteenth-century notions of this relationship.

Armstrong, however, is by no means alone in seeing Victorian domestic fiction as a narrative form most notable for the ways in which it confines both women and other potential sources of disorder to the arena of the household. This indeed is the background assumption that guided the enormously influential assertions of Sandra Gilbert and Susan Gubar in their colossal study of nineteenth-century women writers. Taking Coventry Patmore's "The Angel in the House" as the authoritative account of Victorian gender differences, they conclude that "the madwoman in the attic" symbolizes the estrangement of the woman writer who attempts to deviate from Patmore's vision (22–36). Nina Auerbach's treatment of the monstrous woman, which differs, in its links to archetypal and myth criticism, from the psychoanalytic view propounded by Gilbert and Gubar, likewise depends on the assumption that the boundaries of domesticity are necessarily restrictive. Auerbach's demonic woman is thus associated with the breaking of these bounds (7-9). The Victorian image of the woman outside the family is, for these influential thinkers, the image of a monster, a demon; for Auerbach this is part of a cultural mythos that, constructed in terms of polarities, depended on a reading of women as angels (victims) or monsters.[1] For Gilbert and Gubar this same image represents the thwarted imagination of female authors. Nancy Armstrong's more recent book does not pose a serious challenge to these views, except in her critique of Gilbert and Gubar's assumption that sexuality is always and only about sexuality (165). Such notions of sexuality, for Armstrong, involve acceding to the Victorian idea that middle-class respectability required the repression of female sexuality, of essential aspects of the woman (165). Her theory, by contrast, replaces a notion of repression with the argument that these extrasocial depths in the self were themselves a product of Victorian culture, and that they were produced largely by writing. By transforming cultural material into psycho-sexual terms, says Armstrong, Victorian domestic fiction concealed the political power it exercised in effecting such a transformation (165). She concludes that, once the domestic woman became the representative of the dominant view, rather than the politically oppositional term it had been in eighteenth-century writing, any aspect of female selfhood that resisted acculturation as the "angel in the house" was redefined in terms of individual pathology, a strategy that rendered potential political resistance effectively apolitical (252).

Armstrong's conclusions, like those of Gilbert, Gubar, and Auerbach, depend on the assumption that the life of the household is wholly separate from the political realm of social arrangement, sanction, and distribution. Such accounts see narratives of courtship and marriage as inevitably implicated in the divorce of the public and the private spheres. Indeed, many critics, particularly feminist critics, have taken as axiomatic the notion that, as Rachel Blau DuPlessis argued, *Bildung* and romance could not coexist in the resolution of the narrative.[2] On DuPlessis's account, the choice of romance or *Bildung* resulted in marriage or death, respectively. Such resolutions were, for DuPlessis, part of the cultural production of romance, such that marriage rewarded the ability to cope with the demands of sexuality or kinship, while death was the inevitable result of improprieties in this negotiation. In this paradigm, emancipation can only lie in escaping the ends of marriage or death toward which the domestic novel inevitably leads, so that political resistance consists in "writing beyond the ending" to rescript possibilities for women (DuPlessis 3–4). But this paradigm, like many discussions of domestic fiction, locates politicality solely in opposition, and defines opposition narrowly in terms of the resolution of the narrative. Such accounts, which necessarily see the resolution of the romance plot in marriage as nonoppositional, fail to capture the ways in which domestic fiction could and often did function as a mediator in cultural debates. If, after all, DuPlessis is right in arguing that marriage is a reward for successfully meeting the demands of sexuality, then it may also be true that the resolution of an education plot — a form of *Bildung* — in romance and marriage functions to legitimize *Bildung* rather than to exclude it. DuPlessis, I suggest, is unable to make this leap because, predicating her argument on a belief in gendered separate spheres, she cannot perceive *Bildung* and romance as coeval or interrelated.[3] Such arguments, like more recent revisions of the idea of "separate spheres," misunderstand the role of domestic space in the liberal polity.

In the last two chapters, I devoted considerable attention to the ways in which the bourgeois individual depends for its status as a bearer of rights on mental qualities. The political philosophy of the liberal polity figures education as a necessary precondition for the creation of the citizen, insofar as it considers the end of education as the cultivation, in the self, of those mental qualities. Twentieth-century feminist theory has criticized liberal philosophy for its construction of the individual as an abstract bearer of rights, a "generalized other,"[4] but has failed to see the ways in which the fiction of the generalized other, governed, in Cartesian fashion, by self-discipline and reason, likewise depends on an idea of the individual as a being of interior psychological depth. Thus Iris Marion Young argues that liberalism's commitment to impartiality requires the expulsion of desire and feeling from deliberation ("Impartiality" 63):

The construct of an impartial point of view is arrived at by abstracting from the concrete particularity of the person in situation. This requires abstracting from the particularity of bodily being, its needs and inclinations, and from the feelings that attach to the experienced particularity of things and events. Normative reason is defined as impartial, and reason defines the unity of the moral subject, both in the sense of knowing the universal principles of morality and in the sense of what all moral subjects have in common in the same way. This reason thus stands opposed to desire and affectivity as what differentiates and particularizes persons. ("Impartiality" 62–63)

I suggest, however, that Young's critique of liberalism misunderstands its idea of reason. It is true, for example, that Locke represents abstraction much as does Young (*Essay* II.xi.§9–11), but it is also true that abstraction from particular objects and ideas is not the only operation of reason in Locke's analysis. He clearly states that "[i]t is not enough to have a confused Perception of something in general: Unless the Mind had a distinct Perception of different Objects, and their Qualities, it would be capable of very little Knowledge" (*Essay* II.xi.§1). Moreover, should the faculty of discrimination fail, that is, should we fail to consider objects in their concrete particularity, "so far our Notions are confused, and our Reason and Judgement disturbed or misled" (*Essay* II.xi.§2). Far from opposing reason to desire and affectivity, Rousseau for one was willing to allow animals a limited participation in natural right, because, as he pointed out, "they share something of our nature through the sensitivity with which they are endowed" (*Discourses* 96). Far from suppressing affectivity, Rousseau argues that "sensitivity" is the ground of right: "It seems, in effect, that if I am obliged to do no harm to my fellow man, it is less because he is a reasonable being than because he is a sensitive being: a quality that, being common to beast and man, ought at least to give the one the right not to be uselessly mistreated by the other" (*Discourses* 96).

Thus the foregrounding of emotion, which I will show to be the province of domestic fiction, is even in the early Victorian novel a profoundly political gesture. This is so because, in constructing the individual as the bearer of rights, liberal political philosophy consistently assigned those rights only to a self with interiority, capable not only of evaluation but of emotion. In my reading of Wollstonecraft, I showed that "right reason" is not treated according to twentieth-century caricatures of Enlightenment rationality, but depends for its success on the individual's successful integration of thought and feeling. Wollstonecraft believes that such integration, a necessary condition for true citizenship, can only be achieved through right education. In this she is not departing from the liberal or Enlightenment idea of the individual as citizen, but insisting on the extension of such notions to women. Indeed, Wollstonecraft was following such thinkers as Rousseau, for whom sympathy ("pity") is anterior to reason but necessary to its right operation (*Discourses* 128–39). If I am correct in my understanding of Wollstonecraft, then the foregrounding of emotion in domestic fiction does not, as Nancy Armstrong has argued, require the suppression of all that is political in the text (N. Armstrong 218). Armstrong's claim that the psychologizing of the individual (*de facto* if not *de jure*) rules out the possibility of political import misunderstands the ways in which the liberal notion of civil society is predicated on precisely such an idea of the individual. One bears rights, according to this philosophy, to the degree that one is capable of exercising them; it was on these grounds that Wollstonecraft's *Vindication of the Rights of Woman* attempted to prove women capable of exercising the same rights as men. My claim in this chapter is that domestic fiction foregrounds qualities of mind and emotion through the romance plot, not as a means of containment, but as part of an attempt to negotiate personhood for the female self. Moreover, the domestic vocabulary Armstrong finds to be vitiated of its potential for resistance after 1840 remains an important part of this negotiation of personhood, because it not only assumes that value resides in qualities of the mind, but indeed predicates its definition of the fully functioning self-as-citizen on such qualities. Further, it is in domestic fiction that the space in which such a self first comes to be is fixed in its relationship to the other *topoi* of the polity.

This argument has important implications for the widely held idea that social and domestic space were conceptual binaries in Victorian political and moral topographies. If my claim that the notion of interior depth is central to the construction of the bearer of rights is correct, then it is possible that modern critics have misread Victorian attentiveness to the household. It is at least possible, in such a case, that the foregrounding of the domestic, even in political resolutions,[5] is not simply a rhetorical move that privatizes and therefore contains political problems, but one that presents the so-called private sphere as the originary space of civil society. I will show that the foregrounding of emotion, of the character as a discrete individual, is, in the rhetoric of political reform, articulated as a necessary if insufficient condition for the extension of rights. Indeed, this is an extension of my analysis of Wollstonecraft's treatment of Jemima in *The Wrongs of Woman*. But in the light of Nancy Armstrong's claims that such political gestures disappear from the domestic fiction of the 1840s, it seems vital to show, through the work of Gaskell, that this function of psychological characterization remains fundamental to the political arguments in these works. Once this is established, I will attempt to show that such an understanding of character underwrites the conventions of domestic fiction. Indeed, it seems to me the importance of domestic fiction to the history of notions of the female self lies in the fact that the resolution of the narrative requires the kind of exploration of mental qualities I have already shown to be so important in the work of Wollstonecraft, Opie, and Edgeworth.

It should be clear from the foregoing that I take issue with DuPlessis's and others' accounts of the romance plot. I see the negotiation of courtship narratives as a crucial gambit in the elaboration and enlargement of female destinies. This is so not only because these narratives link apparently private matters to the functioning of the community, and therefore of the polity; where marriage for a woman functions to reward appropriate behaviour, it can also sanction behaviour and mental qualities that might be considered dubious for a woman. It is possible, in other words, for a woman to be both wife and citizen. Thus in Charlotte Mary Yonge's *The Clever Woman of the Family*, it is the strong-minded, opinionated, wilful Rachel Curtis who finally achieves marriage, family, and perfect felicity.[6] Bessie Keith, who "took all hearts by storm with her gay good-humour and eager sympathy" (121), "so helpful, so kind, so everything" (127), marries, on the other hand, a man more than twice her age for wealth and position. After neglecting him shamefully in the first year of their marriage, she dies in premature labour brought on by a fall she takes trying to avoid the importunities of an old suitor, who has been inspired to try his luck again by her willingness to tryst with him at a garden party:

[I]t was perilous ground; ladies, however highly principled, cannot leave off self-pleasing habits all at once, and the old terms returned sufficiently to render the barrier but slightly felt. When Lady Keith had spoken of her intention of leaving Timber End, the reply had been the old complaint of her brother's harshness and jealousy of his ardent and lasting affection, and reproof had not at once silenced him. This it was that had so startled her as to make her hurry to her brother's side, unheeding of her steps. (319)

The different fates of Rachel and Bessie may be an unusual case, but I will show that happy marriage owns a similar legitimating function in Gaskell's *Wives and Daughters* and *North and South*. Reading private resolutions as potentially public and political gestures, I will return to notions of the public and private, and attempt to delineate their relationship as other than hierarchical and conceptually separate. For now, however, let me remark that if I am right about this, Armstrong's idea that the vocabulary of domesticity was adopted in the domestic fiction of the 1840s as a means of confining and containing political disorder must be a profound misreading of the very nature of the Victorian political and domestic project.

"Domestic fiction" is concerned with intimate (that is, nonmarket) relationships. Such fiction devotes its attention to the relationships of *philia* (affective relations), whose province, commonly understood, is that of the household or of a set of households (community). I term this province intimate, rather than private, in order to disentangle it from the unsatisfactory notion of separate spheres, and in order to suggest that, while the relations of such space are implicated in and indeed to some extent governed by economic relations, these latter are not the purpose (end) of the relationships of intimate space. Thus, while the negotiation of a romance plot may be the organizing principle of a domestic narrative, and the successful resolution of that plot in a happy marriage may require the successful conclusion of public economic or political aspirations, the getting and spending of the world's wealth is, in the domestic fiction, a means to the end of intimacy, rather than the reverse.[7] Domestic fiction imposes a morally normative order on these relationships only as part of a privileging of intimacy over economy.

The foregoing, however, is not intended to assert that the intimate space of the household and its relationships was represented in domestic fiction as withdrawn from the vagaries of the economic sphere. By describing the household as intimate space, I seek to capture the sense in which the ends of the household were held to be quite different from those of the marketplace: The one occupying, in domestic fiction, a privileged position as the sustained attempt to respond to the question of "how should one live," and the other as a response to the question of "what must one do, since one must live."[8] As I will show with regard to *North and South*, the tension between the means to life and the ends of it becomes most visible in the aristocratic anxiety attending the notion of trade. Without mitigating the elitism of contrasting notions of "gentleman" and "tradesman," I suggest that the idea of incompatibility revealed in this anxiety may have in part to do with an inchoate sense that those who are concerned with the means to life may be barred by that activity from the noble pursuit of its ends, and must therefore remain outside the citizenry as broadly construed.[9] If the foregoing is possible, it may also be possible that the prescriptive withdrawal of the home from public space so many have observed operating in nineteenth-century culture represents an attempt on the part of the middle class to establish a space devoted to the pursuit of the ends of life, and thus to justify their inclusion as full citizens.

There are, as should be clear, two senses of life operating here, and the sense with which the intimate space of the household is concerned entails notions of the good life, while the other involves life as subsistence, or indeed as the means to the first. William James Booth devotes the first section of his excellent book, *Households: On the Moral Architecture of the Economy*, to a scrupulous account of the ancient Greek *oikos*. Booth describes the Homeric household as an economic unit, that is, a production/consumption unit through which the material needs of its rulers were secured (31), indeed, that household Aristotle describes in the epigraph to this chapter. The household comes into being, for Aristotle, because we are not and cannot be — as Opie and Edgeworth indeed discovered — self-sufficient outside of a community. The household exists to free us from scarcity and want, and thus to enable the shared purposes of its rulers (Booth 31–32; 37). The central concept, then, of the household or of the *polis*, conceived of as a set of households, is *autarky*: The greatest possible freedom from constraint, a way of life that stands on its own. It is worth recalling here that this is the self-sufficiency Aristotle calls perfection.[10] The object of household activities is therefore wealth, but this is not to say that the getting of wealth is the *purpose* of the household. Booth, following Aristotle, is clear on this point. He sees wealth, need, and use as closely related in the ancient *oikos*, such that the object of the household, wealth, is something useful for the sustenance of ends beyond that of wealth getting (41). Wealth, the economic, on this account is therefore a means and not an end, a tool in the service of the good life (41).

Elizabeth Cleghorn Gaskell's *Wives and Daughters* (1864–66) provides a liberal analogy to the *oikos*, so described. From the "old rigmarole of childhood" (*Wives* 1) with which the novel opens, the Gibson household and Molly, only child of the house and its widowed master, are at the centre of the fictional universe: "In a country there was a shire, and in that shire there was a town, and in that town there was a house, and in that house there was a room, and in that room there was a bed, and in that bed there lay a little girl" (*Wives* 1). I take this rigmarole as an expression of the *raison d'être* of domestic fiction, which exists to place the household, and the cultivation of the citizen, at the root of the liberal polity. I will expand on this in a moment, but first let me observe that part of the significance of this rigmarole is that neither the household nor Molly may stand alone. Just as Aristotle, in the epigraph that opens this chapter, observes that it is natural for households to join together to achieve their perfect end, the domestic novel, whose centre is the household, rarely indeed confines itself to one home.[11] Molly achieves her *Bildung* — which includes an almost certainly successful resolution of the romance plot — by evaluating and discarding different idioms of living.[12] *Wives and Daughters* thus begins with Molly's visit to The Towers and moves rapidly to her extended stay at Hamley; they are, as we soon learn, two quite different households. This is not insignificant, since the communities within which such households stand are represented in domestic fiction in terms of sets of households and the movement between them.

Each of these households responds differently to the question at the root of their intimate relations: How should one live?[13] Both The Towers and Hamley take as their response an idea of aristocratic status, but the Cumnor notion of status and that of the Hamleys are very different. In what this difference consists remains to some extent unclear, although the Hamleys are an ancient Tory family, while the Earls of Cumnor owe their ascendency to the time of Queen Anne:

Squire Hamley's estate was not more than eight hundred acres or so. But his family had been in possession of it long before the Earls of Cumnor had been heard of; before the Hely-Harrisons had bought Coldstone Park; no one in Hollingford knew the time when the Hamleys had not lived at Hamley. "Ever since the Heptarchy," said the vicar. "Nay," said Miss Browning, "I have heard that there were Hamleys of Hamley before the Romans." (*Wives* 39)

Part of the distinction between the two families is captured by the fact that Molly is at home with the Hamleys (their name is, of course, no accident), but profoundly ill-at-ease on her first visit to the relatively recent Cumnor ("Come-not"?) family. Among the squirearchy Molly is treated as a daughter of the house, whereas among the Cumnors at The Towers she is patronized and condescended to; Squire Hamley and his younger son, Roger, are drawn to Molly's mental worth, while for Lady Cumnor in particular it is enough that Molly is one of "'the Hollingford people,'" villagers, hospitality to whom gives such trouble (*Wives* 7–8; 92). This distinction is not, of course, absolute; Lord Hollingford and his sister Lady Harriet, like Roger Hamley, are impressed by Molly's intelligence, despite their status as Cumnors. Lady Harriet assigns Molly to her brother Hollingford at a dance as "'a good, simple, intelligent little girl, which you'll think a great deal more of, I suppose, than of the frivolous fact of her being very pretty'" (*Wives* 310). And Lady Harriet is right. Lord Hollingford compliments Mrs. Gibson on Molly after the dance, saying, "'[w]hat a charming little lady that daughter of yours is! Most girls of her age are so difficult to talk to; but she is intelligent and full of interest in all sorts of sensible things; well read, too — she was up in *Le Règne Animal* — and very pretty!'" (*Wives* 311). Mrs. Hamley, on the other hand, errs as much as Mrs. Gibson in failing to discern Roger's worth over Osborne's 'sensibility' (*Wives* 65–66).

The question of how one should live is represented in domestic fiction as the proper province of the household, which means that economic considerations, according to such fictions, are instrumental ones. In this sense at least, domestic fiction is Aristotelian in its concerns. Action, in the Aristotelian view, is of two kinds, and it is in relation to this distinction that I have shown two senses of life to be operating in my account of intimate space. Action, in the first sense, is directed toward the satisfaction of necessity, and in the second sense, toward the pursuit of the beautiful or noble. This latter type, which is understood as the proper end of life, is only possible once leisure to pursue these ends has been secured, and is therefore dependent on action of the first kind and on a despotic hierarchy that ensures the master of the *oikos* is freed by the labour of others to pursue his own ends (see Booth 43–44). Booth, therefore, argues most convincingly that central to both the household and the *polis* is a knowledge of the proper use of wealth, which is praxis or free life in the community (66). Moreover, the virtue of a citizen, on Aristotle's account, can only be fully achieved in a regime that provides him with leisure (a result of freedom from economic constraint). Indeed, as Booth indicates, without such freedom, public deliberation is impossible; tyranny, then, "often seek[s] ways in which citizens may be kept busy and without leisure" (47). It is for this reason that when there is an intrusion of economic considerations into intimate space — that is, when fortune and status come to be seen as the ends of life and not as means to those ends, when nobility is misunderstood in terms of status and not pursuit — a disruption occurs. This is clearest in the courtship and marriage of Mr. Gibson and Hyacinth Kirkpatrick, née Clare, former governess at The Towers. Mrs. Kirkpatrick sees marriage wholly in economic terms: "'I wonder if I am to go on all my life toiling and moiling for money? It's not natural. Marriage is the natural thing; then the husband has all that kind of dirty work to do, and his wife sits in the drawing-room like a lady'" (*Wives* 100). It is worth remarking at this juncture that Mrs. Kirkpatrick sees the relationship between man and wife in terms of wholly separate gendered spheres, assigning the "dirty work" of getting and spending to masculine space and perceiving the feminine as "naturally" apart from it. Her account is mistaken, however, and this error contaminates the intimate space of the Gibson household. No sooner do the newlywed Gibsons return to Hollingford than the economy of the household begins to break down. The first sign of this breakdown is the departure of Molly's old nurse, Betty, whose long tenure in the household Mr. Gibson describes as "'a sort of service of the antique world'" (*Wives* 182). Betty is replaced by Maria, former under-housemaid at the Towers, a "'genteel girl!'" who "'always brings in a letter on a salver!'" (*Wives* 183), and who suits Hyacinth's pretensions to 'county' status.

The disruption of the Gibson household consists primarily in the new Mrs. Gibson's confusion as to the means and ends of living. Fortune and status are, for

Hyacinth, not the means to the good life but the essence of such a life, and in order to achieve these ends (which ought to be means), she willingly throws the household into disarray. Mr. Gibson's habit of dining at noon is put aside in favour of the comfort of "high-born ladies, with noses of aristocratic refinement" (*Wives* 183), who might be calling; his ordinary supper of bread and cheese is likewise banished in favour of "badly made omelettes, rissoles, vol-au-vents, croquets, and timbales" (*Wives* 185) that Mrs. Gibson feels won't "scent the house" (*Wives* 184). Such changes are, of course, trifles. While they touch on Mr. Gibson's comfort — he finds it difficult to arrange his doctor's rounds around "this new-fangled notion of a six o'clock dinner" (*Wives* 184) and the staff of the household gives notice — they are significant in that the space of the household is disrupted by them. Mr. Gibson does not combat his new wife on these small changes: "He had made up his mind before his marriage to yield in trifles, and be firm in greater things. But the differences of opinion about trifles arose every day, and were perhaps more annoying than if they had related to things of more consequence" (*Wives* 185). Mr. Gibson perceives these problems as "trifles" because they are confined to the arrangements of household space. But, I suggest, it is because these problems are so confined that they have to do with different responses to the question of how one should live. As such, these "trifles" must eventually affect all of the people who are involved with the Gibson household, although the good doctor does not admit this until it is almost too late:[14] "On the whole, it was as well that Mr. Gibson spent so much of his time from home. He sometimes thought so himself when he heard his wife's plaintive fret or pretty babble over totally indifferent things, and perceived of how flimsy a nature were all her fine sentiments" (*Wives* 337).

Now, it may be argued that my analysis of the Gibson household in terms of the ancient *oikos* fails to recognize the economic revolution that transformed the embedded and contained household into the contractarian liberal household (see Booth 9). My argument about the differing ends of life posited by Hyacinth and Gibson, after all, may be seen as failing to recognize the ways in which this transformation obscured the idea of the ends of economic life and the necessity of private virtue for the *autarky* of the polis. I hope to show, however, that the radical contractarianism on which such a challenge must be based not only misrepresents the project of liberalism, but in fact endangers that project. The transformation of the *oikos* economy into what we now understand as a market economy was coincident with, if not dependent on, a shift from hierarchical despotism to ideas of social order based on consent and contract. The voluntaristic model of political association, put forward in various forms by such thinkers as Hobbes and Locke, involved, at least theoretically, a shift away from status as the basis of all relations of power amongst individuals.[15] This move meant, among other things, that the preferences that governed the pursuit of ends were no longer seen as wholly determined by the master, as they were in the *oikos*, but determinable by all persons, and that the persons so involved in the establishment of ends were conceived of as alike in their freedom and rights. As Booth shows, the newly liberal household was grounded in ideas of equality, consent, and autonomy; in such a household, "persons are self-owners (or Kantian autonomous agents), pursuers of their own abilities, and individuals over whom control can be exercised, or exchanges effected, only through their consent" (9). Now, voluntarist or contractarian accounts of the liberal polity have consistently argued that the equality that is prerequisite to the idea of consent can only be advanced under a political philosophy that views individuals as bearers of rights in the abstract sense. On these accounts, to retain the notion of private virtue, which ancient political philosophers saw as crucial to the well-being of the polis, endangers the contractarian foundations of the liberal state because, in suggesting that there are preconditions for autonomy, it also suggests that individuals are not, in fact, alike in their claims to equality and rights. The implications of this have long been clear. If individuals are not equally self-owners, then the hierarchical despotism that preceded liberal contractarianism may any day return, because individuals can for this reason be stripped of their rights.

The problem is this: Can we advance a version of liberalism that both retains consent (and therefore, freedom and autonomy) and does not depend on a notion of the individuals as *a priori* equal? Can we advance, in such a liberalism, a concept of positive liberty that can bring about equality and not endanger the negative liberty at its heart? Must, as Alisdair MacIntyre has famously claimed, our choice be Aristotle or Nietzsche? I am arguing, in fact, that liberalism in its earliest formulations already contained the answer to this question, and that this answer depends on the place of the household. I have shown that Nancy Armstrong is in fact correct in identifying a discursive displacement of kinship, rank, and fortune (status) in favour of qualities of the mind as the "idiom of living." I agreed with Armstrong that this replacement is a profoundly political gesture, and I am now suggesting that its political import was an inevitable part of the shift of relationships of power from status to contract. Clearly, the idea that relationships of power are founded on consent, however theoretical that idea may be, means they are founded on some other grounds than status; their foundation, in fact, is whatever enables free and full consent. These conditions are qualities of the mind, in Armstrong's sense of the term.

The fundamental precondition for consent in liberal thought is the idea of reason. I have discussed the role of Descartes's assertion that "we should never allow ourselves to be convinced except on the evidence of our reason" (Descartes 30) in early feminist claims for women's education. These claims turned, in Cartesian fashion, on women's obligation to base all decisions, including submission to "male" authority, on rational understanding rather than on blind submission to custom. The republican or social contract model of political authority was advanced in the same way; both arguments have as their starting point a belief in a kind of commonwealth of reason, in and under which all persons are equal and equally able to consent. Significantly, however, the argument for equality of consent (and, by extension, self-ownership), was not based on common (equal and shared) reason, but on equal and shared rationality, which is the *capacity* for reason.[16] If this were not so, if the notion of equality in this sense did not mean capacity but an already existing reason, then the notion of the education of the citizen would not have played such a significant role in the political thought of the major liberal contractarians, Locke and Rousseau.[17]

To be a person, in the juridical sense, is for Locke to be both a self-owner and capable of consent. To be capable of consent is, finally, to reason, but this requires education. Booth usefully explains Locke's treatment of children in this sense:

Though the state of their reason does not yet permit them to be active contracting agents, they are nevertheless persons in a passive sense. That is, they are as equal as all persons with respect to dominion over one another; they are born to equality and freedom and not to thraldom. In its foundations, then, parental government properly understood shares in certain central qualities of all just human associations: the equality and freedom of persons (even if temporarily unequal in the degree to which these attributes have come fully into being) and the absence of enduring and natural relations of subordination among them. The authority of the parents, thus construed, does not derive from a right to rule based on an abiding superiority over their charges but rather from a duty to care for those who are born to freedom and who are not yet able to exercise it.[18]

If we take seriously the liberal account, both of an innate rationality understood as the primordial capacity to reason, and of the significance of education in the training of the citizen, then it is clear that what replaces status in the formulation of liberal relations of power is not consent but its precondition, rationality, which is a quality of the mind. Wollstonecraft makes this clear, as I have already shown. Her contention for juridical personhood on behalf of women, I argued, cannot be considered apart from her claim that virtue stems only from reason, and without repeating my argument, I will recall my claim that in Wollstonecraft's *The Wrongs of Woman* virtue is dependent on right reason, but is also inspired by right feeling. Thus the argument of every revolutionary, which according to Jean-Paul Sartre is "'we too are men'" ("Materialism" 217), is developed in a discourse that intends to show that the other is not in fact other but brother, a like creature, one capable not simply of reason but of virtue, sensibility, feeling. To say that I, too, am a man is in this sense to say that I have the inner complexity, the sensibility, and the capacity for virtuous action that is the philosophical precondition for free personhood in the liberal sense of the term. "Men," for Sartre, are "freedoms in possession of their own destinies" ("Materialism" 229). This is so because consent requires evaluation; the law, with its notion of competence, has long understood this.

Consequently, if feelings — as distinct in such philosophy from passions, which it is the task of reason to suppress[19] — are among the preconditions of evaluation and therefore of consent, then contractarian liberalism misunderstands its own origins in neglecting relations of *philia* alongside those of exchange. Another closely related implication hearkens back to seventeenth- and eighteenth-century claims that public virtue is an aggregate of private virtue. I am suggesting that this is so, indeed must be so, because, as Charles Taylor has shown, we come into selfhood in communities. Taylor argues that the vocabulary we have with which to discuss the good and the just (in other words, to engage in strong or means-end evaluation) we take from the community (e.g., *Papers* 2: 292), but, crucially, the community conceived of in this sense necessarily includes, indeed is predicated on, the household. If we come to be selves, and thus capable of juridical personhood, in the household/community, then that space is not and never can be a wholly private one. Moreover, while household space is distinguished from that of the marketplace partly by the affective relations that constitute both its immediacy and its intimacy, the household, because such *philia* is philosophically necessary to reason and therefore to consent and freedom, stands as the misrecognized foundation of the liberal polity.

I have brought up the displacement of status in favour of qualities of the mind through the transformation of the despotic *oikos* into the liberal household to provide a philosophical background for my claim that in *Wives and Daughters* there are no real "trifles." This means that Hyacinth's mistaken adherence to fortune and rank as the ends of life, rather than to the cultivation of those mental qualities wealth and status may afford, functions in the novel as a danger to the community and its (mutually determined and determining) ends of freedom, equality, and autonomy. In this sense what Mr. Gibson identifies as "trifles" in Hyacinth are not trifles at all, but the conditions of unfreedom. My larger claim, of course, is that this is true of domestic fiction as a genre. Thus Flora May in Yonge's *The Daisy Chain* spends little time in her own home, preferring instead to further her husband's political career; she insists that her infant daughter be kept quiet, without herself undertaking to quiet the child, and swears to her father that all is well, until the child dies of an overdose of opiated syrup. Likewise Bessie Keith's death in Yonge's *The Clever Woman of the Family*[20] is partly brought on by her constant toying with her unwanted suitor: "She had never either decidedly accepted or repelled his affection, but . . . let him follow her like a little dog and amused herself with him in the absence of better game" (318). Anything that touches or distorts intimate space in such fiction is part of a larger pattern of corruption, so that it is, finally, "the small domestic failings — the webs, the distortions of truth" (*Wives* 380) that provoke the conflicts of *Wives and Daughters*.

It must, I think, be said that there are different senses of "trifle" operating here. One sense has to do with minor events and alterations that have little or no direct bearing on the important or noble ends of life, but that signal a disagreement as to the nature of those ends. Another, but related, sense of the term has to do with patterns of error, in which the important is treated as unimportant, and the wholly insignificant treated as wholly significant. Thus Mrs. Gibson's confusions as to the proper use of household space, which is a confusion about the ends and means of life, is "trifling" in this last sense. Cynthia, who is in many ways the most interesting character in *Wives and Daughters*, cannot be faulted, on my account, for "trifling" with the affections of her various lovers, simply because she has not been raised to make these kinds of clear distinctions. Recall that the faculty of discrimination, for Locke, is as important as that of abstraction. That Cynthia's education is at fault is clear in her plea to Molly before leaving for London:

"Would you be my friend if — if it turned out ever that I had done very wrong things? Would you remember how very difficult it has sometimes been to me to act rightly" (she took hold of Molly's hand as she spoke). "We won't speak of mamma, for your sake as much as mine or hers; but you must see she is not one to help a girl with much good advice, or good — Oh, Molly, you don't know how I was neglected just at a time when I wanted friends most. Mamma does not know it; it is not in her to know what I might have been if I had only fallen into wise, good hands. But I know it; and what's more," continued she, suddenly ashamed of her unusual exhibition of feeling, "I try not to care, which I daresay is really the worst of all; but I could worry myself to death if I once took to serious thinking." (*Wives* 460)

In what does this neglect consist?[21] I think it is clear that Mrs. Gibson's error with regard to her own child is the same as her confusion in the Gibson household. And the problem is a grave one. While Cynthia's troubles begin, like Flora May's or Bessie Keith's, with small domestic failings, they almost lead both her and Molly into disaster. Cynthia, at fifteen, was driven to borrow money from a bachelor, Mr. Preston, in her mother's absence. While Hyacinth had written that Cynthia might vacation with friends, Cynthia tells Molly, "'she had never said how I was to get any money for the journey'" (*Wives* 492). Again it is a problem of confusing the really trivial and the important: Cynthia says to Molly,

"I wish I had her letter to show you; you must have seen some of mamma's letters, though; don't you know how she always seems to leave out just the important point of every fact? In this case she descanted largely on the enjoyment she was having, and the kindness she was receiving, and her wish that I could have been with her, and her gladness that I too was going to have some pleasure, but the only thing that would have been of real use to me she left out, and that was where she was going to next." (*Wives* 492)

This omission leads Cynthia to rely on Mr. Preston for help, rather than her mother; she is grateful to him for "'crumbs of kindness'" and "'little by little'" tells him her troubles (*Wives* 493). This vocabulary of the minute echoes, rhetorically, the narrative progress of Cynthia's troubles; just as she reveals her situation to Mr. Preston, so too she is, little by little, drawn into a pattern of deceit that begins with omission and ends in falsehood. Mr. Preston convinces Cynthia to accept the loan of twenty pounds by belittling its significance: Cynthia says, "'[h]e had twenty pounds in his pocket, he said, and really did not know what to do with it, should not want it for months. . . . Twenty pounds would not be too much, I must take it all, and so on'" (*Wives* 493–94). Cynthia accepts the money, telling Molly later, "'that was the beginning! It does not sound so very wrong, does it, Molly?'" (*Wives* 494). But of course the money is soon spent, and once it is gone both the magnitude and the significance of the loan rapidly become apparent to Cynthia. She tells Molly, "'I turned sick at the thought of telling mamma, and knew enough of our affairs to understand how very difficult it would be to muster up the money'" (*Wives* 495), and a letter from Mr. Preston proposing marriage and referring to that "'unlucky debt, which was to be a debt no longer, only an advance of the money to be hereafter mine, if only — '" (*Wives* 495) is eventually answered with the promise of marriage.

The first omissions soon, of course, give way to larger deceits. It is four or five years later when Cynthia confesses to Molly her secret engagement. Still bound by her promise to Preston, Cynthia nevertheless engages herself to Roger Hamley.

"'[I]t seemed,'" she says, "'a way of assuring myself that I was quite free; and I did like Roger'" (*Wives* 497). Now she is threatened with a public revelation of her conduct; Preston holds love letters written to him by Cynthia, which he threatens to reveal unless she acknowledges the engagement. Cynthia enlists Molly to return the unlucky twenty pounds and get the letters back, but swears her to secrecy. Among the consequences of Cynthia's "underhand work"[22] is the tainture of Molly's reputation; the gossips of Hollingford hear of Molly's meeting with Preston, and her standing in the town suffers:

There was a tacit and under-hand protest against her being received on the old terms. Every one was civil to her, but no one was cordial; there was a very perceptible film of difference in their behaviour to her from what it was formerly; nothing that had outlines and could be defined. But Molly, for all her clear conscience and her brave heart, felt acutely that she was only tolerated, not welcomed. She caught the buzzing whispers of the two Miss Oakeses', who, when they first met the heroine of the prevailing scandal, looked at her askance, and criticized her pretensions to good looks, with hardly an attempt at under-tones. (*Wives* 548)

This, too, is a small change; but, again, true trifles in the world of *Wives and Daughters* are rare or nonexistent. This is so because trifles are presented not in terms of their opposition to things of enormous significance, but in terms of gradations, and conflict arises, in *Wives and Daughters*, when we fail to see that small actions can have large and telling consequences. Mrs. Gibson's "small domestic failings" (*Wives* 380) are signs of larger errors of conduct, and her omissions in her letters to Cynthia provoke a series of events that almost sink both Molly and the Hamleys. It is Miss Browning, spinster friend of the Gibsons, who first identifies the nature of the problem, although she erroneously assumes that it is Molly who is at fault: "'As if the poor girl who has been led away into deceit already would scruple much at going on in falsehood'" (*Wives* 541). Likewise, the exchange between Mr. Gibson and Cynthia, when the whole story comes out, suggests that even the most minute events cannot be considered apart from their consequences, and that these consequences are necessarily larger than their immediate purview: "'What faults you have fallen into have been mere girlish faults at first, — leading you into much deceit, I grant.' 'Don't give yourself the trouble to define the shades of blackness," said Cynthia, bitterly. "I am not so obtuse but what I know them all better than any one can tell me'" (*Wives* 578).

I want to suggest that this synecdochal pattern of relationships between the trifle and its largest consequences has some implications for domestic fiction as a mode. In my earlier comments on the subject of "intimate space," I observed that the domain of the household could not be perceived as withdrawn from social and political relationships. This implication of domestic space in social concerns is signaled, in part, by the movement between households that is part of the organization of domestic fiction, and in part by conceptions of the means and ends of life. In my account, the pursuit of the means of life is a necessary precondition for the pursuit of its ends in the space of the household, and the examination of the different ends of life — the province of domestic fiction — is an originary condition for the health of the polity. While the public consequences of Cynthia's deceptions are averted by Molly's steadfastness and Lady Harriet's defense of her honesty, the results of Osborne Hamley's deceits are much graver.

Osborne and Roger Hamley are brothers:

Osborne, the eldest — so called after his mother's maiden name — was full of tastes, and had some talent. His appearance had all the grace and refinement of his mother's. He was sweet-tempered and affectionate, almost as demonstrative as a girl. He did well at school, carrying away many prizes; and was, in a word, the pride and delight of both father and mother. . . . Roger was two years younger than Osborne; clumsy and heavily built, like his father; his face was square, and the expression grave, and rather immobile. He was good, but dull, his schoolmasters said. He won no prizes, but brought home a favourable report of his conduct. . . . It was a great question as to whether he was to follow his brother to college after he left Rugby. Mrs Hamley thought it would be rather a throwing away of money, as he was so little likely to distinguish himself in intellectual pursuits; anything practical — such as a civil engineer — would be more the line of life for him. She thought that it would be too mortifying for him to go to the same college and university as his brother, who was sure to distinguish himself — and, to be repeatedly plucked, to come away wooden-spoon at last. (*Wives* 42)

The great hope of the Hamleys, however, is a failure, and Osborne's error puts the family and the village at risk. Molly's first visit to Hamley is marred by Mrs. Hamley's news that Osborne has "'just passed'" his examinations; he is "'only low down among the *junior optimes*, and not where he had expected, and had led us to expect'" (*Wives* 85). Before long, Molly discovers that Hamley Hall itself is disrupted, that "[s]omething [is] out of tune" (*Wives* 196). The Squire tells Molly their troubles:

"Molly, we are all wrong at home! Osborne has lost the fellowship at Trinity he went back to try for. Then he has gone and failed miserably in his degree, after all that he said, and that his mother said; and I, like a fool, went and boasted about my clever son. I can't understand it. I never expected anything extraordinary from Roger; but Osborne — ! And then it has thrown madam into one of her bad fits of illness." (*Wives* 192)

Osborne's faults have grave consequences. He has run up bills at Cambridge, and borrowed money as well, to bankroll a secret marriage to a French servant-girl. The parallel to Cynthia's behaviour is plain, but the consequences still worse. Without knowing the cause of the debts, the Squire is forced to mortgage some of his land. More, the drainage project the Squire undertook to reclaim barren land is stopped, and the working men laid off (*Wives* 199). In short, it is the brilliant and clever Osborne who endangers not only Hamley Hall, but the tenants for whom the Squire is responsible. If, as for Aristotle, the village is a microcosm of the state, Osborne has clearly led the *micropolis* away from freedom and self-sufficiency. This is the Squire's real grief:

"I know I turned them off — what could I do? I'd no more money for their weekly wages; it's a loss to me, as you know. He doesn't know . . . how it cut me to turn 'em off just before winter set in. I lay awake many a night thinking of it, and I gave them what I had — I did, indeed. I hadn't got money to pay 'em, but I had three barren cows fattened, and gave every scrap of meat to the men, and I let 'em go into the woods and gather what was fallen, and I winked at their breaking off old branches" (*Wives* 357)

To say that the end is enacted through the means is by no means revolutionary. Sartre has shown this:

Indeed all free behavior posits an end. But free behavior is surpassing of Being by a being situated in the midst of Being. The end is *to* come to Being. It transcends it and preserves it within itself. Therefore it envelops an understanding of Being, since in Being it must come to Being. At the same time, as an end, it groups the beings that are present in a meaningful unity; they become means. And . . . the synthesis of *all* the means cannot be distinguished from the end. This means that the end is the illuminating organization of means. (*Truth* 17–18)

Sartre's claim suggests, among other things, that our means are our ends; this is so in the sense that they are mutually determining as well as mutually corrigible, and in the sense that we cannot give up one without the other. It is therefore true, even tautological, to say that the province of domestic fiction is the investigation of our ends and our means. By this I mean that domestic fiction inquires into the conditions of freedom. It does so by considering the proper relationship of our means to life's ends, as I have shown in my discussion of Hyacinth Kirkpatrick Gibson. It also does so by investigating the mental conditions that make possible the virtue of the citizen and the health of the state. I have shown that the thematic organization of "trifles" in *Wives and Daughters* both suggests and defends the province of domestic fiction, conceived in this way. The movement of the young from their confined and unfree state to autonomy and freedom within the community — *Bildung* — is most often the organizational device behind such fictions. This shows, as the contrast between Molly and Cynthia makes clear, that the affective relations of the household are not and never have been withdrawn from the arrangements of the polis. Instead, such relations are an essential (and essentially contested, in a different sense) precondition for the health of that polis in a liberal state that takes as its goal the task of securing the greatest possible freedom for the greatest possible number. If domestic fiction continues to make profoundly political gestures, and I am saying that it does, it does so against a background understanding of the household as the space, more than any other, in which the freedom of its members must be secured. By this I mean that the "old rigmarole of childhood" with which *Wives and Daughters* begins does more than locate the household at the foundation of the polity; it asserts with John Donne that "no man is an island, entire of itself" and with Blaise Pascal that had Cleopatra's nose been shorter, the entire course of history would have changed. That rigmarole, like the one of the horseshoe nail, says that there can be no real trifles just as there can be no way to treat our ends without our means: "For want of a nail, the shoe was lost; for want of a shoe, the horse was lost; for want of a horse, the rider was lost; for want of a rider the battle was lost; for want of the battle the war was lost; for want of the war the kingdom was lost, and all for the want of a horseshoe nail."

The household is, finally, the foundation of the polity; it is so because it is intimate space and thus that space in which we cultivate our selves as rights bearers. And if the household is the root of the liberal *polis*, it is also, because of the affective relations that govern it, the space of liberal fulfillment, of ends rather than market means. Because this is so, both the polity and the household on which — and for which — it stands are imperilled by trifles that ignore the true nature of liberal self-fulfillment by way of positing an archaic vocabulary of self and worth, one predicated on status and show rather than on virtue and reason.

Two formulations on the subject of political fiction are worth recalling at this point. Rosemarie Bodenheimer argues that the task of political fiction is to confront and negotiate the rift between public vocabularies, which theorize social arrangements, and the temporal experience of individual histories (231–32). Victoria Middleton suggests, similarly, that the political novel occurs at the intersection of two fictive worlds: The private world of individual history and character development, and the public one of political conflict (4). My point is *not* that the eruption of the so-called private domain functions to suppress the historical and economic information that constitutes the public domain, but that the rift between these languages or fictive worlds is not properly understood as a rift at all. In this sense the task of confrontation and negotiation, which for Bodenheimer describes and defines political fiction, is one of recognition and diagnosis. And what is diagnosed, to resort to a type of Aristotelian claim, is a species of tyranny to which, in the absence or illness of intimate space, the public domain must always fall prey. Thus, as I will show in my next chapter, domestic fiction sought not to suppress "historical information," as Nancy Armstrong would have it (by which she apparently means economic information), but to represent that dimension of the human condition as instrumental to the task of living a good life.

NOTES

1.   See, in particular, Auerbach, Ch. 3 (63–108).

2.   See especially DuPlessis, Ch. One, "Endings and Contradictions" (1–19), for her argument about nineteenth-century fiction.

3.   For similar views, see Boone; Foster; Yeazell. See Shaffer for an important challenge to the conventional view of nineteenth-century marriage plots.

4.   My use of "generalized other" here is intended to recall Benhabib's discussion of liberalism in *Situating the Self* (148–202). She situates this abstract rights-bearer partly in terms of the "concrete other" posited by Gilligan in her developmental theory of female ethics (*Voice*). For a critique of liberalism in terms of this abstract bearer of rights, see Young, "Impartiality."

5.   My thinking on this matter owes a great deal to Trollope's treatment of the romance plot in his political saga, the Palliser novels. While a discussion of these books in such a context must here remain a promissory note, I will remark that in *Can You Forgive Her?* and *Phineas Finn*, Trollope adopts parallel narratives in order to figure private moral dilemmas as inextricable from the dilemmas of parliamentary politics through which he charts the elephantine progress of reform.

6.   But see Wheatley for a view of Rachel's humiliation and illness as a necessary subordinating device that fits her for marriage to Alick (904). Wheatley emphasizes masculine control of female intellect in Ermine and, ultimately, Rachel; I concur, rather, with Sturrock, who points to Ermine's writing as a mitigation of the anti-public dimension of the novel (39).

7.   Trollope's Pallliser sequence complicates this means-end hierarchy in an investigation of differing notions of the ends of life that I suggest is profoundly disillusioned about the responses he saw to the question of how we should live.

8.   But see Langland for a view of the home as the site in which money entered social signification and consolidated middle-class power, extending and entrenching market structures, through the mediation of women.

9.   I am deeply indebted for this point and for much of what follows to William James Booth's remarkable account of the place of the household in ancient and modern states.

10.   *Politics* I.ii.1252b27. For ease of reference, I have adopted the method most philosophers use for citing Aristotle, by book, chapter, and section.

11.   Charlotte Mary Yonge's *The Daisy Chain* is an important exception. Here, the novel's focus is almost solely on the May household and their enormous brood of children. But even here the May children achieve their *Bildung* through examination and evaluation of other idioms of living; that this is achieved largely through visits to the Mays rather than May visits elsewhere does not, in my view, pose a serious challenge to my argument.

12.   Foster, however, sees Molly as "confine[d] to a small, private arena [which] . . . seem[s] to represent a diminution of female potential" (176) and the romantic ending as "Gaskell's final commitment to conventional womanhood" (181).

13.   I adopt this from Nussbaum, who takes Plato's remark that "[it] is no chance matter we are discussing, but how one should live" from the *Republic* as the starting point for her thesis in *Love's Knowledge* that "certain literary texts . . . are indispensable to a philosophical inquiry in the ethical sphere" (23).

14.   Note that Langland's reading, which quite differently takes Hyacinth Gibson as an "insensitive and selfish" wife and mother but a loyal and discriminating household and status manager in class terms (133–34), likewise asserts the vulnerability to social power created by contempt for details (136).

15.   Booth has also made this point (9).

16.   See, for example, Descartes:

Good sense is mankind's most equitably divided endowment, for everyone thinks that he is so abundantly provided with it that even those with the most insatiable appetites and most difficult to please in other ways do not usually want more than they have of this. As it is not likely that everyone is mistaken, this evidence shows that the ability to judge correctly, and to distinguish the true from the false — which is really what is meant by good sense or reason — is the same by innate nature in all men; and that differences of opinion are not due to differences in intelligence, but merely to the fact that we use different approaches and consider different things. For it is not enough to have a good mind: one must use it well. The greatest souls are capable of the greatest vices as well as of the greatest virtues; and those who walk slowly can, if they follow the right path, go much farther than those who run rapidly in the wrong direction. (3–4)

17.   See Rousseau's *Emile*, esp. Book I, and Locke's *Thoughts*.

18.   Booth 104. See, for example, Locke, *Two Treatises* II.§55–58.

19.   Thus, for example, Descartes says of "philosophers of ancient times" that "[t]heir control of their thoughts . . . was so absolute, that is, they were so accustomed to regulate their desires and other passions, that they had some justification for considering themselves richer and more powerful, more free and happier, than any other man who did not have this

philosophy, and who, however much he might be favored by nature and fortune, had no such control over his desires" (20–21).

20.   Wheatley analyzes Bessie's sensational demise in detail.

21.   Buchanan argues that Mrs. Gibson's neglect of Cynthia, combined with her inability to see her daughter as a distinct individual, "blocks Cynthia's growth into autonomous womanhood," while Molly's "network of surrogate mothers . . . provide[s] the delicate balance between merging and separation [that] can thus more objectively retrieve and reinforce the girl's strengths" (500). While Buchanan's point that shared female experience provides necessary female autonomy in Gaskell (512) is interesting, she does not suggest how this model provides a significant end for Molly's *Bildung*; if Molly will, indeed, "carry her self-reliance into her status as a wife" (512), then surely she will not need to reproduce the shared mothering that made her own autonomy possible.

22.   The term is Molly's (*Wives* 500).

5

"We too are men":
Enacting Revolution in *North and South*

> TROFIMOV: The vast majority of the intellectual people I know, seek nothing, do
> nothing, are not fit as yet for work of any kind. They call themselves intellectual,
> but they treat their servants as inferiors, behave to the peasants as though they
> were animals, learn little, read nothing seriously, do practically nothing, only talk
> about science and know very little about art. They are all serious people, they all
> have severe faces, they all talk of weighty matters and air their theories, and yet
> the vast majority of us — ninety-nine per cent — live like savages, at the least
> thing fly to blows and abuse, eat piggishly, sleep in filth and stuffiness, bugs
> everywhere, stench and damp and moral impurity. And it's clear all our fine talk
> is only to divert our attention and other people's. Show me where to find the
> *crèches* there's so much talk about, and the reading-rooms? They only exist in
> novels: in real life there are none of them.
> — Anton Chekhov, *The Cherry Orchard*, Act II.

We err, as I have said, in assuming a rift between the political and the domestic in
fiction. This assumption fails in part because it oversimplifies notions of the private
and the public, and my reading of *Wives and Daughters* attempts to redress this
problem by attending to the political gestures made even within the most domestic
of fictions. What remains to be shown, however, is the ways in which avowedly
political fiction likewise depends on the originary and intimate space of the household in order to make its claims. I want therefore to turn now to Gaskell's *North
and South* in an effort to counter those readings of this novel that rely, in my view,
too heavily on the notion of prescriptively separated spheres.

Since Louis Cazamian's seminal treatise on the social novel in England (1903),
Gaskell's *North and South* has been read as a social-problem novel in a set of
interpretations that have, on the whole, treated the resolution of its romance plot,
Nancy Armstrong-like, as a retreat from or containment of public and political
problems in a highly romanticized, domesticated, and "individual solution."[1]
Others, such as Miriam Allott, have taken the romance plot as the whole of the

novel, treating Gaskell's account of industrial England and the strike as "look[ing] forward . . . to the emotional entanglements of a later age, when the pattern of society adds new complications to the relationships between men and women."[2] Angus Easson's considered treatment of both *Mary Barton* and *North and South* takes seriously both the industrial and personal issues of the novel, but nevertheless sees them very much as separate strands "held together in Thornton and Margaret" (95).

Catherine Gallagher's analysis in *The Industrial Reformation of English Fiction* complicates the commonplace readings of *North and South* by taking as its thesis the notion that social cohesion can be achieved through introducing the cooperative relations that sustain private life to the public domain (147). She reads the novel, however, as finally implying a break between the two spheres. Thus, the novel, on this account, by giving us versions of the action that are foreign to Margaret's view, and that thus undo the official connections between public good and private behaviour, subverts the assumptions shared by both Margaret and the narrator (169–71). While Gallagher's work has provided a significant corrective to those readings that take individual solutions as a retreat from social responsibility, her final conclusion, that women can maintain their moral superiority only through confinement in the home and isolation from the marketplace (177–78), fails to take into account both Margaret's final status as investor in Marlborough Mills and the significant interpenetration of intimate and market space that marks the novel's resolution.

Rosemarie Bodenheimer's treatment of *North and South*, which builds on Gallagher's foundational work, goes one step further, to argue that Gaskell's interest both politically and domestically is in accommodation, negotiation, and the avoidance of revolt. This is so for Bodenheimer even in the romantic solution that permits Margaret to engage in economic, social, and domestic partnership with Thornton (63). Yet her conviction that Gaskell "dismantles" the separation of spheres that underlies the narrative commonplace of woman as social saviour betrays a belief in the dominance of separate spheres ideology I believe to be false; my claim is that Gaskell, in her treatment of these domains, is extending and expanding liberalism rather than undermining it.

More recently, Dorice Williams Elliott has attempted to redress problems in *North and South* criticism by suggesting, convincingly, that Gaskell is offering a new paradigm for social relations, one in which women inhabit a sphere Elliott calls "social" and that mediates between domestic and political space. According to Elliott, while Gaskell "does not challenge the private arrangements of the domestic sphere where men rule over women legally, sexually, and emotionally," the novel nevertheless claims an independent, autonomous role for women in the social sphere, one modeled on the role of the district visitor (25). While Elliott's claim that marriage stands as a metaphor and model for class relations accords to some degree with my reading of the novel, I am uncomfortable with her description of Margaret's role as a mediator of social relations; such an account, it seems to me, blurs the significance of both Margaret's *Bildung* and the resolution of conflict between master and man that is achieved by Higgins and Thornton. I am similarly uncomfortable even with Barbara Leah Harman's exciting discussion of female public appearance in *North and South*, less because of any flaw in her treatment of the merging of private and public matters than because of her emphasis on private affairs as primarily sexual in nature, and the consequent elision of other ends to which intimate space and indeed intimacy itself may be devoted ("In Promiscuous Company"). I want to suggest that Margaret cannot be seen as the sole mediator of *North and South*, even as the intimate domain of the novel cannot be seen as solely or even largely concerned with sexual intimacy. Moreover, while Elliott's notion of a social sphere for women ably redresses problems with earlier Gaskell criticism, I will show that the blurring of distinctions between private and public space occurs not through some mediatory social sphere, but through the colonization of economic space by the concerns and affective relations of the household.

My first claim, that *North and South* details a contest among cultures, is an uncontroversial one.[3] The heroine, Margaret Hale, moves between two major and three minor *topoi*, and, as in *Wives and Daughters*, this movement is necessary to the investigation of the differing ends of life. In *North and South*, however, the differing ends of life are not figured in terms of individual households, but in terms of sub-cultures: We see the ends of life contrasted through the juxtaposition of the rural and the urban (Helstone and Oxford placed against Milton and London) and of the north (industry) and south (agriculture). This movement is necessary because Margaret's *Bildung* requires her to choose for herself, and from among a variety of alternatives, both the proper ends of life and the means to those ends; nor is she the only character for whom this movement provokes such an investigation. Her father, Mr. Hale, resigns his position as vicar of Helstone because he becomes a dissenter; part of his refusal of hypocrisy in this regard is his relocation of his family to the manufacturing town of Milton-Northern. Mr. Thornton, the manufacturer and the figure who, above all others, is attended by the anxiety surrounding the figure of the merchant or trader, likewise undergoes a refinement of his ideas of the ends of life; while he does so without leaving Milton, this change is provoked by the intrusion of other points of view (particularly Margaret's) into his way of life.

Despite the small role that the southern hamlet of Helstone plays in the plot of *North and South*, it is a major *topos* in the story because it is the major counterpart to Milton-Northern. Helstone is a kind of ideal or fairy-tale world, as Margaret's suitor, Henry Lennox, is aware. When Margaret describes it as "'a hamlet,'" with a "'church and a few houses near it on the green — cottages, rather — with roses growing all over them'" (*North* 42), Lennox is gently mocking:

"And flowering all the year round, especially at Christmas — make your picture complete," said he.

"No," replied Margaret, somewhat annoyed, "I am not making a picture. I am trying to describe Helstone as it really is. You should not have said that."

"I am penitent," he answered. "Only it really sounded like a village in a tale rather than in real life."

"And so it is," replied Margaret, eagerly. "All the other places in England that I have seen seem so hard and prosaic-looking, after the New Forest. Helstone is like a village in a poem — in one of Tennyson's poems. But I won't try and describe it any more. You would only laugh at me if I told you what I think of it — what it really is." (*North* 42–43)

Lennox is right. Margaret adopts here the picturesque terms of her idealization of her home in the New Forest. Because she has been away, living with her Aunt Shaw and her cousin Edith for ten years, Helstone has receded into dream; it has become unreal, the place where her "bright holidays" (*North* 35) are passed. Her memories of the village are marked by a *romanticization* of home without that familiarity that would take them out of the poetic or fairy-tale realm. Thus, Margaret tells Lennox, "'I can't describe my home. It is home, and I can't put its charm into words'" (*North* 43). Indeed, for Margaret, home is not a place but a picture; it is the *picturesque*, more like Richard Payne Knight's "didactic poem," *The Landscape*, than it is like much of Tennyson:

> [T]he retir'd and antiquated cot; —
> Its roof with weeds and mosses cover'd o'er,
> And honeysuckles climbing round the door;
> While mantling vines along its walls are spread,
> And clust'ring ivy decks the chimney's head. (348)

Knight shared with his contemporary, Uvedale Price, a sense of the picturesque as an educated mode of aesthetic vision, an eye and mind educated in the principles, not of landscape, but of the Italian landscape painters who first established the picturesque (Hussey 14). For Knight, "the objects and circumstances called *picturesque* . . . afford no pleasure, but to persons conversant with the art of painting, and sufficiently skilled in it to distinguish, and be really delighted with its real excellences" (*Analytical Inquiry* 349). While Price sought to preserve the notion of picturesque qualities inherent in the object, he, too, asserted the importance of "a cultivated eye" (356), and thus for both thinkers[4] the object of the picturesque gaze, like Helstone in the early chapters of *North and South*, is formed, literally and figuratively, through the human ability to comprehend it as art. This ability, moreover, does not stem from knowledge of the picturesque object itself, but from knowledge of the painterly tradition. Thus Margaret's demurral, "'I cannot tell you about my own home. I don't quite think it is a thing to be talked about, unless you knew it'" (*North* 43), does not suggest the hominess of that supposedly familiar space, but is itself ironic; Margaret does not know her home, and thus cannot talk about it in terms other than those of the picturesque.

Margaret's return to Helstone, after her cousin Edith's marriage to Captain Lennox (Henry Lennox's brother), bears out this tension between appearance and reality:

This life — at least these walks — realized all Margaret's anticipations. She took a pride in her forest. Its people were her people. She made hearty friends with them; learned and delighted in using their peculiar words; took up her freedom amongst them; nursed their babies . . . resolved before long to teach at the school, where her father went every day as to an appointed task, but she was continually tempted off to go and see some individual friend — man, woman, or child — in some cottage in the green shade of the forest. Her out-of-doors life was perfect. Her in-doors life had its drawbacks. With the healthy shame of a child, she blamed herself for her keenness of sight, in perceiving that all was not as it should be there. (*North* 48–49)

There are several interesting dimensions to this passage. First, it is clear that Margaret's fairy-tale home, which we have already seen evading any description other than that of the picturesque, can retain its picturesque quality only outside the walls of the parsonage. I suggest that this is so because the enforced familiarity of the household, the even hypertrophied intimacy of that space (although here I use the term "intimate" to denote proximity rather than a quality of life chez Hale) intrudes itself on Margaret's view, and reduces the distance necessary for her mis-perception of it as ideal. That Margaret's response to her mother's dissatisfaction with Helstone[5] is to "try to tempt her forth on to the beautiful, broad, upland, sun-streaked, cloud-shadowed common" (*North* 49) bears out my notion that the qualities Margaret associated, while in London, with "home" can only be found outside, where the distance necessary for her chronic confusion of appearance and reality remains uninterrupted.

Second, Margaret's pride in the forest, and in its people, is revealing; that "[i]ts people were her people" (*North* 48) calls to mind the privileging of the gazing subject in the paradigm of the picturesque. Because, as a mode of viewing, the picturesque required a knowledge of art, the picturesque, and indeed aesthetic vision generally, was largely the province of the educated and monied classes and was thus predicated on material prosperity. An analogy may thus be drawn between the control of the phenomenal world in the service of art, and politico-economic control over the nonmonied classes.[6] Margaret's role among "her people" is as a Lady Bountiful, visiting the sick, reading to the aged, and nursing the babies. Any other role, such as that of teacher, that would remove "her people" from their position as peasants is indefinitely postponed.[7]

Margaret's treatment of "old Isaac" in the sketching scene with Henry Lennox may, however, pose a problem for my claim that the people of the forest are, for Margaret, valued primarily in terms of their role as figures in a picturesque landscape. Lennox comes to visit Helstone parsonage, and he and Margaret go out sketching. Their subject is a pair of tumbledown cottages, built by squatters half a century before (*North* 57). The foresters are planning on taking them down, Margaret tells Lennox, when the old man who remains in one is dead (*North* 57). She goes to speak to the "'poor old fellow'" (*North* 57), and Lennox sketches the pair: "Mr Lennox hastily introduced the two figures into his sketch, and finished up the landscape with a subordinate reference to them" (*North* 57). Such figures would not have been unusual in picturesque landscapes of the time; indeed, the figures considered most appropriate to a picturesque landscape were those of the peasantry, who, as objects of the gaze, are valued in terms of our ability to comprehend them as art.[8] To be sure, in this instance, it is Lennox rather than Margaret who introduces old Isaac into his sketch,[9] but Margaret, like her father, admires Lennox's work. Indeed, Margaret so admires the sketch of Isaac and herself that she resolves to try one herself: "'I wonder if I could manage figures? There are so many people about here whom I should like to sketch'" (*North* 58). I suggest that Margaret's desire to sketch the local yeomanry, as part of her avowed admiration of local simplicity and naturalness, is indicative of her refusal to see them on their own terms, a refusal that will characterize Margaret's dealings with those she perceives as her inferiors through much of the novel.

This scene, like Margaret's attempt to describe Helstone to Lennox and her disillusionment with life at Helstone parsonage, is part of a tension between appearance and reality that pervades the novel. Even the urbane Henry Lennox is drawn in; the "aspect of home" as the two return from their sketching expedition is "all right and bright" (*North* 57), and after dinner he echoes her earlier description of the place:

"What a perfect life you seem to live here! I have always felt rather contemptuously towards the poets before, with their wishes, 'Mine be a cot beside a hill,' and that sort of thing: but now I am afraid that the truth is, I have been nothing better than a Cockney. Just now I feel as if twenty years' hard study of law would be amply rewarded by one year of such an exquisite serene life as this — such skies!" looking up — "such crimson and amber foliage, so perfectly motionless as that!" pointing to some of the great forest trees which shut in the garden as if it were a nest. (*North* 60)

Lennox is, as the reader knows, misled; the parsonage at Helstone is no comfortable nest, and the life of the Hales is far from hearty. Nor can the out-of-doors life, which remains perfect, properly compensate for the tainture of intimate space by Mrs. Hale's dissatisfaction and ambition, since both Margaret and Lennox misapprehend the *topos* of the New Forest by viewing it solely in terms of surface appearances. The vocabulary of apprehension and misapprehension that Gaskell adopts to characterize these impressions, moreover, ironizes them from the very beginning. If home is "all right and bright," this is only one of its aspects, and that the picturesque one; "aspect" is, after all, a painterly term that suggests the brightness, like the rightness, here, is only on the surface.

Margaret, of course, largely encounters the surface. She moves through her own home as a stranger, reintroduced after ten years to a fairy-tale nest with which she is rapidly disillusioned; she moves through the New Forest like a tourist, viewing the landscape rather than becoming implicated in it. Her initial reaction to the North is much the same. Mr. Hale has resigned his ministry, and accepted a new position as tutor in Milton-Northern; to make the move easier for Mrs. Hale to bear, the family is established first at the seaside town of Heston, near Milton. The town

has a character of its own, as different from the little bathing-places in the south of England as they again from those of the Continent. To use a Scotch word, everything looked more "purposelike." The country carts had more iron, and less wood and leather about the horse-gear; the people in the streets, although on pleasure bent, had yet a busy mind. The colours looked grayer — more enduring, not so gay and pretty. There were no smock-frocks, even among the country-folk; they retarded motion, and were apt to catch on machinery, and so the habit of wearing them had died out. (*North* 95)

As readers, we know why there are no smock-frocks in the north; Margaret, however, is struck only by the differences between north and south (*North* 95). The seaside town remains, for her, a series of "unusual scenes moving before her like pictures, which she cared not in her laziness to have fully explained" (*North* 96). Thus, despite the family's move to the north, Margaret remains unimplicated in her surroundings. She remains, that is, an immigrant, one who migrates, or even a tourist, journeying toward a scene but never becoming part of it.

I take this notion of the tourist from Janet Giltrow's account of travel narratives, which she says always advance toward the denouement of homecoming (132). When, as is true of the Hale's migration northward in *North and South*, the one-way journey of permanent emigration structures the narrative, that ideal of the round trip nevertheless structures the writer's account in terms of a "poignant disappointment" and "unresolvable alienation" (Giltrow 132). Characteristically, the kind of pleasure in landscape that typifies the tourist's reactions does not, as in Giltrow's account of Susanna Moodie, readily anticipate incorporation into the scene she observes (133). I would suggest that this may be an apt description of Margaret's reactions as well. Like Moodie's account of Canada in the early stages of *Roughing It In the Bush*, Margaret's willingness to neglect concrete details — explanations of these unusual scenes — is "that of genteel sightseeing – and a quick, unimplicating view of foreign sites" (Giltrow 133).

I introduce this discussion of the tourist in order to capture some of the reasons for the distinction between appearance and reality Gaskell lays out in her treatment of the conflicting subcultures of *North and South*. To know a place, in the terms set out in this fiction, one must be implicated in it. This is perhaps clearest in the initial conflict between the northern-bred manufacturer, Thornton, and Margaret, the southern aesthete. Thornton says

"I would rather be a man toiling, suffering — nay, failing and successless — here, than lead a dull prosperous life in the old worn grooves of what you call more aristocratic society down in the South, with their slow days of careless ease. One may be clogged with honey and unable to rise and fly."

"You are mistaken," said Margaret. . . . "You do not know anything about the South. If there is less adventure or less progress — I suppose I must not say less excitement — from the gambling spirit of trade, which seems requisite to force out these wonderful inventions, there is less suffering also. I see men here going about in the streets who look ground down by some pinching sorrow or care — who are not only sufferers but haters. Now, in the South we have our poor, but there is not that terrible expression in their countenances of a sullen sense of injustice which I see here. You do not know the South, Mr. Thornton," she concluded. . . .

"And may I say you do not know the North?" asked he. (*North* 122–23)

But if Margaret does not know the north, neither does she know the south; if, as she says, in the south "'there is not that terrible expression . . . of a sullen sense of injustice,'" it is partly, as she later admits, because "'the sameness of their toil deadens their imagination; they don't care to meet to talk over thoughts and speculations, even of the weakest, wildest kind, after their work is done; they go home *brutishly* tired, poor *creatures*'" (*North* 382, emphases mine). The existence she insisted on seeing as idyllic, as picturesque, is indeed far from it, because if the men of the north are "'ground down by pinching sorrow and care'" (*North* 123), the agricultural labourers of the south are, by her own account, little better than brutes. Indeed, if the agrarian lifestyle is idyllic at all, it is so only for those who toil not, neither spin, for "'the slow days of careless ease'" (*North* 122) Thornton describes are not the province of labour and never have been. Margaret's protegé, Nicholas Higgins, knows perhaps best of all that neither of these subcultures proposes any kind of haven for the underside of society: "'God help 'em! North an' South have each getten their own troubles. If work's sure and steady theer, labour's paid at starvation prices; while here we'n rucks o' money coming in one quarter, and ne'er a farthing th' next'" (*North* 382). I will return to this point shortly, but for now let me observe that the conflict between north and south, as Gaskell lays it out here, is provoked by misapprehension and misunderstanding. Neither Margaret nor Thornton really know each other's place, and without the necessary familiarity or even intimacy that, as I have shown, brings knowledge, both have recourse only to what Giltrow has described as "an abstract plane of diffuse enthusiasm" (133). Neither see the whole of their own place, because they will not recognize the Higginses and Bouchers of these places; Thornton can speak of those "'toiless and successless'" only because he is not among them and knows little of them.

It is, I think, significant that Gaskell casts the process of becoming familiar with the new place in terms of language. Mr. Hale remarks that he "'hardly know[s] as yet how to compare one of these houses with our Helstone cottages. . . . One had need to learn a different language, and measure by a different standard, up here in Milton'" (*North* 212). We saw in my earlier treatment of Opie how the question of conventions is cast in terms of private and public languages, and indeed, as others before me have remarked, the conflict of vocabularies is foregrounded in *North and South* (Elliott 39–40). Thus Margaret, on her return to Helstone, made friends with "her people" partly by learning their "peculiar words" (*North* 48), and, as she becomes increasingly familiar with Milton-Northern, defends the new vocabulary to her mother, who complains of its "'vulgarity'":

"[I]f I live in a factory town, I must speak factory language when I want it. Why, mamma, I could astonish you with a great many words you never heard in your life. I don't believe you know what a knobstick is."

"Not I, child. I only know it has a very vulgar sound; and I don't want to hear you using it."

"Very well, dearest mother, I won't. Only I shall have to use a whole explanatory sentence instead." (*North* 302)

I want to argue that with this defense of factory language, Margaret ceases to become a tourist or even an immigrant; she has become part of the north. It is a change prompted by her deep involvement with the Higgins family, not as figures in a landscape, nor even, at the end, as objects of her benevolence, but as human, if not like her, then like enough.[10] The subcultures of north and south that categorize (but do not, I suggest, polarize) the different domains of experience in this novel are distinguished from one another partly by experience, and it has become commonplace to observe that language cannot conveniently express experiences that are foreign to it. This is not to say that such experiences are inexpressible in other languages, but that without the word, the perfect word which expresses the exact nature of the new experience, one must, as Margaret has finally learned, "'use a whole explanatory sentence instead'" (*North* 302).

Moreover, I want to argue that Margaret's defense of factory slang and her adoption of its terms is a phenomenon different both in intent and operation from her acquisition of the "peculiar words" (*North* 48) of the New Forest. There, Margaret persisted in seeing herself as separate from "her people" (*North* 48); the role in which she cast herself, in "the important post of only daughter in Helstone parsonage" (*North* 36), meant that she learned their language much as she sketched their cottages. Such linguistic aerobics do not represent an attempt to fuse her horizons with theirs by learning a different language, and measuring by a different standard, but rather to capture the quaintness and picturesqueness of a people who remain, for her, figures in a landscape.

I said above that the investigation of subcultures in *North and South*, like the representation of households in *Wives and Daughters*, is part of a sustained investigation of the noble ends of life. In the major *topoi* of the novel, Helstone and Milton-Northern, this investigation proceeds through complex analogies among masters and hands, gentlemen and men, and differing representations of suffering. The minor *topoi*, Oxford and London, however, are treated more simply as explicit representations of the goods and ends of life. This is clear, first of all, in the debate over the acquisitive life that attends Margaret's godfather's visit to Milton. Mr. Bell, although born and bred in Milton, "glor[ies]" in Oxford (*North* 410), and for him the good life is not "the bustle and the struggle" of Milton (*North* 410), but the Aristotelian contemplation of the citizen. It is not one of busyness, but of "sitting still, and learning from the past, or shaping out the future by faithful work done in a prophetic spirit" (*North* 410). In other words, for Bell the good life is the life of the *oikos*, as Booth describes it; I will not rehearse here what I have already discussed at length, but I will reiterate Booth's claim that in the ancient Greek *oikos*, wealth is only an instrument in the service of the good life (Booth 41) and that for Aristotle, the virtue of a citizen can only be achieved in a regime that provides him with the leisure to pursue the beautiful and the noble (Booth 43, 47). Now, it is clear from Bell's defense of Oxford's "'beauty and its learning, and its proud old history'" (*North* 413) that Gaskell identifies the praxis of the Aristotelian citizen with the praxis of the academy. The problem is that one can only engage in such praxis once freedom from scarcity has been achieved. Mr. Hale at least is aware of this. When Bell complains of "'this bustle. Everybody rushing over everybody, in their hurry to get rich'" (*North* 409), Hale is quick to point out that Bell owns the rare leisure to engage in noble action: "'It is not every one who can sit comfortably in a set of college rooms, and let his riches grow without any exertion of his own. No doubt there is many a man here who would be thankful if his property would increase as yours has done, without his taking any trouble about it'" (*North* 409–10).

Bell criticizes what he perceives as lives wholly given over to the acquisition of wealth; like the Greeks of the ancient *oikos*, he sees wealth as a means rather than an end, and argues against Thornton the Oxonian position that the manufacturers of the north have forgotten that wealth is not and can never be an end in itself. "'I wonder,'" says Bell, "'when you Milton men intend to live. All your lives seem to be spent in gathering together the materials for life'" (*North* 412). In this remark Bell captures the essence of the Aristotelian critique of the acquisitive life. William James Booth articulates this critique in terms of the radical transformation of the art of acquisition from its proper place as subordinate to the purposes of the household or the polity into an end-in-itself (Booth 50). Once detached from the preexisting ends of the household, and thus from the conception of the good life that defines its praxis, once detached from needs and thus from the idea of sufficiency, acquisition becomes detached from its own limits, "that it provide sufficient things for life and the good life" (Booth 50). Bell's rhetorical question, "'I wonder when you Milton men intend to live,'" treats life in this context as the good life, and it is the point of his remark that the getting of wealth cannot be life in this sense because it is not properly an end but a means. Indeed, the debate between the two men goes on to investigate the nature of life in this sense:

> "By living, I suppose you mean enjoyment" [Thornton said].
> "Yes, enjoyment, — I don't specify of what, because I trust we should both consider mere pleasure as very poor enjoyment."
> "I would rather have the nature of the enjoyment defined."
> "Well! enjoyment of leisure — enjoyment of the power and influence which money gives. You are all striving for money. What do you want it for?" (*North* 412)

"Enjoyment," in this passage, must be seen as to some degree coincidental with the ends of life. It is not, significantly, to be confused with pleasure. Both men appear to dismiss "mere pleasure" as "very poor enjoyment" in this sense, although they resist the imputation of slavishness and brutishness Aristotle makes to the life that sees pleasure as an end in itself: "The many, the most vulgar, would seem to conceive the good and happiness as pleasure, and hence they also like the life of gratification. Here they appear completely slavish, since the life they decide on is a life for grazing animals" (*Ethics* I.v.1095b16–20). Gaskell does not go nearly as far as Aristotle in this regard, but it is clear that the life of mere pleasure, which she associates with London, with the Shaws, and especially with Margaret Hale's cousin Edith and her husband, Captain Lennox, can in no wise be seen as a virtuous life.

If an emphasis on outward appearances in *North and South* is, as I have shown, a sign of misapprehension, is, in fact, noncommittal, then it is clear from the London chapters that it is likewise unvirtuous. And here we see a link to the liberal politics of a Wollstonecraft, for example, that critiques the prizing of outward signs over mental qualities. In London, "[e]very talent, every feeling, every acquirement; nay, even every tendency towards virtue, was used up as materials for fireworks; the hidden, sacred fire, exhausted itself in sparkle and crackle" (*North* 497). Such a life is not one of rational enjoyment, but one of the senses and thus an animal life, and unfree. Indeed, it may be said that for Gaskell the problem with a life that spends itself on concern with outward appearances alone is that it is sensuous, and therefore animal: "They talked about art in a merely sensuous way, dwelling on outside effects, instead of allowing themselves to learn what it has to teach" (*North* 497).

But if the life of unlimited pleasure is animal, and therefore slavish and unfree, so, too, is the life of unlimited acquisition. The debate between Thornton and Bell partly captures the notion that a life in which means are mistaken for ends — a life of unlimited wealth-getting — is, in a real sense, an unfree life. Some elaboration may be necessary here. Booth directs our attention to Aristotle's *Nicomachean Ethics*[11]: "[T]he money-maker's life is in a way forced on him [not chosen for itself]" (I.vi.1096a6; add. Irwin). It is thus a slavish life because it is constrained, that is, involuntary: "What is forced has an external origin, the sort of origin in which the agent or victim contributes nothing — if, e.g., a wind or human beings who control him were to carry him off" (*Ethics* II.ix.1110a1–3). Since only those actions that originate with the agent can be virtuous or noble, the life of acquisition can be neither; it is, moreover, unfree because it is an unleisured life, as Mr. Bell points out. It is unleisured because it is limitless, "an occupation as endless as its object [wealth]" (Booth 51).

Bell's elaboration of the notion of leisure, however, highlights a different valence of this passage, and one that undermines his critique of the life of acquisition. He clarifies "'enjoyment of leisure'" as "'enjoyment of the power and influence which money gives'" (*North* 412). This can be read in two ways. First, it can simply be seen as an allusion to the virtues of the citizen in the Aristotelian sense, for whom political praxis and political excellence both require leisure (Booth 47; *Politics* II.viii.1269a34 and V.xi.1313b16–31); such a reading would be consistent with Bell's unabashedly Aristotelian position. But Bell's comment is also consistent with the Aristotelian position that the leisure necessary for virtuous praxis must be procured through a despotic hierarchy, in which subordinate groups are servile and without leisure so that the master may have the time to devote to his own ends. Thus it is that tyrants depend on keeping the people busy, without leisure to determine their own ends (Booth 47; *Politics* V.xi.1313b16ff), a point I take up at more length in chapter 6. In other words, Bell can lead the virtuous life of an Aristotelian citizen only because his wealth accumulates without him, and because this wealth earns him "the power and influence" (*North* 412) that help to ensure that his riches continue to grow through the exertions of others. It is open to Bell to achieve virtue only because others are constrained to procure his freedom from scarcity; in this sense he is a tyrant and a hypocritical one, because he uses his leisure in part to despise as unfree those whose labour has procured his freedom.

Mr. Bell is an anachronism in the sense that the life of virtue he defends belongs properly to the hierarchical despotism of the *oikos* economy, and not to the industrial liberal economy, which is predicated at least theoretically on ideas of consent and contract. It is Thornton who points this out:

"Remember, we are of a different race from the Greeks, to whom beauty was everything, and to whom Mr Bell might speak of a life of leisure and serene enjoyment, much of which entered in through their outward senses. I don't mean to despise them, any more than I would ape them. But I belong to Teutonic blood; it is little mingled in this part of England to what it is in others; we retain much of their language; we retain more of their spirit; we do not look upon life as a time for enjoyment, but as a time for action and exertion. Our glory and our beauty arise out of our inward strength, which makes us victorious over material resistance, and over greater difficulties still. . . . If we do not reverence the past as you do in Oxford, it is because we want something which can apply to the present more directly. It is fine when the study of the past leads to a prophecy of the future. But to men groping in new circumstances, it would be finer if the words of experience could direct us how to act in what concerns us most intimately and immediately; which is full of difficulties that must be encountered; and upon the mode in which they are met and conquered — not merely pushed aside for the time — depends our future. But no! People can speak of Utopia much more easily than of the next day's duty; and yet when that duty is all done by others, who so ready to cry, 'Fie, for shame!'" (*North* 413–14)

I have quoted Thornton's defense of the Milton men at length because it is here, I suggest, that Gaskell unpacks in detail the implications for the polity of the transformation of the ancient economy of the household into the voluntaristic economy of the liberal state. That it is a liberal state, of course, is clear from Bell's response to Mr. Hale's jest that Thornton and Bell "'must try and make each other a little more liberal-minded.'" "'I don't want to be more liberal-minded, thank you,'" says Bell (*North* 410).

In Thornton's treatment, the notion of enjoyment departs from the sense of the ends of life that it had in Bell's slightly earlier account, with which Thornton appeared to agree. Here, enjoyment is largely, if not wholly, synonymous with "mere pleasure," which is the gratification of the "outward senses." This idea, as we have seen, is associated in Gaskell with the unfree life of the London hedonist, but for Thornton the slavishness of the sensual life is also characteristic of the life of the citizen in the *oikos* economy. That Oxford stands in for that economy in Gaskell's topography is explicit in Thornton's argument; he, unlike Bell, is aware of the implications of the transformation of that economy into the voluntaristic associations of the industrial age. Against this idea of leisured enjoyment he poses "'inward strength'" as virtue ("'our glory and our beauty'"), a virtue that exists in and through not leisure but "'action and exertion.'" Moreover, action and exertion must be directed both publicly and personally; our concerns, which for Thornton are emphatically shared concerns, are "intimate" and "immediate." Thus, they are shared, and public, but they also arise from the intimate domain, and must be felt affectively if they are to impact politically.

This said, it is not clear that Thornton and Bell are as rigidly opposed as the polarities of Gaskell's title would suggest. Both are opposed to the kind of life in which "beauty [is] everything"; both believe the ends of life ought to be noble ones. But Thornton sees, as Bell apparently does not, the hypocrisy of a stance that despises as unfree those whose unfreedom secures one's own freedom. He is aware at this point, if he has not been so throughout the novel (and I would argue that he has not), that the prosperity of the Milton manufacturers, and thus their freedom (in this respect alone, Thornton is Aristotelian indeed), is achieved through the labour of those who are not free and cannot be freed if that prosperity is to remain. Moreover, I argue that it is one of the implications of Thornton's final assertion — "'People can speak of Utopia much more easily than of the next day's duty; and yet when that duty is all done by others, who so ready to cry, "Fie, for shame!"'" — that Milton is to Britain as a whole (and therefore to Oxford, Helstone, and London) what the millhands are to the manufacturers. If Milton is not the picturesque idyll of the New Forest, nor the seat of beauty and learning that is Oxford, nor even the sparkle and fireworks of London, it is because it is engaged in securing the wealth necessary to these *topoi*, and to the pursuit of their varied ends.

Thornton's response to Bell is emphatic in part because he is the figure, more than any other in the novel, in and through whom the nineteenth-century unease regarding the figure of the merchant or trader is developed and interrogated. In chapter 4 I remarked that the tension between the means and the ends of life, which is clearly articulated here in Bell's critique of the acquisitive life, is visible in part in the aristocratic anxiety attending this figure. I suggested that this anxiety might have to do with a sense that those who are concerned with the means to life are barred by that activity from the pursuit of noble ends. I want now to put this notion to the test.

Margaret, on her return to Helstone, rejects out of hand the idea that she might make acquaintances of a not-so-distant wealthy family, the Gormans. She asks her mother, "'[a]re those the Gormans who made their fortunes in trade at Southampton? Oh! I'm glad we don't visit them. I don't like shoppy people'" (*North* 50). She prefers "cottagers and labourers, and people without pretence" (*North* 50), that is, those resigned to their slavish role of producing wealth for others to enjoy, and who reveal no inclination to pursue the life that, for Margaret, is the hereditary property of the aristocracy and the learned professions. Her objection to the Gormans, whom she knows either very little or not at all, has to do both with their having engaged in trade, and with their having disassociated themselves from it; "pretence" is a key word in this passage, suggesting both the Gormans' desire to withdraw from the instrumental sphere of getting wealth, and the ways in which, for Margaret at least, this activity is an essentializing, though not essential, one.

I am suggesting that Margaret's character, at the beginning of the novel if not the end (she is on this point much altered by the end of *North and South*), is very much a conservative one; class is inherited, and has its own peculiar privileges, such that any attempt to move between classes or to blur their distinctions by acquiring the privileges of, for example, the learned professions is "pretension" and therefore despicable. Thus, in the pivotal scene between Mr. Hale and Margaret, in which he announces his intentions to leave the Church and move to Milton-Northern as a private tutor, she is wholly contemptuous: "'A private tutor!' said Margaret, looking scornful: 'What in the world do manufacturers want with the classics, or literature, or the accomplishments of a gentleman?'" (*North* 72). Not only does her reaction highlight the degree to which she considers a classical education (that is, the "liberal arts") the province of the leisured classes, it likewise betrays the ways in which the middle classes were, even at mid-century, outside the domain of the citizenry as narrowly construed. Manufacturers cannot be gentlemen; the importance of this term to Margaret has already been signaled on the occasion of Lennox's visit, when, viewing her father with her suitor's eyes, she notes that "[h]e looked a complete gentleman in his rather threadbare coat and well-worn hat" (*North* 58). Note here that the category of gentleman is not identical with that of wealth; it represents, rather, freedom from the pursuit of wealth. While Nancy Armstrong contends that the institutionalization of a vocabulary that enshrined qualities of the mind over the external signs of wealth and status had been thoroughly accomplished in domestic fictions by the 1840s, this account neglects the anxiety surrounding characters like Thornton, anxiety that continues to call into question such a system of evaluation. While it is fair to say that Margaret's idea of the gentleman captures the dominant perspective at the level of the literary imagination, it is also true that the anxiety I am documenting continues to permeate such novels. This persistence suggests that this institutionalization could not have been nearly so general as Armstrong would like to argue. Moreover, it is worth noting that in *North and South*, as in *Wives and Daughters*, qualities of mind and behaviour continue to be signaled through external signs and symbols.

While Mr. Hale, according to Margaret's view, "favourably . . . impressed every stranger" (*North* 58) as a gentleman, Margaret's initial reaction to Thornton is manifestly one of scorn. She sees a man about whom there is "'nothing remarkable — not quite a gentleman; but that was hardly to be expected'" (*North* 102). He "'seems made for his niche . . . sagacious, and strong, as becomes a great tradesman'" (*North* 102), but these, we are led to believe, are not the qualities of a gentleman. At the same time, however, it becomes clear shortly after this first meeting that her view is a mistaken one. The wallpaper at their new house, which Margaret despises for its "vulgarity and commonness" (*North* 102), has been replaced, but the landlord's relaxation of his determination not to repaper is not due to any influence of the gentleman: "[W]hat he did not care to do for a Reverend Mr Hale, unknown, in Milton, he was only too glad to do at the one short sharp remonstrance of Mr Thornton, the wealthy manufacturer" (*North* 103). This exchange, which remains secret from all the Hales, is the reader's first indication that "Mr Hale was no longer looked upon as Vicar of Helstone, but as a man who only spent at a certain rate" (*North* 109). I will return to the wallpaper presently, but for now I will only observe that this scene shows the supposed influence of the gentleman giving way in this new environment to the real influence of "'that man'" (*North* 101). Indeed, Mr. Hale does not "favourably impress" true strangers, only those who are already versed in the signs that mark the southern British "gentleman."

Paradoxically enough, while Margaret clearly resents the supposed "pretensions" of the manufacturers to the culture of gentlemen, she likewise criticizes their deference. When Thornton tells the Hales that he believes "'if a good customer chose to come at midnight, I should get up, and stand hat in hand to receive his orders,'" Margaret's "lip curl[s]" (*North* 124). Significantly, however, it is not deference to those she supposes to be his betters that Margaret resents; indeed, Thornton shows little sign of recognizing the Hales as his betters, and herein lies his pretension. Deference to customers, however, represents a kind of enslavement to the acquisitive life; it is not out of respect for qualities of the mind, or culture, that Thornton stands "hat in hand," but to wealth and money. We are returned here to the notion of the acquisitive life as constrained and unfree; because, as Booth points out, the life of acquisition requires entry into the marketplace, it is a dependent life (Booth 52). On the classical Greek view, withdrawal from the autonomy of the household into the marketplace necessarily implies a loss of autonomy; it is "to subject oneself, indirectly, to the wills of others and to the vagaries of the commercial life" (Booth 52). Thornton's deference, then, is dependence in this sense; it is, for Margaret, contemptible because it is a wilful dependence, chosen (on her reading) out of the desire for unlimited wealth rather than forced on him.

Moreover, for Margaret, much of the problem of the acquisitive life is that, in taking the means of life as its end, it infects the nature of the man engaged in it. Thus her "first impression"[12] is that it is "'a pity such a nature should be tainted by his position as a Milton manufacturer'" (*North* 129). There are several possible readings of Margaret's claim here. One is simply that class is both inevitable and entire; Thornton's status as manufacturer (tradesman) is, on this reading, his only identity, not simply part of it. Such a reading might concur with Margaret's earlier condemnations of "'shoppy people,'" although here her references to tainture suggest that Thornton's nature is not, in fact, entirely coincident with his occupation. Another is that a life devoted entirely to acquisition, for its own sake rather than for the sake of furthering the ends of life, a life, in fact, that confuses its ends and its means, contaminates and infects that portion of life that ought to be devoted to other ends. I incline toward the latter reading. Margaret explains her use of the term "'taint'" to her father as "'that testing of everything by the standard of wealth. When he spoke of the mechanical powers, he evidently looked upon them only as new ways of extending trade and making money. And the poor men around him — they were poor because they were vicious — out of the pale of his sympathies because they had not his iron nature, and the capabilities that it gives him for being rich'" (*North* 129–30). Clearly, the tainture to which Margaret refers is not simply confined to Thornton himself; she links her critique of the merchant here to a critique of the consequences of the wholly acquisitive life for the community.

Nor is this a particularly controversial claim, either on my part or Margaret's; Gaskell has set up a complex relationship of analogies in *North and South* that, I suggest, not only permits but requires the synecdochal relationship of the individual to the community, and in so doing, refutes the notion of separate spheres. In other words, Thornton's wholesale withdrawal from the contained and embedded economy of the *oikos*, associated here, as we have seen, with the agrarian south, both allows him to stand for Milton and has important consequences for that community. Margaret criticizes, first of all, what she sees as Thornton's misrecognition of the new inventions in industry; while what these inventions represent for her is ambiguous (an intrusion into the picturesque landscape, an emblem of human achievement?), she clearly rejects Thornton's treatment of them as instrumental to the acquisitive life. Still more marked is her rejection of Thornton's social

Darwinism; the poor play an interesting role in Margaret's description of Thornton's tainture. She criticizes Thornton for his contractarian, voluntaristic account of poverty (a point to which I will return), but also links the poor — the conjunction that begins this assertion, "'And the poor men,'" is crucial here — implicitly with the "'mechanical powers'" in order to criticize Thornton's treatment of the poor as means to his mistaken end of making money. In Booth's terms, Margaret sees Thornton's replacement of the affective bonds of the community, because of his desire for wealth without limit, with the "ephemeral" bonds of self-interest (Booth 53) as a blow to the relations of the community. While Margaret is to some degree mistaken about Thornton's ideas of the ends of life (it is fair to say that Thornton undergoes a type of *Bildung* parallel to Margaret's), it is clear from the structure of the novel that Gaskell shares Margaret's condemnation of the purely acquisitive life. Indeed, the strike and the consequences that attend it are significant markers of the rupture to community, both in terms of affective bonds and autonomy (Thornton is constrained to bring in strikebreaking labour from Ireland), and Gaskell's account of the strike, as I will shortly demonstrate, locates its cause in precisely this type of misapprehension of the role of the labourer.

I have just remarked that Margaret is mistaken about Thornton's allegiance to the acquisitive life, and intimated that her realization of this error is a fundamental part of her growth. Certainly, her reaction when her brother, Frederick, mistakes Thornton for one of the shopmen indicates that her views have changed: "'Oh, only,'" said she, reddening and looking straight at him, "'I fancied you meant some one of a different class, not a gentleman; somebody come on an errand.'" "'He looked like some one of that kind,'" said Frederick, carelessly. "'I took him for a shopman, and he turns out a manufacturer'" (*North* 324). Not only does the careless and off-hand nature of Frederick's remarks here parallel Margaret's "quick, unimplicating views" earlier, and her "lazy" reluctance to describe Thornton to her mother after their first meeting (*North* 102), but Frederick, like Margaret, is uninterested in the distinction between tradesmen and manufacturers. She had "'appl[ied] the word [tradesman] to all who have something tangible to sell'" (*North* 102); for Frederick, all those in any way engaged in trade are "'of that kind.'" Likewise, Frederick takes Thornton's appearance as the incontrovertible sign of class, as Margaret did, adhering to his old, southern notions of "gentleman." Part of the irony of Margaret's change in this respect stems from the complex relation between external signs and qualities of mind in this notion of gentlemen. The very idea of the gentleman is supposedly predicated on notions of qualities of mind and behaviour; it is thus ironic, if not paradoxical, that both Margaret and Frederick have consistently taken the term to apply to those whose inward qualities are manifested in what are to them the recognizable outward signs of the "gentleman." Such irony is emphasized by the resolution of Frederick's troubles in a Spanish merchant house, "her preux chevalier of a brother turned merchant, trader!" (*North* 425).

Indeed, much of the anxiety surrounding the figure of the tradesman-manufacturer-merchant in *North and South* is represented by Gaskell in terms of the vexed question of the "gentleman." This dimension of the novel is first introduced in Margaret's reflection that her father "looked a complete gentleman" (*North* 58); the conflict between appearance and reality that marks not only the sketching scene in which this observation appears, but much of the novel besides, poses the question of what it means to be a gentleman. Similarly, Margaret's scornful inquiry as to what manufacturers might want with "'the classics, or literature, or the accomplishments of a gentleman'" (*North* 72) suggests, as I have already shown, that these two spheres, which may be distinguished as the sphere of leisure and noble action, and the sphere of busyness and acquisitive action, are very much separate from each other. But it is also clear that such a polarization of these two spheres, which may have suited the more rigid social stratification of the south, is inadequate in Milton-Northern. Both Margaret and the faithful family retainer, Dixon, are astonished by the "impertinence" of the Milton girls, who, in applying for the job of servant, express doubts "as to the solvency of a family who lived in a house of thirty pounds a-year, and yet gave themselves airs, and kept two servants, one of them so very high and mighty" (*North* 109). Significantly, while Margaret is "repelled by the rough uncourteous manners of *these people*" (*North* 109; emphasis mine), it is not they who are guilty of pretension but the Hales. This, I think, is clear in Gaskell's description of the "fastidious pride" with which Margaret shrinks from the "hail-fellow accost" of the Milton-Northerners (*North* 109); it is the same pride with which she holds herself aloof from Thornton's handshake (*North* 127). The handshake is "the frank familiar custom of the place," but Margaret is unaccustomed to the social democracy of both greetings in the street and shaking hands, and "simply bow[s] her farewell" (*North* 127). In this case, while Margaret's aloofness is attributed not to fastidiousness or pride but to ignorance of local custom, and she immediately regrets her ignorance, I want to suggest that the close thematic relationship between these two scenes indicates a continuity between them, such that Margaret's pride is a kind of ignorance in Gaskell's account, and thus a species of pretension.

Indeed, the difficulty all Hales encounter in Milton is the apparent inability of the Milton-Northerners to recognize their worth, an inability better understood in terms of the Hales' inability to demonstrate that worth in a manner comprehensible to the North. Thus Mr. Hale, invited to lecture to the working men at a local Lyceum, chooses Ecclesiastical Architecture as his subject, "rather more in accordance with his own taste and knowledge than as falling in with the character of the place or the desire for particular kinds of information among those to whom he was to lecture" (*North* 191). While ecclesiastical architecture may be a fitting subject for a gentleman, in the southern sense or in the sense Margaret suggests when she circumscribes the classics and literature as the province of gentlemen, it is also true in the fiction that the qualities of the gentleman must be publicly recognized. This is the real import of Margaret's pride in her father's appearance in that early scene with Henry Lennox; it is also a significant dimension of both Margaret's and Frederick's initial reactions to Thornton. Thus, even if one's identity as a gentleman (or, for that matter, a lady, as we shall see in a moment) is predicated on mental qualities, these are manifested in part in accomplishments and behaviour, and both of these last may be differently valued in different cultures.

Bessy Higgins, the dying daughter of the workman Nicholas Higgins and object of Margaret's "Lady Bountiful" role in Milton, recognizes that these categories may vary. Bessy becomes "quite roused up" at the news that the Hales will dine with the Thorntons, saying, "'[b]ut they visit wi' a' th' first folk in Milton'" (*North* 199). She tries to explain herself further to Margaret by pointing out that "'they thinken a deal o'money here; and I reckon yo've not getten much'" (*North* 199). Margaret is uncontroversially Victorian in pointing out that education is a superior measure of gentility than wealth: "[W]e are educated people, and have lived amongst educated people. Is there anything so wonderful, in our being asked out to dinner by a man who owns himself inferior to my father by coming to him to be instructed?" (*North* 199). The irony of Margaret's response lies in her assumption of Thornton's "inferiority"; Mr. Hale has, from the first, both liked and admired Thornton, and treated him as a friend and an equal. Margaret, too, by the time of this dinner, has come to have considerable regard for Thornton, but the difference between her view of him and her father's is that Hale takes Thornton's abilities as a businessman as indicative of his mental qualities, while Margaret takes those same abilities as a necessary detraction from quality in that sense.

Interestingly enough, the very term "gentleman" is a significant category for Margaret as it is not for Thornton. He tells her,

"I am not quite the person to decide on another's gentlemanlikeness, Miss Hale. I mean, I don't quite understand your application of the word. But I should say that this Morison is no true man". . . .

"I suspect my 'gentleman' includes your 'true man.'"

"And a great deal more, you would imply. I differ from you. A man is to me a higher and a completer being than a gentleman."

"What do you mean?" asked Margaret. "We must understand the words differently."

"I take it that 'gentleman' is a term that only describes a person in his relation to others; but when we speak of him as 'a man,' we consider him not merely with regard to his fellow-men, but in relation to himself, — to life — to time — to eternity. A cast-away, lonely as Robinson Crusoe — a prisoner immured in a dungeon for life — nay, even a saint in Patmos, has his endurance, his strength, his faith, best described by being spoken of as 'a man.' I am rather weary of this word 'gentlemanly,' which seems to me to be often inappropriately used, and often, too, with such exaggerated distortion of meaning, while the full simplicity of the noun 'man,' and the adjective 'manly' are unacknowledged — that I am induced to class it with the cant of the day." (*North* 217–18)

Thornton's casting of this discussion in terms of conflicting vocabularies is important for my purposes. First, to return to the vocabulary I have already established, it highlights a distinction between the idioms of living in Darkshire and in the southern parts of England. Second, Thornton's remark that "gentleman" describes a person in, and only in, the public dimensions of his character — "'his relation to to others'" — coincides with my claim above that for a gentleman to be a gentleman his claim in this respect must be publicly recognized. Cast in these terms, then, it is Thornton rather than Margaret who, paradoxically enough, erects qualities of the mind as superior to external signs and symbols; his notion of a "true man" is the Rousseauean idea of one whose mental quality requires no external recognition.

It must, however, be observed at this point that Gaskell allows no major character in *North and South* any kind of firm moral high ground. After all, as we later discover, Thornton hopes that "all men should recognise his justice" (*North* 403), a quality we may fairly assume is for him one of the attributes of a true man as it is for Margaret characteristic of the "gentleman." And justice, if it is justice at all, is a term that can only apply to men in their relations with others. This, alone, does not counter Thornton's definition of a "man," since his term is intended to encompass both relations with others and those with oneself, but it is significant here that the public dimension of the just act exists not simply in its applying to ethical relations amongst individuals, but in the others' recognition of that act; recognition, here, I suggest, is a species of assent to the act as just.

It is because recognition of one's goods is a species of assent that Thornton is swayed by Margaret's argument to go down and face the mob of strikers who have descended on the house. Margaret here adopts Thornton's own idiom, ordering him: "'[G]o down this instant, if you are not a coward. Go down and face them *like a man*. Save these poor strangers, whom you have decoyed here. Speak to your workmen *as if they were human beings*. Speak to them kindly. Don't let the soldiers come in and cut down poor creatures who are driven mad. I see one there who is. *If you have any courage or noble quality in you, go out and speak to them, man to man!*'" (*North* 232; emphases mine). The notion of a "man," as Margaret uses it here, is profoundly indebted to the definition of the term Thornton propounded earlier. It relies both on fair and just relations with others — which, significantly, necessarily requires seeing those others as men as well as oneself — and on qualities which are primarily if not wholly internal, like courage. Courage is a public virtue, like what we perceive as justice, but it is also an internal one, a quality of mind and will that affects behaviour, rather than an external sign of status. Margaret may have erred in convincing Thornton to face the mob "'like a man,'" and indeed she does apologize to him for "'having said thoughtless words which sent [him] down into the danger'" (*North* 252), but her error is in misreading the crowd as men, and thus believing that relations "man to man" are possible among them. In becoming a mob the strikers have given up reason and therefore personhood: Their noise is "as the demoniac desire of some terrible wild beast" (*North* 232), they are "gaunt as wolves, and mad for prey" (*North* 233). She does not err in the substance of her plea to Thornton, however, and indeed learning this lesson will prove to be the significant point in Thornton's *Bildung*. While the mob is "mad," this is so, as Margaret intuits, because they have been driven so. Indeed, as this scene shows, Gaskell's take on the workers parallels Wollstonecraft's characterization of Jemima, through whom, as I have shown, Wollstonecraft documents her claim that personhood requires treatment *as* a person and not as a brute or animal.

It should be clear from the foregoing that the vexed question of the "gentleman" versus the "man" in *North and South* requires a careful distinction between two types of external manifestation. Thornton's complaint that Margaret's notion of the "gentleman" deals only with man in his relationship with others highlights the significance of internal qualities to our categories of the self, and can be read, as I have been reading it, as a condemnation of metonymical readings of character. This, indeed, is the point of Margaret's reaction to the speech of the ladies at the same dinner party that poses the question of men and gentlemen. She observes to her father that their conversation "'reminded me of our old game of having each so many nouns to introduce into a sentence,'" that is, that "'they took nouns that were signs of things which gave evidence of wealth, — housekeepers, under-gardeners, extent of glass, valuable lace, diamonds, and all such things; and each one formed her speech so as to bring them all in, in the prettiest accidental manner possible'" (*North* 221). Margaret fairly articulates the kind of vocabulary these ladies have taken as their idiom of living; it depends on the symbols of wealth and power to indicate value, and in this respect can be seen as anachronistic in the sense that Armstrong has described. But it is also true that Margaret has herself depended on external symbols for her recognition of the "gentleman," and it is this dependence that Thornton criticizes in the extended passage quoted above. Thus Margaret's playful remark, "'I felt like a great hypocrite tonight'" (*North* 221), while apparently denoting her appearance at the dinner party in her "'white silk gown'" with her "'idle hands before [her]'" after having spent the day in "'good, thorough, house-work'" (*North* 222), can be read as self-reflexive mockery of her own evaluations of character. Appearances are misleading; this is the point not only of this passage but of the misreadings of events that provide both impetus and obstacle to the romance plot of the novel.

It is important to note, however, that the "reality" against which "appearances" are posed in *North and South* is not wholly an internal reality. By this I mean that the evaluation of a character must depend, for Gaskell, not only on such internal qualities as courage but also on our relations with others. In Gaskell's articulation the good must be associated not simply with the moral — what it is good to be — but with the ethical, which may by contrast be understood, in Charles Taylor's terms, as what it is right to do.[13] And the difficulty of disentangling these notions has in part to do with the fact that our notions of what it is right to do have everything to do with our ideas of what it is good to be, that is, with our ideas of the ends of life. This problem, which is a problem for the theorist rather than for the novelist, as Gaskell's work makes clear, comes through clearly in the confrontation between Thornton and Margaret that follows the strike scene.

Margaret is offended by Thornton's thanks for protecting him from the rage of the mob; her offense originates in the meaning Thornton and his entire household have placed on the event, that is, in her words, "'a personal act between [them],'" and therefore that Thornton

"may come and thank [her] for it, instead of perceiving, as a gentleman would — yes! a gentleman," she repeated, in allusion to their former conversation about that word, "that any woman, worthy of the name of woman, would come forward to shield, with her reverenced helplessness, a man in danger from the violence of numbers."

"And the gentleman thus rescued is forbidden the relief of thanks!" he broke in contemptuously. "I am a man. I claim the right of expressing my feelings." (*North* 253)

Margaret seems here to be arguing that Thornton was right in concluding that the "gentleman" is a term that applies only to a man in his relations with others, that is, that it has to do with his behaviour and not his moral sense. Moreover, on her account, the behaviour of the gentleman must not only be other-directed but established by others, independently of one's own moral sense. Such a prescription recalls Rousseau's Sophie, whose subjection to the will of others I discussed in chapter 1. Thornton, on the other hand, "claims the right" not only to express his feelings, but to determine for himself his own behaviour. The problem here, as it is for both Margaret and Thornton throughout the novel, is that, as readers of the behaviour of others, we rarely have access to anything other than behaviour. The evaluative process that determines our actions — the moral sense in terms of which we refine our ethics — is unknown.[14] Thus, Thornton mistakes Margaret's motivation in shielding him from the mob as a personal and romantic one; he likewise misreads her lie and her apparent tryst, which the reader knows to be with her brother, and thus draws his conclusions from appearances, which are in Gaskell's oeuvre notoriously untrustworthy.

Gaskell's solution to this problem, one that Cazamian has fairly cast as part of the "idealist interventionist reaction," is to propound a kind of intimacy that will increase our knowledge of the other and redress our misunderstandings. For example, Frederick can act as a milepost of Margaret's progress by confining his comments on Thornton to appearance alone — "'[h]e is an unprepossessing-looking fellow'" (*North* 331) — while Margaret has become aware of more than his "aspect": "'You would not have thought him unprepossessing if you had seen him with mamma'" (*North* 331). Here the distinction between aspect — *superficiae* — and other types of externals is clear. An even more significant marker of Margaret's growth is Mr. Bell's treatment of Henry Lennox, whom Margaret "'liked . . . long ago'" (*North* 460). Bell claims he was unable to form an opinion of Lennox's character, because "'[h]e was so busy trying to find out who I was, in the first instance, and what I was in the second, that he never let out what he was; unless indeed that veiled curiosity of his as to what manner of man he had to talk to was not a good piece, and a fair indication of his character'" (*North* 461). "Busy" is, of course, a loaded term in Bell's idiom, but here the busyness of which he accuses Lennox is not that of the acquisitive life but that of one busy about another's business; it is the busyness of one who seeks to acquire all of the "nouns" that convey evidence of wealth and status, of the "gentleman" in the old sense. As in Margaret's telling remark to Mr. Bell, "'I want you to *see* Edith; and I want Edith to *know* you'" (*North* 464; emphases mine), the distinction being made here is one between superficial and therefore unreliable appearances, and a more reliable — but more difficult — knowledge of the other. Edith, who is "a great beauty," "all softness and glitter" (*North* 464), offers much to see and little to know; she is a fitting emblem of that London that presents only its bright and superficial aspect to the world.

Significantly, Gaskell suggests that part of what makes London superficial is the rigid distinction between the labourers and the masters, so much so that the workers are invisible: "[T]he very servants lived in an underground world of their own, of which she knew neither the hopes nor the fears; they only seemed to start into existence when some want or whim of their master and mistress needed them" (*North* 458). This invisibility, I want to argue, has two significant effects. First, it means that no one — or no thing, if, as here, the servants are a type of automaton — emerges from "underground" to interrupt the sparkling London life. Second, the distance between surface society and the Morlock-like workers creates a seemingly unbridgeable gap between the masters and the servants that makes the latter unknowable. As the site of this invisibility, London is sharply distinguished from Milton-Northern, where public space at least is governed by a kind of democracy. As I will show, however, the republicanism that rules public space in the North is a necessary but, importantly, insufficient antidote to the ignorance of each other that keeps the classes in the constant state of war described by Thornton (*North* 125). Thornton's idea of a battle between the two classes is predicated, in part, on his Hobbesian notion of industrial society as a struggle that allows only the survival of the fittest. This link is drawn by Thornton himself; he responds to Mr. Hale's question, "'[i]s there any necessity for calling it a battle between the two classes?'" by saying,

"[i]t is one of the great beauties of our system, that a working-man may raise himself into the power and position of a master by his own exertions and behaviour; that, in fact, every one who rules himself to decency and sobriety of conduct, and attention to his duties, comes over to our ranks; it may not be always as a master, but as an overlooker, a cashier, a book-keeper, a clerk, one on the side of authority and order." (*North* 125)

Thornton is here clearly ignorant — perhaps wilfully — of what will later become clear in his debate with Bell, that it is in the interests of those "on the side of authority and order" to keep the working men unfree. He is likewise mistaken in placing authority and order *de facto* in the right; I suggest that the point of the Frederick Hale subplot of mutiny and exile in *North and South* is to highlight this notion of wrongful and tyrannical authority.

Frederick is in Spain after years of exile in South America because he rebelled against the captain of his ship. From the beginning of his service with Captain Reid, Frederick had "'look[ed] forward with apprehension to a long course of tyranny,'" a tyranny that manifested itself in "impatience with the men" and "imperiousness in trifles" (*North* 152). He is finally provoked to mutiny with the rest of the crew when a sailor is injured during a race down the rigging ordered by the captain on a whim, a "freak" that recalls Edgeworth's condemnation of Harriot Freke. Margaret, with her mother, believes Frederick acted rightly; she says that "'[l]oyalty and obedience to wisdom and justice are fine; but it is still finer to defy arbitrary power, unjustly and cruelly used — not on behalf of ourselves, but on behalf of others more helpless'" (*North* 154). In this regard, as elsewhere, Margaret appears to be arguing the contractarian liberal view that we have the right to consent to and to reject authority through the use of right reason. The government, of course, does not and cannot take this view of their navy, as Mr. Hale is aware; he believes the government must "take very stringent measures for the repression of offences against authority, more particularly in the navy, where a commanding officer needs to be surrounded in his men's eyes with a vivid consciousness of all the power there is at home to back him, and take up his cause, and avenge any injuries offered to him, if need be. Ah! it's no matter to them how far their authorities have tyrannised, — galled hasty tempers to madness, — or, if that can be any excuse afterwards, it is never allowed for in the first instance." (*North* 265)

Hale may deplore a system in which, like the military courts, "'authority weighs nine-tenths in the balance, and evidence forms only the other tenth'" (*North* 326), but he stops far short of critique, just as, while he supports Mrs. Hale and Margaret in their attempts to relieve the wants of one of the strikers, he takes the authority of the masters as his general rule:

[H]e made an unsatisfactory compromise. His wife and daughter had not only done quite right in this instance, but he did not see for a moment how they could have done otherwise. Nevertheless, as a general rule, it was very true what Mr Thornton said, that as the strike, if prolonged, must end in the masters' bringing hands from a distance . . . why, it was clear enough that the kindest thing was to refuse all help which might bolster them up in their folly. (*North* 211)

The relationship between masters and men, in *North and South*, as should be clear from the foregoing, turns on the vexed question of authority. For Thornton, it is enough for authority to know that it is acting reasonably; it need proffer no account of its reasons to those affected by it. In effect, his complaint that "'because we don't explain our reasons, they won't believe we're acting reasonably'" (*North* 163) amounts to a denial of personhood to those he tellingly refers to as the "hands" in a synecdoche that strips them of mind and reason. Margaret questions his refusal, and Thornton counters her argument on behalf of the workers by asking, "'[d]o you give your servants reasons for your expenditure, or your economy in the use of your own money?'" (*North* 164). It is, I think, revealing that the woman who pleads that the workers have "'a human right'" (*North* 164) to question authority is the same one who told Dixon "'you forget to whom you are speaking'" (*North* 83) when Dixon criticized Mr. Hale's decision to move the family to Milton-Northern, the same one who "severely resented" the "impertinence" of prospective servants (*North* 109). However right Margaret may be in claiming Thornton should treat the workers as persons, and the relationship of authority among them, therefore, as contractual, she subscribes to a far different view of hierarchical social relations. Her idea of hierarchy has little to do with the constant struggle Thornton sees waged amongst masters and men; rather, it is divinely ordered. Thus, Thornton's view of authority is dynamic, fluid, mutable; Margaret's, on the other hand, is essential, static, immutable. She reminds Bessy Higgins not to be impatient with her life, to "'[r]emember who gave it you, and made it what it is!'" and in almost the same moment tells Nicholas Higgins that "'God . . . ordered what kind of life it was to be'" (*North* 133). Indeed, in this supranatural account of the class structure may lie the key to Margaret's distaste for "pretension"; believing one's social place is divinely ordered, she likewise believes any attempt at ameliorating or changing one's lot is necessarily a misguided attempt to alter the divine order by evading one's essential (God-given) nature. While I do believe Margaret changes her mind about the aprioristic nature of social class, indeed, that this is the end of her *Bildung*, her response to Thornton on the issue of authority is not part of this change.

Her notion of the worker's "human right" to know the reasons for their hardships, indeed, makes this clear; she meant, she tells Thornton, "'that there seemed no reason but religious ones, why you should not do what you like with your own'" (*North* 164). Much like her father, Margaret is at this point still confusing charity with justice. She is not concerned with the consensual bases of authority, but with its paternalistic duties: "'[T]here is no human law to prevent the employers from utterly wasting or throwing away all their money, if they choose; but that there are passages in the Bible which would rather imply — to me at least — that they neglected their duties as stewards if they did so'" (*North* 165). Despite the paternalistic foundations of Margaret's plea for the master as "steward" of his men, however, there is much in her argument against Thornton that speaks to a liberal, if not a republican, stance. She argues that "'the masters would like their hands to be merely tall, large children — living in the present moment — with a blind unreasoning kind of obedience'" (*North* 166). As such, of course, they are incapable of virtue, as I have shown in earlier chapters; virtue, properly understood, can be practiced only by those who are juridical persons and thus free to be virtuous. This is likewise clear in Thornton's adoption of her metaphor:

"In our infancy we require a wise despotism to govern us. Indeed, long past infancy, children and young people are the happiest under the unfailing laws of a discreet, firm authority. I agree with Miss Hale so far as to consider our people in the condition of children, while I deny that we, the masters, have anything to do with the making or keeping them so. I maintain that despotism is the best kind of government for them . . . I will use my best discretion — from no humbug or philanthropic feeling, of which we have had rather too much in the North — to make wise laws and come to just decisions in the conduct of my business — laws and decisions which work for my own good in the first instance — for theirs in the second; but I will neither be forced to give my reasons, nor flinch from what I have once declared to be my resolution." (*North* 167)

Thornton can take this stance because he reads the interdependence between masters and men as meaning that "'[his] interests are identical with those of [his] work-people, and vice-versa'" (*North* 166). He does not, however, mean to argue for a true coincidence of ends, as should be clear from the passage quoted above, but rather to suggest that, as in the Greek *oikos*, the ends of the community must be those ends determined by the master. Like Margaret's idea of "gentlefolk," Thornton's idea is revealed as inadequate and anachronistic. His claim is interesting because, as we have already seen, Thornton rejects the Greek model of community and household; if this is so, and if it is also so that Thornton is advocating, above, a despotic hierarchy, then in what does his rejection of the *oikos* consist?

I suggest that Thornton's liberalism consists, finally, in his disavowal of the paternalistic model of government advocated by Margaret. His despotism, by his own account, is restricted to the time when his men are in the mills; outside of that space, which is not public in the same sense as the space of the streets, nor private in the sense that a drawing-room or parlour is, the hands are justifiably self-owners, and therefore men: "'Because they labour ten hours a-day for us, I do not see that we have any right to impose leading-strings upon them for the rest of their time. I value my own independence so highly that I can fancy no degradation greater than that of having another man perpetually directing and advising and lecturing me, or even planning too closely in any way about my actions'" (*North* 168). The problem that Thornton identifies with Margaret's analogy between masters and men and parents and children is that paternalism is an inadequate model for governance. By this I mean that subordinance in the mill cannot, on Thornton's account or indeed on the accounts of such liberal thinkers as Locke, be taken as equivalent to infancy; the men are not, as he tells Margaret, "'puppets of dough, ready to be moulded into any amiable form we please'" (*North* 170). His form of despotism is marginally preferable to Margaret's apriorism because it is contained and embedded, pretending to no influence or control outside of the space over which he is master; hers, on the other hand, is limitless simply because it is transcendental. This is the implication of her claim that "'God has made us so that we must be mutually dependent. We may ignore our own dependence, or refuse to acknowledge that others depend upon us in more respects than the payment of weekly wages; but the thing must be, nevertheless'" (*North* 169).

At the same time, I would be mistaken in arguing that Gaskell is erecting Thornton's political economy as any kind of moral touchstone. If his model of governance is preferable, because contained and embedded, to Margaret's aprioristic and essentialist paternalism, it is likewise problematic because it depends on the radical separation of spheres. Gaskell's warning is clear. The liberal polity is fundamentally betrayed if, in that polity, industry is allowed to retain the classical despotism of the *oikos*, and this is the threat of the separation of the various liberal *topoi* . And, as we have already seen, it is this separation — the invisibility, for example, of the "toilers and moilers" in London (*North* 458) — which presents the most difficult obstacle to intimacy between the classes. In this regard Thornton's refusal to give reasons to his hands, that is, his treatment of them as brutes, is what causes both the strike and the riot; Margaret's insistence that Thornton "'[g]o down and face them like a man'" (*North* 232) is not only an argument for treating the "hands" as men, as I have shown, but a plea that the enormous distance between the classes be bridged.

Without the kind of mutual knowledge that Gaskell is advocating, Thornton and others like him will continue to assume that the side of the masters is necessarily the side of "authority and order," and therefore that they are justified in their treatment of the workers. It is interesting in this regard to note that Bessy Higgins describes the goal of the strikers as correcting just this kind of impression. The union committee, according to Bessy, had "'charged all members o' th' Union to lie down and die, if need were, without striking a blow;'" they are, indeed, as distressed as Thornton by the riot, because their intent is to "'show the world that th' real leaders o' th' strike were not such as Boucher, but steady thoughtful men; good hands, and good citizens, who were friendly to law and judgement, and would uphold order; who only wanted their right wage, and wouldn't work, even though they starved, till they got 'em; but who would ne'er injure property or life'" (*North* 259–60). Significantly, the strikers' argument is the same one that Sartre has described as the seed of every revolution, which is to say that the strike is itself a declaration that "we too are men" ("Materialism" 217). By this I mean that the strikers' demands proceed from a set of claims about their qualities as citizens and as men: That they are hard-working, honest, loyal, law-abiding. Some of these claims have to do with the strikers in terms of their relationships with their masters, first of all, but also with one another — and others have to do with their internal qualities, or with what Thornton calls man's relationship to himself (*North* 218). But because even our notions of what it is right to do must proceed from our ideas of what it is good to be, because questions of morals and ethics can never be thoroughly disentangled from each other, except in terms of the idealizations of theory, all of the strikers' demands can therefore be seen as issuing from the claim that they are certain kinds of beings, and as such must be considered bearers of rights. This is clearest in the mind of Nicholas Higgins, who condemns a book on political economy in exactly these terms: "'Lord bless yo', it went on about capital and labour, and labour and capital, till it fair sent me off to sleep. I ne'er could rightly fix i' my mind which was which; and it spoke on 'em as if they was vartues or vices; and what I wanted for to know were the rights o' men, whether they were rich or poor — so be they only were men'" (*North* 292–93).

I have been arguing that juridical persons in a liberal polity derive their status as bearers of rights from mental qualities. I have likewise argued that because rights are assigned on such a basis, the twentieth-century notion of the liberal individual as an *abstract* bearer of rights represents a misreading of liberal political philosophy. This is so, I said, because the rights that attend the juridical person in this philosophy proceed from a notion of the self as a creature with interiority, capable of emotion and evaluation; in short, capable of living a virtuous life. I am now arguing that Gaskell's insistence on knowledge of the so-called other — in *North and South* both masters and men, intriguingly enough — is a profoundly political and pragmatic gesture, rather than an idealist and interventionist one. By her account, unless we come to recognize the other as a man, and therefore as like us, those others are forever barred from their rightful[15] status as persons in the juridical sense. Recognition, as I said before, must here be considered as a species of assent; the assent involved in such recognition is assent to the other's status as a bearer of rights.

I call Gaskell a pragmatic interventionist rather than an idealist one because *North and South* does not merely put forward a call for such knowledge, figured by her as a necessary condition for recognition, but proffers a model of how the fusion of horizons must proceed. And this model has important implications for my claim that public and private space are not radically separate topographies in Victorian thought. I argued in my discussion of *Wives and Daughters* that the movement between households that is the province of domestic fiction affords a means of considering the differing ends of life. The heroine of such fictions undergoes such movement in order to determine for herself what the ends of life ought to be, and in so doing illuminates the relationship between the intimate space of the household and the public space whose condition is determined by our ideas of the ends of life. I have gone on to show that in *North and South* the contest among differing ends of life does not occur through contrasting households, but through contrasting subcultures. The narrative movement of *North and South*, however, is not simply among the three major and two minor *topoi* of the novel, but between what are conventionally perceived as public and private space. I am arguing, indeed, that the private plots of *Bildung* and romance are not subsidiary or indeed even separate from the public plot of the strike and relations between masters and men, but that the two inform each other. Indeed, it is my contention that the interpenetration of intimate space and public space is, for Gaskell, both an inevitable part of the transformation of society by the industrial revolution, and a necessary condition for knowledge of the other, which knowledge, as I have shown, is for her a crucial precondition for the extension of rights. I want now to illustrate this claim by turning to Gaskell's representations of household space in *North and South*.

I have already mentioned the vulgarity perceived by Margaret and Mr. Hale in the wallpaper that adorns their new house in Milton-Northern. It is worth noting that "the atrocious blue and pink paper and heavy cornice" (*North* 98) adorn the room that is to be the drawing room, that is, that part of the home that Speare admits to his otherwise narrow description of the political domain[16] and that I have already described as the locus of both household intimacy and the household's negotiations with outsiders. As such, the drawing room bears considerable weight as emblem of the ends of life to which a particular family adheres, and thus it is not surprising that Gaskell figures part of the contrast between the Thorntons (north) and the Hales (south) in terms of these chambers. When Thornton first comes to the little house at Crampton (a suburb of Milton-Northern) for tea, he observes this himself:

The drawing room was not like this. It was twice — twenty times as fine; not one quarter as comfortable. Here were no mirrors, not even a scrap of glass to reflect the light, and answer the same purpose as water in a landscape; no gilding; a warm, sober breadth of colouring, well relieved by the dear old Helstone chintz-curtains and chair covers. An open davenport stood in the window opposite the door; in the other there was a stand, with a tall white china vase, from which drooped wreaths of English ivy, pale-green birch and copper-coloured beech-leaves. Pretty baskets of work stood about in different places: and books, not cared for on account of their bindings solely, lay on one table, as if recently put down. . . . It appeared to Mr Thornton that all these graceful cares were habitual to the family. (*North* 119–20)

I have quoted the bulk of Thornton's impressions here because of his own perception that these "graceful cares" are habitual to the Hales; that is, I am suggesting that, as the sign of intimate space, the drawing room is intended to capture the Hales' views of the ends of life. This account explains, first of all, why the "vulgarity and commonness" (*North* 102) of the pink and blue wallpaper was so distressing, not only to Margaret but to her father; it also explains the most obvious differences between Thornton's home and the "cramped" little house in the suburbs. For the Hales the space of intimacy, which is also the space of negotiation with the outside world, must reflect the family's actions: Thus the drawing room is background to "baskets of work" and to books, to family pursuits that are action and not mere appearances. In Thornton's household, on the other hand, the drawing room is a kind of landscape, a picture intended to be gazed upon and not lived in. Indeed, it is only on the occasion of the Thornton's dinner party that "[e]very cover was taken off, and the apartment blazed forth in yellow silk damask and a brilliantly-flowered carpet" (*North* 213). In other words, the luxuriousness of the Thornton drawing room is not directed at the family or their pleasure, but at their guests; as such, it has to do with the appearance of wealth and power, with the demonstration of success rather than the enjoyment of it. With its "[e]very corner ... filled up with ornament, until it became a weariness to the eye" (*North* 213), in no way does it mitigate the portrayal of the Thorntons as acquisitive in the sense I have been describing.

Interestingly, however, the Thornton drawing room has as its view "the bald ugliness of the look-out into the great mill-yard" (*North* 213). Mr. Hale is surprised at this, asking Mrs. Thornton, "'[d]on't you find such close neighbourhood to the mill rather unpleasant at times?'" (*North* 214). He means, as he explains, "'the smoke and the noise — the constant going out and coming in of the work-people might be annoying!'" (*North* 214). I want to suggest that the proximity of the marketplace to the intimate space of the Thornton household, however, is not part of Gaskell's critique of the purely acquisitive life, but a counter to the kind of hypocrisy shown by such as Bell in rendering invisible and despising the sources of his wealth. This indeed is the substance of Mrs. Thornton's response to Hale: She says, "'I am not become so fine as to desire to forget the source of my son's wealth and power'" (*North* 214). Likewise, the conversation of the men at the dinner party attracts Margaret because it ignores the division between drawing room and market-place: "She was glad when the gentlemen came ... because she could listen to something larger and grander than the petty interests which the ladies had been talking about" (*North* 217). Both cases represent a division between public and private as negative, the first because it is hypocritical and pretentious, the second because it leads to a kind of pettyness, of "trifling" in the sense I used the term earlier.

It is not enough for Gaskell's purposes, however, to show the intervention of the public sphere in the domain of the private. More importantly, she is arguing — and this, I contend, is the pragmatism of her interventionist claims — that the space of the marketplace will always be one of unlimited acquisition, with everything that entails, unless the intimate space of the household is brought into the market itself. This is so for two reasons. First, because, as we shall see, the knowledge of the other that is a necessary precondition for the extension of rights is impossible without the affective bonds that can only be forged in intimate space, and second, because the acquisitive life can only be contained, and therefore limited and made instrumental rather than an end-in-itself, when the concerns of intimate space are brought into it.

It may be that the strikers' march on Thornton's home, which soon becomes a riot, is an attempt to represent the terrors that may arise when the interrelationship of intimate and economic space must be forced; it is certainly the case that Thornton's visit to the home of the unemployed worker, Higgins, illustrates my point in this regard.   Thornton had already refused Higgins work that morning, accusing him of lies, impudence, and labour agitation.   It is only by entering Higgins's home that he can be convinced of the truth of what he had called "'a very unlikely story'" (*North* 398), that Higgins had taken on the guardianship and support of the orphaned children of one of his fellow strikers.   Just as it is Margaret's movement among different spaces that allows her to acquire knowledge of those she had considered entirely other — the working class, manufacturers — Thornton can only begin to perceive his workers as men rather than "hands" once he has seen them in the context of their private lives.

In these terms Thornton's dining room in the mill can be seen as final proof of the success of his *Bildung*. He tells Bell, "'I'm building a dining-room — for the men. I mean — the hands'" (*North* 444). His hasty correction of his new term for the workers — "men"   — for his old term, "hands," indicates, of course, a significant change in his habits of thought, but there is more going on here than a simple change of idiom.   The dining-room scheme, which both Thornton and Higgins take credit for, is simply a cooperative meal plan for the employees; Thornton supplies the provisions at wholesale, along with a housekeeper-cook and kitchen, and the workers pay him rent for the whole as well as for his costs.   This is not a recreation of affective bonds in terms of the despotic hierarchy of the *oikos*: Thornton visits his dining room only by invitation, and indeed, tells Bell, "'[i]f they had not asked me, I would no more have intruded on them than I'd have gone to the mess at the barracks without invitation'" (*North* 446). Indeed, there is nothing in the dining-room scheme that abrogates in any way the vaunted independence of the workers; Thornton is aware that should the plan "'fall into a charity'" the "'simplicity of the whole thing'" would be spoiled (*North* 446).

At the same time, the dining room succeeds partly because it brings the intimate space of the household into the marketplace, where it may then serve as a site of negotiation and compromise rather than as an extension of the busyness of the mill. Thornton believes that by eating with the men occasionally, he is "'getting really to know some of them now, and they talk pretty freely before me'" (*North* 446). It is Bell who suggests that this could only be possible in intimate space: "'Nothing like the act of eating for equalising men'" (*North* 446). It is, then, this penetration of intimacy into the public sphere that finally teaches Thornton that these, too, are men: "Once brought face to face, man to man, with an individual of the masses around him, and (take notice) *out* of the character of master and workman, in the first instance, they had each begun to recognise that 'we have all of us one human heart'" (*North* 511).

William James Booth has argued most convincingly that the industrial revolution replaced the affective bonds and despotic hierarchy of the *oikos* economy with the alienation of labour and voluntarism of liberalism. He points out that Marx sought, unsuccessfully, to redress the alienation of contractarian liberalism, but ultimately found no solution to that problem that did not bode a return to the despotism of feudal life (272–75). I have been arguing that, remarkable as the work of Booth and other political philosophers of liberalism has been, they have erred in taking for granted the abstraction of the liberal individual, conceived as a juridical person, and that this error consists in failing to see that the very status of the bearer of rights depends on the claim that "I, too, am a man," a claim that is backed up by the exegesis of the other in terms of psychological depth. The profoundly political gesture made in Victorian fictions consists in precisely such exegesis, and this explication of the other's claims to rights necessarily occurs in the context of the household, because the intimate space of the household is the domain of emotion, evaluation, and interior qualities — that is, the domain of the ends of life. *North and South* is significant for my argument because it is here that Gaskell acknowledges the need for intimate knowledge of the other, which she figures as a precondition for that recognition of and assent to the status of that other as a bearer of rights. If this is so, it is also true that the so-called liberalism of the utilitarians, or hardline contractarians, is finally shown up by Gaskell as inadequate liberalism because it is not capable of the extension of rights that is its avowed purpose. This is the end of Thornton's *Bildung*. He says, at last, "'[m]y only wish is to have the opportunity of cultivating some intercourse with the hands beyond the mere 'cash nexus.' But it might be the point Archimedes sought from which to move the earth, to judge from the importance attached to it by some of our manufacturers, who shake their heads and look grave as soon as I name the one or two experiments that I should like to try'" (*North* 525). Thornton is right, of course; the reconstruction of public space to accord with liberalism, properly conceived, would involve another kind of revolution. It would, indeed, move the earth, but without this reconstruction, the republicanism from which liberalism grew and toward which it must always tend is radically endangered. This is so, as I have said, because it requires relations not between abstract bearers of rights but between juridical persons, who are bearers of rights by virtue of the fact that they reason, and whose ability to reason is grounded on, among other things, affective interiority. This is likewise the end of Margaret's *Bildung*:

[S]he had learnt, in those solemn hours of thought, that she herself must one day answer for her own life, and what she had done with it; and she tried to settle that most difficult problem for women, how much was to be utterly merged in obedience to authority, and how much might be set apart for freedom in working. . . . So Margaret gained the acknowledgement of her right to follow her own ideas of duty. (*North* 508)

It is true that my attention to the revolutionary claim "we too are men" in *North and South* has been largely, if not quite wholly, involved in demonstrating the significance of this claim for the workers-as-other. But, as I observed above, Gaskell's exegesis of this point proceeds in *North and South* through a complex system of analogies, and I will conclude by pointing out that to the degree that Margaret's *Bildung* parallels that of Thornton — as indicated partly by the fact that the romance plot between these characters cannot be satisfactorily resolved until they have both reached that point of recognition, which is assent and therefore acknowledgment — her status as a person (citizen) also parallels that of Higgins. That is, like the workers', Margaret's right to submit to authority only when the validity of that authority has been confirmed by her own reason is, finally, the point of Gaskell's novel. That shame she garners, which is partly public, by her lie to Thornton about her meeting with her brother, briefly and secretly in England, is a necessary part of this point; it may be worthwhile to recall here Wollstonecraft's argument that virtue is only possible if we are free to err. Viewed from this angle, Margaret's investment of her inheritance in Thornton's mill is not simply the instrument of the necessary happy ending, but a prerequisite for her marriage because it establishes Thornton and Margaret as partners, figuratively in marriage as economically in Marlborough Mills. And partnership, of course, is only possible between agents who are also self-owners and therefore bearers of rights.

NOTES

1.   Cazamian says Margaret's marriage to Thornton "symbolizes the social reconciliation" (214) but thinks "the problem of industry" is a linked subplot rather than part of the same plot (215). Deirdre David sees the romantic plot as the dominant one, and takes it to contain the potentially explosive class relations of the novel outside the political domain (41). Here David's argument is similar to that of Yeazell. Arnold Kettle finds "the emotion generated by the conflict between Margaret and Thornton . . . kept within the bounds of compromise, a compromise confirmed by the marriage at the end of the book" (183). Margaret Ganz, in *Elizabeth Gaskell: The Artist in Conflict*, similarly reads the romance plot as the "true climax" of the novel (104), arguing that after Margaret and Thornton's confrontation with the strikers, the social-problem aspect of the novel is "dwarfed" by "the intricacies of romantic misunderstandings" (101), despite her awareness that it is "personal considerations and circumstances — private trials, individual shocks to the conscience — [that] effect solutions to social conflicts" (103). A somewhat less critical view is advanced by biographer Winifred Gérin, who accepts on faith Gaskell's happy ending as "a possible solution to jarring cultures, standards, prejudices — in a truce between conflicting interests, in a victory for both sides in the conciliation of Masters and Men" (152). Raymond Williams, somewhat differently, is more concerned with the legacy Margaret brings to Thornton than with their marriage; for Williams, this is a move typical of Gaskell, whom he says "works out her reaction to the unsupportable situation by going — in part adventitiously — outside it" (92).

2.   Allott 19. Allott disagrees, however, with the A.B. Hopkins's 1952 categorization of *North and South* as "a Victorian *Pride and Prejudice*" (Hopkins 139; Allott 19) that takes the reeducation of both Margaret and Thornton as its central thread, and the industrial theme as providing the antipathy between them (Hopkins 140). A similar reading is offered by Gerald DeWitt Sanders, for whom "the invincible love of a man and a woman" is "the story itself" to which Hale's religious dissent, Margaret's lie, and the vicissitudes of labour and capital must be subordinated, although he places it, like many others, as the last of Gaskell's trilogy of social-problem novels (74). Sharps, only somewhat differently, argues that *North and South* is a "middle-class romance" that shouldn't be placed with Gaskell's first two novels, both written with a social purpose (207). More compelling is Wainwright's 1993 assessment of the novel in terms of Millian liberalism and the conditions through which the individual attains both autonomy and "authenticity"; I differ from Wainwright in taking

Margaret's *Bildung* as a longer progress, and in my emphasis on the role of *topoi*.

3.   I take the idea of culture, in Ulf Hannerz's terms, to involve three dimensions: ideas and modes of thought, that is, "the entire array of concepts, propositions, values and the like which people within some social unit carry together, as well as their various ways of handling their ideas in characteristic modes of mental operation"; forms of externalization of these meanings, which are the ways in which they are "made public;" and social distribution, that is, "the ways in which the collective cultural inventory of meanings and meaningful external forms . . . is spread over a population and its social relationships" (7). "Subculture," then, refers to a smaller unit of this "collectively carried meaning" within a wider culture, and to which wider culture the subculture is not entirely homogeneous (Hannerz 37).

4.   See Ross for a treatment of the debate between Price and Knight.

5.   Mrs. Hale believes her husband should seek episcopal preferment, and expresses her dissatisfaction with their simple life in Helstone by castigating the place as unhealthy (*North* 49).

6.   Bermingham's *Landscape and Ideology*, for example, makes such a connection, between the rustic tradition in landscape painting and the enclosure movement. See, in particular, her discussion of the aestheticization of rural poverty in the picturesque (73–83).

7.   Margaret's relationship with Nicholas and Bessy Higgins proves salutary in this regard. See also Dorice Williams Elliott's account of Margaret's unofficial role as "district visitor."

8.   For a discussion of figures appropriate to a picturesque landscape, both human and animal, see Hussey 118–19; Bermingham 68–69; and Fabricant 61–70.

9.   That Lennox likewise includes Margaret as part of his landscape is, I think, a telling comment on his view of her, and one that is commented on much later by Mr. Bell in a different context. He says to Thornton, "'You can speak of her in that measured way, as simply a "beautiful creature" — only something to catch the eye. I did hope you had nobleness enough in you to make you pay the homage of the heart'" (*North* 444).

10.   Margaret's visit to Bessy Higgins's deathbed, and her subsequent invitation to Nicholas Higgins to join the Hales for tea, announces this change (*North* 277–97).

11.   I am indebted to William James Booth for drawing my attention to certain pertinent passages from Aristotle.

12.   The tea with Thornton is not, of course, Margaret's first meeting with him, and her relation of her impressions in the following chapter are not her first impressions, as we have already seen; however, chapter 11, in which Margaret's present account is related, was titled "First Impressions" by Gaskell.

13.   *Sources* 79. Taylor is not suggesting that the moral and the ethical are not overwhelmingly intertwined, but proffering a conceptual distinction.

14.   I do not mean to suggest by this that our evaluative processes are unknowable; indeed, it is much of the point of *North and South* that they are knowable, in principle at least, but that there are always obstacles to our knowledge. In this respect Gaskell's treatment recalls Opie's *Adeline Mowbray*, although Gaskell's account is less pessimistic.

15.   I use this term in the sense both of "bearer of rights" and "right to."

16.   "[A Political Novel] *is a work of prose fiction which leans rather to "ideas" than to "emotions"; which deals rather with the machinery of law-making or with a theory about public conduct than with the merits of any given piece of legislation; and where the main purpose of the writer is party propaganda, public reform, or exposition of the lives of the personages who maintain government, or of the forces which constitute government. In this exposition the drawing-room is frequently used as a medium for presenting the inside life of politics*" (Speare ix).

6

The Economy of the Household: Liberalism and Intimate Space in Dickens and John Stuart Mill

> The only freedom which deserves the name, is that of pursuing our own good in our own way, so long as we do not attempt to deprive others of theirs, or impede their efforts to obtain it.
> — John Stuart Mill, *On Liberty*

Alasdair MacIntyre argues in his groundbreaking treatment of moral theory, *After Virtue*, that those who try to analyze the moral condition of our culture have only two real theoretical alternatives: Nietzsche or Aristotle (see esp. 109–20). And from my observations so far it may well seem that I have thrown my lot in with MacIntyre and chosen Aristotle. But for reasons I hope will shortly become clear, this is not the case, nor, indeed, do I agree with MacIntyre that our choices are limited in quite this way. His impoverished vision of our moral-theoretical condition is, to be fair, necessary on his analysis. Having sought (apparently in vain) for an epistemological grounding for the discourse of rights, he is forced to dismiss the Enlightenment claim to reason, in Nietzschean fashion, as the masking of will, and consequently must retreat to a philosophical time before the Enlightenment in order to defend rights at all. Rights cannot, for MacIntyre, be grounded in reason because, according to a rights-based moral theory, other persons are ends-in-themselves, not means-to-ends, and as MacIntyre rightly points out, "[q]uestions of ends are questions of values" (26). The problem arises with his consequent claim that "on values reason is silent; conflict between rival values cannot be rationally settled. Instead one must simply choose — between parties, classes, nations, causes, ideals" (26).

The problem, quite clearly, is MacIntyre's narrow conception of rationality. He buys here into a rigid distinction between the objective (the known), which for him is properly the domain of the rational, and the subjective (the knower), which for him is given to "sentiment and feeling" (26) and is therefore nonrational.[1] Like those feminist epistemologies Mary Hawkesworth complains of in "Knowers, Knowing, Known," MacIntyre's rigid fact/value dichotomy ignores centuries of philosophical debate about the nature of reason, rationality, and knowledge in order to "conflate all reasoning with one particular conception of rationality, that of instrumental reason" (Hawkesworth 542). Not only is such a conception of reason, as I have shown, a misreading of the Enlightenment project, it also necessarily leads to MacIntyre's miscasting of human relationships and, by consequence, his dismissal of the discourse of rights. Unable to accommodate feeling or sentiment in his thin notion of rationality, MacIntyre is likewise unable to accommodate values in his consequently malnourished idea of the operations of reason. And without the possibility of reasoned discourse about values, rights (themselves a value, not a property) cannot be. Moreover, conceptions of the ends of life likewise depend on an idiom of living that can accommodate values, because it is only through such an idiom that we can articulate our ideas of the good, on which the ends of life, however defined, must depend. I suggest, then, with Charles Taylor that the concept of rights is fundamentally linked to ideas about values, the good, and the ends of life: Taylor says that "[t]he sense that human beings are capable of some kind of higher life forms part of the background for our belief that they are fit objects of respect, that their life and integrity is sacred or enjoys immunity, and is not to be attacked" (*Sources* 25). Thus, MacIntyre says that for Kant, a human relationship informed by morality is "one in which each treats the other as an end" rather than as a means to one's own ends (23):

To treat someone else as an end is to offer them what I take to be good reasons for acting in one way rather than another, but to leave it to them to evaluate those reasons. . . . It is to appeal to impersonal criteria of the validity of which each rational agent must be his or her own judge. By contrast, to treat someone else as a means is to seek to make him or her an instrument of my purposes by adducing whatever influences or considerations will in fact be effective on this or that occasion. . . . *this distinction is illusory*. For evaluative utterance can in the end have no point or use but the expression of my own feelings or attitudes and the transformation of the feelings or attitudes of others. I cannot genuinely appeal to impersonal criteria, for there are no impersonal criteria. I may think that I so appeal and others may think that I so appeal, but these thoughts will always be mistakes. The sole reality of distinctively moral discourse is the attempt of one will to align the attitudes, feelings, preference and choices of another with its own. *Others are always means, never ends*. (23–24; emphases mine)

And this — that others are means, not ends — is so for us, according to MacIntyre, and must be so, in the absence of an aprioristic ground for thinking of them as ends. Significantly, however, insofar as others are means to our ends and not ends-in-themselves, they are not "fit objects of respect" in Taylor's sense; they are not fully bearers of rights. But no deontological conception of the person as end is, in MacIntyre's reading, possible, because rule-bound injunctions to treat the other as end always depend on what he calls "the ghost of conceptions of divine law" (111) — that ghost he must choose Aristotle in order to revive.

But in this, too, he errs. MacIntyre claims that we can, "without any inconsistency," refuse Kant's injunction to treat the other as an end rather than a means: "'Let everyone except me be treated as a means' may be immoral, but it is not inconsistent and there is not even any inconsistency in willing a universe of egotists all of whom live by this maxim" (46). Yet conceptual incoherency is, indeed, inconsistency; I cannot seriously, if treating my own self as an end-in-itself, will MacIntyre's universe of egotists because I cannot seriously will that another should treat me as a means.[2] And it is interesting that precisely that nineteenth-century novel that engages in a fundamental critique of such a starved and utilitarian conception of the rational is likewise engaged, both figuratively and literally, with a critique of that social and political solipsism that sees the other not only as irremediably other, but as a means to its own ends. I am speaking, of course, of Charles Dickens's 1854 *Hard Times*.

"The key-note" (*Hard* 60) of *Hard Times*, as Dickens makes clear, is not the economic-utilitarian dependence on fact-based rationality that for Patricia E. Johnson is manifested through the factory and its metonym, fact (130), though this is clearly central. Rather, it is the consequences of this materialist conception for our view of the other,[3] that working-class other whom Dickens seeks to erect, *pace* Josiah Wedgewood, as both man and brother[4] that Dickens sounds again and again. And these distasteful consequences are very like those MacIntyre arrives at, that "others are always means, never ends" (MacIntyre 24). Thus Dickens's Coketown, with its interchangeable streets, is "inhabited by people equally like one another, who all went in and out at the same hours, with the same sound upon the same pavements, to do the same work, and to whom every day was the same as yesterday and to-morrow, and every year the counterpart of the last and the next" (*Hard* 60). It need hardly be said that this is not the sameness of recognizably shared humanity, of recognition of the self in the other on which the reformists of the nineteenth century depended, however naively, but of cogs in the great machinery of fact: "So many hundred Hands in this Mill; so many hundred horse Steam Power" (*Hard* 104). Indeed, the synecdoche we first noticed in *North and South* and that reappears so notably in *Hard Times* emphasizes this analogy; they are "the multitude of Coketown, generically called 'the Hands,' — a race who would have found more favour with some people, if Providence had seen fit to make them only hands, or, like the lower creatures of the seashore, only hands and stomachs" (*Hard* 99). The labourers, this "multitude," are in other words interchangeable insofar as they can be imagined or conceived as without an inner life, without that psychological depth I have already shown is a key feature of the discourse of rights. As Martha Nussbaum points out, "[d]ehumanize the worker in thought, and it is far easier to deny him or her the respect that human life calls forth" (*Poetic Justice* 34).

It is because they are Hands, and, for the Bounderbys and Gradgrinds of the world, *only* Hands, that the multitude of Coketown can be seen as means to another's ends and in no other way. As Hands, they are susceptible to calculation, to the 'rational' evaluation of impersonal criteria on which MacIntyre — and the utilitarians — depend for their sole understanding of reason. Significantly, these criteria are both market-based and market-driven; the facts that for Bounderby are "the one thing needful" (*Hard* 41) are "everywhere in the material aspect of the town; . . . everywhere in the immaterial. . . . and what you couldn't state in figures, or show to be purchaseable in the cheapest market and saleable in the dearest, was not, and never should be, world without end, Amen" (*Hard* 61). The Hands, then, reduced in this inhuman calculus to material, saleable, facts, are the objects of the calculation of reason, and not the subjects; they cannot, themselves, reason, on market criteria or indeed on any other. It is because this is so that Bounderby can advise Stephen Blackpool to ignore the public sphere, which is "'not [his] piece-work'" (*Hard* 110); as an unreasoning Hand, not a reasoner, Blackpool is incontrovertibly not a citizen, able to grant or withhold his consent to authority. Thus is the last province of patriarchal political authority, of "Divine Right," the factory, maintained (*Hard* 114); thus are the labouring multitudes stripped of personhood, of ends in the Aristotelian sense, to become means to the ends of others.

It should be clear from the foregoing that I am treating utilitarian liberalism as the final frontier of despotism, despite what may appear at first glance to be its Enlightenment (if not enlightened) reliance on reason and rationality. Insofar as the idea of reason is used, not merely to legitimate the individual intellect, but to refuse this legitimation to others and to *rationalize* this refusal, it licenses despotism rather than posing a republican challenge to it; insofar as utilitarian "rationalization" takes the marketplace and workplace as its originary spaces, rather than the household, it depends on a confusion of inner virtue with outer value that is alien to classical liberalism's idea of freedom and rationality. The figure of Bounderby foregrounds this dimension of Dickens's liberal critique of *utilitarian* "liberalism." And critique it is. Where George Orwell proffers up grudging approval of that Dickensian radicalism he believes is genuine (414) but moral rather than social (416), I suggest that Orwell has misread what he describes as Dickens's "'message'": That "[i]f men would behave decently the world would be decent" (417). I suggest that the point of Dickens's moral criticism is that it *is* social, and that Orwell failed to understand the social import of his own view of Dickens. Orwell points out that "[if] you hate violence and don't believe in politics, the only major remedy remaining is education. Perhaps society is past praying for, but there is always hope for the individual human being, if you can catch him young enough" (423). Education may have been, for Orwell, an individual solution, but for Dickens it is a profoundly social and institutional one. It is not true, in other words, that Dickens "utter[ly] lack[s] . . . any educational theory" (Orwell 426), but that Dickens's educational theory, relying as it does on the rearticulation of the affective dimension of liberal rationality and the reemphasis of the intimate domain that is its foundation, is unintelligible to Orwell. Thus, according to Orwell, "Dickens sees human beings with the most intense vividness, but he sees them always in private life, as 'characters,' not as functional members of society; that is to say, he sees them statically" (442) and the domestic conclusions of Dickens's novels, in which "[h]ome life is always enough" are finally "the strange, empty dream of the eighteenth- and nineteenth-century bourgeoisie" (446). I contend, however, that this very sufficiency of the domestic life comprises both Dickens's critique of utilitarian rationalism, and his promise of a human decency that might someday become innate. Indeed, for Dickens, the home is not the locus of purposelessness, as Orwell seems to contend (448), but of the most significant purposes of all.

We have already seen the consequences for Stephen Blackpool of Bounderby's dependence on the market as a political model. It remains to examine the consequences, in many ways more far-reaching, of this utilitarian philosophy for Bounderby's own household. Crucially, Bounderby makes little distinction between marketplace and intimate space; he does not make love to Tom Gradgrind's daughter, although "[l]ove was made . . . in the form of bracelets; and, on all occasions during the period of betrothal, took a manufacturing aspect. Dresses were made, jewellry was made, cakes and gloves were made, settlements were made, and an extensive assortment of Facts did appropriate honour to the contract. The business was all Fact, from first to last" (*Hard* 139). And, of course, for Bounderby the betrothal *is* business, an extension of that acquisitive life he has been leading, to which there is neither end nor ends. Louisa is no Hand, of course, no mere means to endless acquisition, but herself acquired and a sign of the success of Bounderby's acquisitive life. Thus, like the Hands she is a victim of the despotism of the market and with them is finally unfree, object and not subject.[5] But it is also true for Dickens that Bounderby is unfree, a victim of the despotism of means. Bounderby, of course, never achieves the recognition of his own unfreedom that Louisa does, "'curs[ing] the hour'" she was born to this starved and barren "rational" conception of human life: "'How could you give me life, and take from me all the inappreciable things that raise it from the state of conscious death? Where are the graces of my soul? Where are the sentiments of my heart? What have you done, Oh father, what have you done, with the garden that should have bloomed once, in this great wilderness here!'" (*Hard* 240–41). Louisa's lapsarian despair is significant here because she has, after all, avoided the sexual fall with Harthouse toward which she has been tending; such a sexual fall, however, is impossible because the Garden of Eden "that should have bloomed once" has never existed. There is no place to fall from, because the "garden" of sentiment and grace, of the affective and the affections, has indeed never existed. In its place has been the "great wilderness" of utilitarian despotism and the acquisitive life. And this seems to me a crucial point, because it is through the absence of any edenic space that we may acquit Dickens of the charge of nostalgia for a sentimentalized, aristocratic, Aristotelian polity. Indeed, Harthouse, who might be seen to represent this garden (heart-house), dwells likewise in the wilderness; he is one of those "fine gentlemen who, having found out everything to be worth nothing" (*Hard* 156), finds a natural allegiance with the "Gradgrind school" (*Hard* 156): "Where was the great difference between the two schools, when each chained [Louisa] down to material realities, and inspired her with no faith in anything else?" (*Hard* 195). For Dickens this link between utilitarianism and fine-gentlemanism points not to a longing for a more gracious past, but to the desire for a possible future, one in which — paradoxically — Louisa and others may achieve their freedom by binding themselves to the proper ends of life.

As I have already shown, the acquisitive life is unfree not simply because it has no end, but because it mistakes the means to life *for* its ends. It remains to observe that in this error Bounderby has fallen prey to the tyranny of the outer life. His "windy boastfulness" (*Hard* 53), his "pervading appearance . . . of being inflated like a balloon" (*Hard* 53), his "balderdash and bluster" (*Hard* 313-314), all point to the poverty, even the vacuity, of his inner life, and it is this vacancy that forces Bounderby to rely on the signs and symbols of the outer life for his value. The means, then, that he has devoted his life to acquiring function for Bounderby as do the rank and status of the aristocracy he aligns himself with, in the figures of Harthouse and Mrs. Sparsit. Bounderby's pride in his assumed stature as a "self-made man" (*Hard* 53) points to his slavish belief in the efficacy of such symbols. If, as he claims, he has been first "'a nuisance, an incumbrance, and a pest'" (*Hard* 55), then his progression through "'[v]agabond, errand-boy, vagabond, labourer, porter, clerk, chief manager, small partner'" to the "'culmination'" that is "'Josiah Bounderby of Coketown'" (*Hard* 55) is, in his view and in the view even of strangers, ample sign of his status: "the Royal arms, the Union-Jack, Magna Charta [sic], John Bull, Habeas Corpus, the Bill of Rights, An Englishman's house is his castle, Church and State, and God save the Queen, all put together" (*Hard* 80). He becomes, for himself and others although only ironically for Dickens, an emblem of the English polity, a kind of bull-beef heir of the sturdy yeoman of an earlier time. Bounderby's emblematic history, despite or perhaps because of being itself manufactured, is like those other acquisitions of Bounderby's, Mrs. Sparsit and Tom Gradgrind's daughter, an external sign of rank in the utilitarian polity. And Bounderby's allegiance to the values ("facts") of the industrial marketplace, again revealed in his pride in his personal history, does not counter but merely disguises his dependence on kinship and other, external signs.

In this light the bedfellows of utilitarian politics, the morally bankrupt aristocracy represented through that "fine gentleman" (*Hard* 156), James Harthouse, and the starveling rationalizers represented through Gradgrind and Bounderby, are not strange at all; there is no difference between the two schools. As the narrator indicates, the despotism of utility derives from the despotism of "material realities" (*Hard* 195) of the external over and against the internal; it is this emphasis on the outer sign that links, for Dickens at least, Bounderby's utilitarianism to the vanishing vocabulary of aristocratic worth. But it might fairly be argued against this conception of utilitarian political theory that Dickens's representation is a mistaken one, and indeed John Stuart Mill's defense of utilitarianism on liberal humanist grounds, seven years after the publication of *Hard Times*, is directed at least in part against "the common herd, including the herd of writers" (*Util.* 209). Indeed, Mill's utilitarianism looks quite different from that tyrannical economy of the material in which Bounderby is both master of his own ends and slave to means.

Like MacIntyre, Mill recognizes that "[q]uestions of ultimate ends are not amenable to direct proof" (*Util.* 207), but unlike him, Mill lays claim to a conception of rationality that not only admits of the *possibility* of questions of ends, but contends for the *necessity* of such questions to the moral faculty (*Util.* 206). Like MacIntyre, Mill recognizes that "little progress . . . has been made . . .

respecting the criterion of right and wrong" (*Util*. 205), but unlike him, Mill does not conclude that "one must simply choose" (MacIntyre 26). *Utilitarianism* takes as its subject, in fact, that "larger meaning of the word proof" (*Util*. 208) that depends on reason, not the senses (*Util*. 206), but that cannot justly inhabit the narrow rooms of MacIntyre's rationality. In particular, Mill's "moral faculty" — and the feeling and sentiment on which it depends — is a branch of reason; it is because this is so that Mill can contend against MacIntyre's universe of egotists. And Mill does so contend; it should be clear that I take issue with MacIntyre's claim that "*either* one must follow through the aspirations and the collapse of the different versions of the Enlightenment project until there remains only the Nietzschean diagnosis and the Nietzschean problematic *or* one must hold that the Enlightenment project was not only mistaken, but should never have been commenced in the first place" (118). He sees no third alternative; explicitly, he sees no third alternative in John Stuart Mill (118); I argue, however, that it is only through the alternative posed by Mill that the Enlightenment project can be preserved from collapse.

Let me explain. I observed earlier that Maria Edgeworth anticipates John Stuart Mill in her insight that, though "the most ignorant person in the world assert that he is happier than you are," we are not bound to believe him, because "though he can judge of his own pleasures, he cannot judge of yours; his are common to both, but yours are unknown to him" (11: 225-226). For neither Edgeworth nor Mill does this require a purely quantitative view of pleasure. Mill tells us that utility can admit of what he takes to be fact, "that some *kinds* of pleasure are more desirable and more valuable than others" (*Util*. 211). We are recalled here to Aristotle's notion of the noble and the good, an ethics of ends that is inadmissible in the purely consequentialist ethics of a Bounderby — or a MacIntyre. Mill is explicit, in other words, about the immorality, indeed the *nonutility*, of the universe of egotists:

As little is there an inherent necessity that any human being should be a selfish egotist, devoid of every feeling or care but those which centre in his own miserable individuality. Something far superior to this is sufficiently common even now, to give ample earnest of what the human species may be made. Genuine private affections, and a sincere interest in the public good, are possible, though in unequal degrees, to every rightly brought up human being. (*Util*. 216)

It is worth recalling at this point Bounderby's delimitation of the public domain: It is not Stephen's piece-work, and therefore he is barred from interest in it. This pointed demarcation of the hand from the citizen parallels Bounderby and Gradgrind's line between "fancy" and "fact." The connection between "fancy" and "fact" and the idea of the other-as-citizen is central to Martha Nussbaum's defense of the literary imagination in *Poetic Justice*, where she mourns the loss of "the capacity to see each other as fully human" in contemporary political life (xiii) and argues that "an ethics of impartial respect for human dignity will fail to engage real human beings unless they are made capable of entering imaginatively into the lives of distant others and to have emotions related to that participation" (xvi). Fancy, or "the metaphorical imagination," in which it is possible to see other things and significances in the immediately perceptible (*Poetic Justice* 36), is thus for Nussbaum "a morally crucial ability" (*Poetic Justice* 37), because our perceptions of humans as humans are "a going beyond the facts, an acceptance of generous fancies, a projection of our own sentiments and inner activities onto the forms we perceive about us (and a reception from this interaction of images of ourselves, our own inner world)" (*Poetic Justice* 38). This for Nussbaum is the central point of Dickens's claim that "there is an unfathomable mystery in the meanest of [the workers], for ever" (*Hard* 104): She sees it as an appeal to go beyond the facts, beyond the visible.[6]

I want to observe, moreover, that not only does Mill here argue, precisely as Dickens does and as Nussbaum resurrects Dickens in order to do, for the centrality of private affections, of the intimate and affective domain, to our notions of the good, but that, again like Dickens, Mill *conjoins* these affections to "a sincere interest in the public good" (*Util.* 216). The impartiality for which Mill contends, then, is not that cramped objectivity of "impersonal criteria" that leads MacIntyre to assert that "[t]he sole reality of distinctively moral discourse is the attempt of one will to align the attitudes, feelings, preference and choices of another with its own" (MacIntyre 24). Nor is it the tabulative rationality of Dickens's "deaf honourable gentlemen, dumb honourable gentlemen, blind honourable gentlemen, lame honourable gentlemen, dead honourable gentlemen" (*Hard* 126). Neither impersonal criteria nor tabulative rationality are for Mill capable of adjudicating happiness, or ends of any kind. Rather, Mill's impartiality of judgment, for him constitutive of that version of utilitarian ethics I see as liberally humanist, exists *in order* to make possible the judgment of happiness, between one's own and that of others. Thus the utilitarian polity is impossible for Mill if its laws and social arrangments fail to place the happiness of the individual in harmony with the whole, and likewise if both education and opinion fail to conjoin and cultivate, in the individual, personal happiness and the good of the whole (*Util.* 218).

Mill does not contend, as I do not, that human selves own some kind of transparent "essence" that education allows them to fulfill. While he sees moral feelings as natural, this is because they are an outgrowth of our nature but nonetheless themselves acquired and not innate; they are "susceptible of being brought by cultivation to a high degree of development" (*Util.* 230). And I suggest that what we acquire — that which our education cultivates — points to our ideas about what is valuable or necessary in a self, conceived as a citizen. Thus Dickens's condemnation of M'Choakumchild's "system" in *Hard Times*: Selves and citizens are not for Dickens "vessels . . . ready to have imperial gallons of facts poured into them until they [are] full to the brim" (*Hard* 42), but those whose rich inner lives allow them, as with Sissy, a "'wisdom of the Heart'" (*Hard* 248). Sissy's wisdom is, significantly, not innate; it too must be cultivated if it is to be garden and not Louisa's "great wilderness" (*Hard* 241). Education is cultivation, for Dickens, and in *Hard Times* as in the later, domestically focused *Great Expectations*, he depends on that education Orwell saw as an individual solution to remedy the ills of a social rationality too narrowly conceived, just as — through Bitzer, for example, or *Great Expectations*'s Estella — Dickens recognized the power of education to further the starved utilitarian conception of human life. Bitzer, indeed, like Estella, recognizes the success of his teaching; he responds to Mr. Gradgrind's prayer for aid by saying, "'[w]hat you must always appeal to, is a person's self-interest. . . . I was brought up in that catechism when I was very young, sir, as you are aware'" (*Hard* 306). Estella, as we shall shortly see, also lacks the wisdom of the Heart, and Bitzer's words to Gradgrind are recalled by her reproaches to Miss Havisham: "'Who taught me to be proud? . . . Who praised me when I learnt my lesson?'" (*Great* 301). And yet the wisdom of the heart cannot, again, be withdrawn from the wisdom of the head, as the "[g]enuine private affections" of the individual, conceived not as a "selfish egotist" (*Util.* 216) but as one who shares in the public good, are not withdrawn from but joined to that public good.

I have been maintaining that there is a complex intersection between the public and the private in Victorian domestic fictions, as in political fictions like *Hard Times*, and that this intersection is not an interruption or an obviation of the political dimension, but crucial to the political claims of such works as *Great Expectations*. If, in this 1860–61 Dickensian vision of the polity, "'a Englishman's ouse is his Castle'" (*Great* 460), it is so because it is the domain of these private affections, affections that derive from, and are cultivated in, the space of ends rather than those market means with which Bounderby's affections are confused. We see the household, in *Great Expectations*, as the foundation of the liberal polity, a polity that, in what I hope to show is Millian fashion, seeks to ensure the self's right to pursue and realize its own ends, its own vision of the good. As such it is the foundation of the liberal state: The so-called private space of the household can be neither withdrawn nor separated from the public and political domain; indeed, it is only when it is so withdrawn that the household, and consequently the state, become tainted by the confusion of ends with means. And *Great Expectations*, concerned as it is with intimate and nonmarket relationships, provides ample illustration of this tainture.

Remember that Bounderby's business, his busyness, which extends the vocabulary and the conduct of the marketplace even over his betrothal, is a species of unfreedom, according to Aristotle. While the household, in *The Politics*, exists to free us from scarcity and want, Bounderby has confused these matters. He does not, in other words, achieve that self-sufficiency that Aristotle calls perfection (*Politics* I.ii.1252b27), because for him the getting of wealth does not procure the household, but is its purpose; he is, I suggested, therefore both slave and master to the despotism of means in the narrow utilitarianism Dickens attacks. Pip's own confusion of means and ends, in *Great Expectations*, is likewise central to the novel; it is a key signal that he cannot escape the spell of Satis House. Returning from Miss Havisham's house, "more than ever dissatisfied" with, as he says, "my home and with my trade and with everything," he takes refuge from his dissatisfaction in "looking in disconsolately at the shop windows, and thinking what I would buy if I were a gentleman" (*Great* 114). To be a gentleman — a man of means — is, for Pip, an end in itself, and not a means to the end of self-sufficiency. The forge, after all, offers him "sufficient means of self-respect and happiness"

(*Great* 130), but the destructive influence of the manor means this sufficiency is not, after all, sufficient. Pip, when he leaves for London to prepare for his expectations is no different from the boy who confesses to Joe after his first visit that "I knew I was common, and that I wished I was not common, and that the lies had come of it somehow" (*Great* 69), and like this boy the older Pip should be reminded that "'[i]f you can't get to be oncommon through going straight, you'll never get to do it through going crooked'" (*Great* 70).

And yet Pip *does* understand there is a distinction, and an important one, between the good life and the life of necessity. His expectations make the good life possible, at least in his view; they are not, themselves, the good life. He sees them, indeed, as the means to an end, as the means to Estella, and thus to the restoration of the household. In his dreams at least, Satis will be sufficient once again: He believes Miss Havisham had "reserved it for [him] to restore the desolate house, admit the sunshine into the dark rooms, set the clocks a going and the cold hearths a blazing, tear down the cobwebs, destroy the vermin" (*Great* 229). And yet, crucially in *Great Expectations* — and this is the finer irony of the name of Satis — the household alone, in and of itself, is not and never can be sufficient. It is Pip's failure to understand this, as he fails to understand so many things, that renders his notion of the distinction between means and ends — and thus the whole notion of the gentleman, whose ends are met by his means and his means alone — so problematic here.[7] The idea of incompatibility revealed, for example, in his assertion to Herbert that "'a gentleman may not keep a public-house'" — although, as Herbert points out, "'a public-house may keep a gentleman'" (*Great* 178) — may have in part to do with that same sense we noted in *North and South*, that those who are concerned with the means to life cannot engage in the noble pursuit of its ends, and are therefore neither fully virtuous nor fully citizens. In other words, Pip's idea of means and ends, like his idea of the household, is illiberal because it insists on their separation even as it insists on the separation of household from market space. In this it is opposed to that emblem of liberal possibility, the forge, which becomes under Biddy and Joe the ideal marriage of domestic and commercial, intimate and civic space.

The discourse of means in *Great Expectations* is important precisely because the household cannot be sufficient. The good life, after all, is not the idle life, the life of mere pleasure, whatever else it may be, and if self-sufficiency is freedom from want, it is not, in the *liberal* state, freedom from work. And here I dissent from Orwell's claim that Dickens's dream, like that of the rest of his age, was a dream of "*complete idleness*" (Orwell 446). Work may indeed for Dickens happen largely "off-stage" (Orwell 441), but it is nonetheless central to his notion of the sufficiency of the home in *Great Expectations*. Thus, for example, the dangerous *insufficiency* of the Pocket household: Mrs. Pocket, "brought up from her cradle as one who in the nature of things must marry a title, and . . . guarded from the acquisition of plebian domestic knowledge," is thus "highly ornamental, but perfectly helpless and useless" (*Great* 187). Pip, too, having set up as a gentleman, is not only perfectly useless but perfectly miserable: "We spent as much money as we could, and got as little for it as people could make up their minds to give us. We were always more or less miserable, and most of our acquaintance were in the same condition. There was a gay fiction among us that we were constantly enjoying ourselves, and a skeleton truth that we never did" (*Great* 270–71).

In this sense at least, *Great Expectations* is Aristotelian in its concern with action. Pip's action, like Mrs. Pocket's, is inaction, directed neither toward the satisfaction of necessity, nor toward the pursuit of the beautiful and the noble — an Aristotelian distinction in which mere pleasure is not freedom but its opposite: "The many," says the *Nicomachean Ethics*, "the most vulgar, would seem to conceive the good and happiness as pleasure, and hence they also like the life of gratification. Here they appear completely slavish, since the life they decide on is a life for grazing animals" (*Ethics* 1.v.1095b16–20). Pip and Mrs. Pocket err in precisely the same way. Both see leisure itself as noble, and fail to recognize that it must be ennobled, as the self must be ennobled, through noble pursuits. Mere pleasure, however, is ignoble, slavish; it is inaction because it is divorced from both means and ends. But in the polity means and ends are linked: the pursuit of the beautiful and the noble, which is private virtue and understood as the proper end of life, is only possible once leisure to pursue these ends has been secured, and therefore depends, in the classical household, on the satisfaction of necessity and, as we have already seen, on a despotic hierarchy that ensures the master of the *oikos* is freed by the labour of others to pursue his own ends.[8]

That his freedom depends on the labour of others — on transported, convict labour, despotic indeed — doesn't occur to Pip, of course, until Magwitch reveals himself: "'I lived rough, that you should live smooth; I worked hard, that you should be above work. What odds, dear boy? Do I tell it, fur you to feel obligation? Not a bit. I tell it, fur you to know as that there hunted dunghill dog wot you kep life in, got his head so high that he could make a gentleman — and, Pip, you're him!'" (*Great* 315). But Pip's idea of the gentleman — and, indeed, Magwitch's — is anachronistic. He wants an outmoded and illiberal, even classical, leisure, secured by others whom he fails to recognize, even while he fails to recognize the pursuits proper to that leisure. And his frenzied fear and dislike in response to Magwitch's declaration of himself as the despised ground of Pip's leisure time,[9] his immediate dissociation of himself from Magwitch's "portable property," points up a key dimension of the discourse of means in the nineteenth-century liberal state. Because it is in the nineteenth century that the concept of leisure, for the working classes, comes into play; what, after all, is the Ten Hours Movement if it is not a recognition that free life in the community depends on action of both kinds? Yet Pip is not freed by the labour of others, but chained; he is chained because he refuses both action directed toward the satisfaction of necessity, and — his necessities secured — action directed toward the pursuit of the beautiful and the noble. And here Angus Calder's point, that during his fine-gentleman stage in London Pip is governed by his own servants and harrassed by traders, seems pertinent; Calder observes that "Pip's 'leisured' life is tormented by the people whose work for him makes his leisure possible" (25). That his chains are gold and silver, as Pip himself recognizes (*Great* 318), rather than Magwitch's iron, does not remove him from the taint of the prison that has haunted him all his life. And Pip's chains are the stronger since he has come, like *North and South*'s Mr. Bell, to despise as less than citizens those who have secured what ought to have been his freedom, Magwitch and Joe.[10] This too is illiberal, because it involves a classical sense of the self and of intimacy, in which only those whose leisure has been secured are recognizable as selves and citizens. Liberalism, as I hope is becoming clear, lays claim quite differently to a ground in which the free life is possible for all.

And this ground, as my epigraph makes clear, is not one in which the question of goods, and therefore of ends, must be dismissed out of hand, as it is for MacIntyre, but one that is dedicated to protecting and preserving the space of ends for others. It is a central tenet, moreover, of John Stuart Mill's *On Liberty* that this life cannot be purchased at the cost of the freedom of others, as is revealed in Mill's attack on Samuel Pope, who defended prohibition to Lord Stanley on the grounds that the drinking of others violated his own social rights. This "monstrous" principle (*Liberty* 288) is so because it is based not on provable harm to others, for Mill the only acceptable limit on the freedom of the individual, but on Pope's idea of a social right of the individual to the right behaviour of others: "The doctrine ascribes to all mankind a vested interest in each other's moral, intellectual, and even physical perfection, to be defined by each claimant according to his own standard" (*Liberty* 288). Clearly, Millian liberalism cannot demand that another give up his right to determine his own ends — his own idea of the pursuit of happiness — in service of our ends, either by "extend[ing] the bounds of what may be called the moral police" (*Liberty* 284) or, as in *Utilitarianism*, excluding the happiness of some from the calculus of the polity (*Util.* 218). As such it is clearly incompatible with Pip's dependence on the labour of others, even of Magwitch's labour, which is "freely" given. Because Magwitch, by enslaving himself to the acquisitive life in order to secure Pip's freedom, has given up his own, it is outside the bounds of what for Mill is allowable: "The principle of freedom cannot require that he should be free not to be free. It is not freedom, to be allowed to alienate his freedom" (*Liberty* 300). Nor, significantly, can the principle of freedom require of others that they give up their liberty to secure our freedom; whatever else Millian liberalism may be, it is not a doctrine of "selfish indifference" (*Liberty* 276).

The problem with Pip, then, is not the ends he chooses, but the means by which those ends are secured. And this is a key point, since, as *On Liberty* asserts, in my epigraph, "[t]he only freedom which deserves the name, is that of pursuing our own good in our own way" (*Liberty* 226). Nor may "our own way" justly include "injuring the interests of one another" (*Liberty* 276); like the Hippocratic oath, the first premise of Millian liberalism is to do no harm. But it is not compatible with this freedom that we take it upon ourselves to adjudicate the ends of others. This is because liberty, for Mill, is about the good, and the ability to determine that good for oneself; *On Liberty*, as Ronald Dworkin points out, defends here a complex notion of liberty as independence that constrains us all to respect the goods of others, as well as to defend our own (Dworkin 263–64). Now, it may seem here that Mill's idea of liberty begins to resemble MacIntyre's, insofar as Mill opposes so vociferously the constraints on freedom that the preferences of others place on us. But Mill is not, as MacIntyre is, contending that the question of ends is not amenable to reason; far from it. Indeed, he criticizes people for believing "that their feelings, on subjects of this nature, are better than reasons, and render reasons unnecessary" (*Liberty* 220). It is not that reason cannot be brought to bear on the question of ends; the arbitrary assertion of one set of values over another, which MacIntyre fears, is not for Mill the result of the poverty of reason but of the poverty of feeling uninformed by reason, that "feeling in each person's mind that everybody should be required to act as he, and those with whom he sympathizes, would like them to act" (*Liberty* 221).

On Liberty therefore presents a sustained defense, not only of ends, but of the compatibility of reason with questions of ends, a compatibility Mill does not use to further the interests of adjudication, but to defend the necessity of ends. Thus, where MacIntyre invokes Ronald Dworkin as having argued that since "the central doctrine of modern liberalism is the thesis that questions about the *good life for man* or the ends of human life are to be regarded from the public standpoint as systematically unsettlable. . . . The rules of morality and law . . . are not to be derived from or justified in terms of some more fundamental conception of the good for man" (MacIntyre 119), he misjudges both Dworkin and modern liberalism. Dworkin's argument that questions of ends *need not* be settlable is not synonymous with MacIntyre's version of it, and indeed Dworkin criticizes at some length those "utilitarian" legal theorists who presume that all standards can be treated as rules, and are only settlable if treated in this way (Dworkin 14–45). And modern liberalism, at least in John Stuart Mill's view of the matter, while it does not demand that we settle this vexed question of ends, grounds its idea of *political* morality at least in the notion that human ends are worthy of protection. This is the "more fundamental conception of the good for man" that MacIntyre argues does not exist: That free life in the community is itself a good, and that it is perhaps the highest good of all to protect that free life by refusing to allow another to determine our ends. And insofar as Mill's doctrine cannot, in his view, be applied either to children or to "those backward states of society" wherein humanity has not "attained the capacity of being guided to their own improvement by conviction or persuasion" (*Liberty* 224), it is clear that reason, in its fullest sense, is a necessary precondition for this free life. Absent reason, we are all unfree.

It is because reason is a crucial precondition for freedom that, as I argued above, the discourse of rights in the nineteenth century depends on the household, on the affective relations that constitute that space, and on the leisure to fulfill the promise of reason that is necessary to the free citizen. This is the proper use of wealth — praxis, or free life in the community (Booth 66). Moreover, as we have seen, the virtue of a citizen, on Aristotle's account, can only be fully achieved in a regime that provides him with leisure, so that tyranny often thrives on depriving its citizens of leisure (Booth 47). This, indeed, is the real tragedy of Mrs. Joe, who confuses busyness with virtue, a tyrant in this sense to herself as well as to Pip and Joe as much through the emblem of the apron she swears she has never had off (*Great* 8–9) as through Tickler.[11]

Recognizing the tyrant in Mrs. Joe, recognizing as he does the insufficiency of this household in its failure of intimacy, Pip must uncover a model for living that will be sufficient, an *idiom* in the sense that I used the term earlier. Pip achieves his *Bildung*, as do Gaskell's heroines, by evaluating and discarding certain idioms of living, certain answers to the question of how one should live. *Great Expectations* thus opens with an account of Mrs. Joe's household: Capricious, violent, coercive, unjust, under the rule of one whose confounding of means with ends creates moral timidity in Pip at least (*Great* 62), that moral timidity that may explain his inaction. Only when Mrs. Joe's passions are forcibly contained may the forge become a model for living. By then, however, Pip has fallen under the sickening influence of Satis House.

Unlike the forge, the brewery on which Satis was founded is idle (*Great* 54); Miss Havisham, in opposition to Mrs. Joe, is also idle, all the time, as Mrs. Joe is busy all the time.[12] The contrast here is between Miss Havisham's classical and despotic sense of the good life, for which she need not labour, and Mrs. Joe's sheerly industrial sense, which, like Bounderby's and Bitzer's, is labour without leisure and without limit. Neither is consistent with that liberalism which sought to extend and enlarge the good life so that all might share in means and ends. It is no wonder, then, that Miss Havisham's idleness exhausts her, as the despotism on which it is based is exhausted: "'I am tired,'" she tells young Pip, "'I want diversion, and I have done with men and women. Play'" (*Great* 57). But leisure — play, or any other kind — cannot be ordered in this way. Leisure is praxis, as I have shown, only when it is virtuous action, that free pursuit of the beautiful and noble in private space that develops and extends one's ability to act, intimately and therefore civically. Indeed, in *Great Expectations* virtue is the wedding of the intimate and the civic domains; no longer the aggregate and foundation of public virtue, as it was in Wollstonecraft, for Charles Dickens virtue consists in the necessary union of private and public, of means and ends. This is the reason Mrs. Joe is Miss Havisham's own double, and that they err in precisely the same way. Both mistake the part for the whole, and therefore play in Satis House is not playful, not free, and not virtuous. Satis has been so much remarked that it is unnecessary to go into details here,[13] but I will observe that Estella's education in that house is a miseducation, its influence on Pip shameful, and that it is Miss Havisham's withdrawal from the world that nearly ruins them all: "[I]n shutting out the light of day, she had shut out infinitely more; . . . in seclusion, she had secluded herself from a thousand natural and healing influences; . . . her mind, brooding solitary, had grown diseased, as all minds do and must and will that reverse the appointed order of their Maker" (*Great* 394). Miss Havisham is finally consumed, both literally and figuratively, by her own mania in the conflagration of her bride-clothes, and her immolation, which is self-immolation, stands with and for the self-destruction of the withdrawn and separate private sphere.

And here Dickens anticipates the criticism of the feminized private sphere that John Stuart Mill was to publish in *On the Subjection of Women* in 1869. Mill contends there that the power of women in the home, so lauded in prescriptions for separate spheres from Rousseau onward, is finally both barren and perverse. He says, "neither in the affairs of families nor in those of states is power a compensation for the loss of freedom. [A wife's] power often gives her what she has no right to, but does not enable her to assert her own rights. A Sultan's favourite slave has slaves under her, over whom she tyrannizes; but the desirable thing would be that she should neither have slaves nor be a slave" (*Subjection* 290). Here, of course, Mill is talking about the patriarchal despotism that governs relations between husbands and wives, not the matriarchy of Satis House, but his argument is pertinent nonetheless; Miss Havisham may not be guilty of "entirely sinking her own existence in her husband" (*Subjection* 290) but this is true only because the potential patriarch never *became* her husband. Everything in Satis House, as is Miss Havisham's entire existence, remains bound up with that absent male figure, and it is because this is so that "everything in the room had stopped, like the watch and the clock, a long time ago. . . . Without this arrest of everything, this standing still of all the pale decayed objects, not even the withered bridal dress on the collapsed form could have looked so like grave-clothes, or the long veil so like a shroud" (*Great* 59). Miss Havisham's power in the home, which extends even over time, is in this sense both *enslaved* and *enslaving*; it is no wonder then that her matriarchal family, like Mill's patriarchal one, is "a school of despotism, in which the virtues of despotism, but also its vices, are largely nourished" (*Subjection* 294–95). This is the school in which Pip learns to despise his "coarse hands and [his] common boots,"[14] and is first enslaved to Estella's beauty and his own "expectations." This, too, is a species of decay, the decay, I suggest, of the promise of free life, as Pip recognizes in his "alarming fancy" that he and Estella "might presently begin to decay" (*Great* 88).

Pip's fancy, however, is no imaginative flight. It is no accident that Estella's retort to Miss Havisham, uttered in the literal wilderness of Satis House, recalls so clearly Louisa Gradgrind's lapsarian reproach to her father, discussed above: Estella says,

[i]f you had brought up your adopted daughter wholly in the dark confinement of these rooms, and had never let her know that there was such a thing as the daylight. . . . if you had taught her, from the dawn of her intelligence, with your utmost energy and might, that there was such a thing as daylight, but that it was made to be her enemy and destroyer, and she must always turn against it, for it had blighted you and would else blight her; — if you had done this, and then, for a purpose, had wanted her to take naturally to the daylight and she could not do it, you would have been disappointed and angry? (*Great* 301–2)

Estella's "daylight" world does exist, but as she recognizes, it has become the conscious enemy of the nightmare world of Miss Havisham and Satis House. Clearly the "ruined garden" (*Great* 236) over which Satis presides is ruined precisely because of this turn away from the "daylight" of intimacy and affection. And it is this refusal of the intimate that has blighted Estella; where Louisa, mourning the "garden that should have bloomed once" (*Hard* 241), nevertheless recognizes in Sissy "the graces of [the] soul" and "the sentiments of [the] heart" (*Hard* 241), for Estella such "'sentiments, fancies'" as love are unutterably foreign, "'a form of words; but nothing more'" (*Great* 358). And Pip is right when he exclaims that such hardness, such pride, "'is not in Nature'"; it is, rather, as Estella tells him, "'in the nature formed within me'" (*Great* 358).

But the "daylight" here stands for more than simply that intimacy of the household, that private good from which Miss Havisham has turned Estella. Ultimately the refusal of the private good, of intimacy, becomes for both Miss Havisham and Estella a refusal of the public good as well; it is, in other words, a refusal of or withdrawal from the life of the community. I have already remarked that Estella's pride is connected to the withdrawal of Satis House from the world; this is so because such a withdrawal is not compatible with the idea of virtue, in the liberal and Dickensian sense, which requires the wedding of public and private, of means and ends. I will return to this point, but for now let me remark that Satis fails because its radical separation from the community involves, indeed requires, a refusal to recognize that community and a concomitant refusal to recognize the good(s) of others. The irony of Satis House, and of Miss Havisham's despotic subjection, then, lies in what appears in Dickens as the artificial withdrawal of the household from life in the community. It is worth noting here that Miss Havisham's "sick fancy" (*Great* 58) of bringing Pip in to "play" is not reaching out into the community, but rather, like her adoption of Estella, a further separation of the community from its parts. The divorce of the household from its surroundings, clearly in the case of Satis House a kind of disease that even Miss Havisham's quarantine cannot prevent from spreading, contaminates everything it comes into contact with, as Pip recognizes: "What could I become with these surroundings? How could my character fail to be influenced by them?" (*Great* 94). This notion — that it is through the attempted quarantine that the infection spreads — is only apparently a contradiction. If we take seriously the idea that the household is the foundation of civil society, of life in the community, then any attempt at separating one from the other, as with Satis House or with Wemmick's Castle, will necessarily fail. And even this failure must have far-reaching consequences, as we have already seen in the figuratively sickening influence of Miss Havisham and Satis House on both Pip and Estella.

It might be argued against my position here, as Kate Flint does in her introduction to the Oxford edition, that Jaggers and Wemmick flourish, as Flint says, "since they are able to separate their private lives from the ruthless, compassionless efficiency of their public ones" (xxi). While she does not claim (it would be impossible to claim) that *Great Expectations* endorses this separation, Flint nevertheless assumes it to be necessary in the newly urbanized England. Here she recalls Booth's description of the "watershed transformation" (9) of the embedded and contained household into that of the contractarian liberal state. I noted earlier that this newly contractarian emphasis meant that the preferences that governed the pursuit of ends came to be seen as equally determinable by all, and that all were thus seen as alike in their claims to freedom and to rights. Thus is the project of the *oikos* democratized, and yet still definitive of the liberal citizen.

We have seen that many thinkers contend that this equality is only possible when the liberal citizen can be conceived in abstract terms alone, as a bearer of rights; private virtue, then, in the Aristotelian sense, endangers the contractarian foundations of liberalism because it erects preconditions for autonomy and thus dilutes the individual's claim to equality and rights. And without the claim to equal self-ownership, hierarchical despotism is never very far away. This would, indeed, be an ominous consequence; my point, however, is that the contractarianism that fails to recognize (or works to obscure) the grounds of autonomy is a contractarianism in which individuals may fail to lay claim to equality and rights. Self-ownership, in my admittedly Lockean sense of the concept, is in principle and in potential, and is recognized as the ground of rights as such; it depends, significantly, on the achievement of autonomy, in the household, in order to fulfill its potential and remain the forming principle of civic life.

Thus, it is because persons are equally self-owners that the idea of leisure and virtuous action in the household must be retained, and it is because our status as bearers of rights, in the abstract, depends on our particularity, affectivity, individuality, that Wemmick and Jaggers are far from models for success in the liberal polity. Both represent a division between the public and the private as negative, and both, I argue, indicate that the space of the market-place will always be one of unlimited acquisition, of getting without end and without ends, unless the intimate space of the household is brought into the market itself. This is so for two reasons. First, because, as we see writ large in *Hard Times* and in the "ruined garden" (*Great* 236) that is the withdrawn Satis House, the knowledge of the other that is a necessary precondition for the extension of rights is impossible without the affective bonds that can only be forged in intimate space. Second, the acquisitive life can only be contained, and made instrumental rather than an end-in-itself, when the concerns of intimate space are brought into it. Thus, for Jaggers the household itself is contaminated by market knowledge, which here is Newgate knowledge. As a result it is nonintimate, as we know from Pip's response to Estella's question, "'Are you intimate?'": "'I have dined with him at his private house'" (*Great* 266). Privacy is no guarantee of intimacy, then, and Jaggers's private house is without affection and without affectivity, not (like the forge) where the best in man makes him "oncommon" (*Great* 70) but where Jaggers "wrench[es] the weakest part of our dispositions" out of his guests (*Great* 211). Crucially, the interpenetration of *topoi* in Jaggers's home has not brought the intimate into the market, but the market into the intimate, and even his disastrous attempt to save Estella from being "took up, took up, took up"[15] like her father cannot redeem him from his twilight world.

Wemmick's Castle, at first glance, might seem to pose an idyllic counterpart to Little Britain. Separated from the rest of London, separated even from Walmouth by a moat and drawbridge, and separate even in the kinds of capacities and opinions that Wemmick holds there, the Castle, for Frances Armstrong, "fulfils almost every Dickensian ideal" precisely through this rigorous separation.[16] Yet I want to argue that Wemmick's Castle is Dickens's most radical critique — if not his most dramatic — of the prescription for separate spheres. This is so, not because even outside Little Britain "'there *are* Newgate cobwebs about'" (*Great* 292), but because the rift between necessity and virtue, work and leisure, market and home, means that the morals Wemmick holds in his "'private and personal capacit[y]'" have no impact on the nonmoral sphere of his trade; as he himself notes, they are "'extra official'" (*Great* 364). Little Britain, the place of work, therefore remains unredeemed by intimacy and the virtue to which it gives rise, even by Wemmick's marriage, which must remain "'altogether a Walmouth sentiment'" (*Great* 449). Nor do the affective relations of the household — and Wemmick's affection for the Aged Parent at least is incontrovertible — pose any effective limit to the acquisitive life. Wemmick's obsession with "portable property" (see, e.g., *Great* 199), like the life of idleness or unlimited pleasure, is slavish and unfree, because it is uncontained and thus without limit; indeed, the getting of wealth beyond the already achieved self-sufficiency of the Castle serves to limit the leisure time and moral space of the household. So radically does it pose this limit that Wemmick's only response to Pip's "wish[ing] him joy" on his wedding day is to say, "'[s]he's such a manager of fowls you have no idea'" (*Great* 449). Even here, then, property is the effective limit to the household's moral space. Even in the triumph of intimacy, in the triumph of Wemmick's successful separation of spheres — for even Pip doesn't know this is a wedding party until they reach the church — that intimacy fails, and it is the failure of intimacy in the very moment of its achievement that Dickens posits as the inevitable end of the doctrine of separate spheres. This is so because the attempted separation of market means from the ends of life entails, for Wemmick as for Jaggers, a fundamental confusion about the nature of means and ends; like Pip's contempt for the means to his own leisure, we see in Wemmick's Castle the disavowal of the means through which it came to be. Without acknowledgment of its means, the Castle can be no end but only further means, and it is for this reason that Wemmick's obsession with portable property — with means beyond limit — stands as emblem of the destruction of intimate life.[17]

Like Louisa Gradgrind, like Miss Skiffins, Wemmick's bride, Estella's situation in the novel as an object of acquisition, a means to the ends of others, signals the consequences of this failure of intimacy. That Estella is a means, and no end in herself, is unmistakable; not only is she, as Pip notes, "set to wreak Miss Havisham's revenge on men" (*Great* 298), and only as the tool of this revenge the object of Miss Havisham's "dreadful" and "devouring" fondness (*Great* 298), but for Pip, too, Estella is object and not subject. Even as Pip contends, in his outrage that Estella might "stoop" to "that hound," Bentley Drummle, that his pain is "referable to some pure fire of generosity and disinterestedness in [his] love for her," (*Great* 305), he sees Estella as a "prize . . . reserved for [him]" (*Great* 298–99). I have noted that the recognition of the other as end and not means is a necessary precondition for the extension of rights, and that this recognition is impossible without the affective bonds that can only be forged in intimate space; crucial to this analysis is the point that private space is not, in and of itself, intimate space, just as Miss Havisham's dreadful fondness for her tool is not that affectivity that enjoins upon us a recognition of the citizen-subject in the other. It remains only to point out that, herself a means to the ends of others, Estella can only treat others as means, as she has been taught; in this sense Miss Havisham's repeated question to Pip, "'How does she use you?'" (*Great* 237, 298) is an insightful one, since she does indeed use Pip "to tease other admirers" (*Great* 296), as she uses Drummle, ultimately, to escape the ornamental life she had been leading, which has grown tiresome and charmless (*Great* 359). This is a key point. Enslaved to Miss

Havisham's ends, Estella herself seeks to enslave others; even as she claims her marriage to Drummle as her "own act" (*Great* 359), her own end, she has become identified entirely with her role as means to the ends of others. Slavish, enslaving, Estella thus reveals the consequences of that radical utilitarian individualism we saw posited in MacIntyre's universe of egotists. In joining her will to Miss Havisham's will, Estella's ends become Miss Havisham's ends, which is to say that Estella ceases to be an end-in-herself (if indeed she ever was) and becomes a means, treating others as means, as incomprehensibly alien figures speaking an idiom of sentiment and affectivity that remains foreign to her tongue. It matters that the immediate consequence of the fulfillment of this egotism is the conflagration that destroys both Miss Havisham and Satis House; the universe of egotists, which enables neither private virtue nor public good, cannot be sustained.

Does Pip learn this? Perhaps. *Great Expectations*, uncontroversially, is the tale of Pip's education, of his cultivation, of his fulfillment as a person in the liberal sense of the word. In the sense that he comes to recognize the shared significance of work and of virtuous leisure, and only in this sense, are his noble expectations fulfilled; thus it is that he is redeemed only when, in the attempt to save Magwitch, he behaves not like the gentleman he once pined to be, but like his earliest friend and benefactor, that "'gentle Christian man'" (*Great* 458), Joe. It is, then, in his affective relations with Magwitch, and, importantly, in his acting on that affection in the larger civic space, that Pip is finally ennobled. Here he abandons at last his view of Magwitch as inconquerably other, "Prisoner, Felon, Bondsman" (*Great* 334), with "Convict in the very grain" (*Great* 333), and sees him as man and brother, who might, indeed, "have been a better man under better circumstances" (*Great* 450). Thus he comes to see him, affectively, as a liberal self; as I have been arguing, it is only when Pip's education permits this affective understanding, through the conjoining of intimate and civic space, that the project of liberalism is fulfilled.

Too much of recent liberal theory betrays its Enlightenment roots by perceiving the affective bonds of the despotic *oikos* as fundamentally at odds with the voluntarism that enables liberalism. This, for example, is the point of Booth's treatment of Marx, whom he says finally could not see how to ameliorate the alienation of the liberal economy without threatening a return to feudalism (Booth 272–75). But the problem so posed is not, in fact, posed by liberalism itself; it is posed by liberal — and anti-liberal — theory that has made so much of the abstract nature of the liberal citizen. Yet, as I have shown, such theory errs by failing to see that the very status of the bearer of rights depends on the claim that Sartre tells us is always the claim of revolution: That we, too, are men. This claim is backed up — must be backed up, as it is even in Rousseau's defense of the animals — by the revelation of the other in terms of psychological depth. It is in intimate space that this revelation takes place, as it is through intimacy that such a self comes to be. This, for example, is the importance of Magwitch's tale of having "'grow'd up took up'" (*Great* 342); if he is a "'mere warmint'" (*Great* 314), it is what he was brought up to be (*Great* 326).

The claim that Magwitch is or could have been more than this, more than

"Prisoner, Felon, Bondsman, plain as plain could be" (*Great* 334) comes through the gradual revelation of his affective self in the intimate space of the household, just as his story highlights the failure of the household for Magwitch. He, like Estella, that "'stock and stone,'" that "'cold, cold heart'" (*Great* 300), remains unfree because he had no intimate space in which to cultivate the virtues of the citizen, capable of emotion as well as reason and evaluation. Magwitch far more than Estella achieves this in the end, with his "dear boy" (*Great* 442). Pip, likewise, does finally manage to cultivate these qualities in himself, and while it may be too late for him, it is not for Young Pip, who will come to selfhood in the liberalized and democratized forge, where means and ends are both fulfilled and where the intimately liberal space of the household partakes of both. And this insight, indeed, is the central assumption of my remarks here. The claim to rights is made through a revelation of the other as a self in the liberal sense; when Pip recognizes himself in Young Pip, by the fire, just such a revelation takes place. If he is redeemed when he recognizes Magwitch as a self, this redemption comes to fruition in his recognition of himself as such. And this recognition is only possible because of the intimate space of the household, refigured as the space of means and ends, in which the political rights-bearer is disclosed.

NOTES

1.   MacIntyre is not alone in characterizing reason as opposed to feeling and sentiment, as I have already shown. See, for example, Judith Butler, "Contingent Foundations."

2.   John Stuart Mill disagrees, saying, "that a rule even of utter selfishness [MacIntyre's universe of egotists] could not *possibly* be adopted by all rational beings — that there is any insuperable obstacle in the nature of things to its adoption — cannot be even plausibly maintained" (*Util.* 249). I do, however, maintain it, on the grounds adduced above, and it is worth noting that Mill's comment on the Kantian imperative here adds that in order for Kant's principle to have meaning, it must mean "that we ought to shape our conduct by a rule which all rational beings might adopt *with benefit to their collective interest*" (*Util.* 249). Since it cannot benefit my own interest that others should treat me as a means, it cannot therefore benefit the collective interest that we should all, collectively, be seen as means to each other's ends; herein lies the insuperable obstacle, though perhaps not "in the nature of things."

3.   I don't mean to suggest that Johnson hasn't taken these consequences seriously; indeed, her treatment of Stephen and Louisa as the real "coke," both fuel and waste product, of the factory system, is a strong one. Johnson is primarily concerned with economic systems, however, where I am interested in the political consequences of the utilitarian view of the other.

4.   Here I depart from the critical tradition noted by Stephen Spector, which indicts Dickens for his failure to depict the psychological depth and interiority of industrial workers convincingly (Spector 365–66; see Sheila Smith for a more general treatment of the issue). If Stephen and Rachael remain psychologically alien, and I agree that they do, I contend that this is Dickens's *subject* more than it is his *failure*.

5.   Gallagher argues, quite differently, that the family-society metaphor of *Hard Times*, in which workers and children share a common oppression, breaks down when Tom and Louisa Gradgrind become adults, because their interests are opposed to those of the workers (150–55).

6.   Spector, on the other hand, takes these same lines as implicating Dickens himself, contending that Dickens's knowledge, observation, and reportage are all governed by the tyranny of the visible and therefore by the same facts he condemns (375).

7.   For a biographical account of Dickens's appreciation of the problem of the gentleman, see Gilmour 103–9. The problem, for Gilmour, is twofold; it involves both a characteristic Victorian "ambivalence" about the rival merits of blood and achievement, in the sense I have been treating, and an ironic sense that the concept of the gentleman requires exclusion, the separation, as Gilmour points out, "of gentlemen from non-gentlemen" (109). Both Calder (27) and Raphael (405) have noted that Compeyson represents Dickens's attempt to work out this ambivalence.

8.   Booth 43–45. Critics from Lionel Trilling to Gail Turley Houston have noted this novel's concern with the unacknowledged ground of civilization, the underwriting of, as Houston notes, the powerful by the powerless (23; Trilling 211).

9.   Rawlins notes that Pip is barred from learning a profession by "Magwitch's twisted sense of what makes a gentleman" (176), a key point, but one that ignores Pip's own perversions of the idea of the gentleman, already established in part through the influence of Estella's disdain for the signs of labour: "coarse hands" and "thick boots" (*Great* 59).

10.   It should be clear from the foregoing that I differ from Gilmour's claim that *Great Expectations* is "an exemplary life-history, the genesis of a Victorian gentleman out of a poor self-helping blacksmith's boy," a history that on Gilmour's account is "not just a snobbish aspiration out of one's class, but was also a desire to be a gentle man, to have a more civilised and decent life than a violent society allowed for most of its members" (129). Gilmour's point about the Victorian effort to distance contemporary life from the perceived violence and despotism of the past is well taken, but neglects the fundamental allegiances between the tyrannies of the past and of the present, allegiances that render Pip's idea of the gentleman anachronistic, which I see as central to an understanding of the novel.

11.   "Tickler was a wax-ended piece of cane, worn smooth by collision with my tickled frame" (*Great* 9).

12.   Houston reads this quite differently. While she recognizes Satis House as "unsatisfying, unnourishing, and barren," she links its sterility to the infiltration of Satis House by the market, through the brewery (20). Her conclusion, however, that Satis thus represents "a fundamental contradiction of the Victorian economy . . . that abundant wealth is founded on deprivation" (20), concurs with my account, although I see this contradiction largely in terms of the despotic household's willingness to ignore its own foundations, rather than in terms of any incursion of market into intimate space. Frances Armstrong likewise seems to suggest that it is the failure of the "private mytholog[y]" to remain private that creates the barren wilderness of Satis House (131–39). Linda Raphael differs again, taking the ruins of the bridal feast (*Great* 82–83; 87) as emblematic of Miss Havisham's failure to realize her "private dream" publicly, in the marriage ceremony (Raphael 402), although Raphael is primarily interested in ideas of feminine entrapment.

13.   See Houston 20; Raphael 401–2; Frances Armstrong 131–33, in particular.

14.   *Great* 61. See Cohen for the argument that Pip's acquired distaste for the "embodied signs of labor" — "[h]umiliation over the laboring (productive) hand" — is connected to shame, in this case "shame over the autoerotic . . . [hand]" (224). While Cohen's treatment of masturbation in the novel is, finally, unconvincing, his claim that "Pip's *Bildung* is an aggressive repudiation of the labor inscribed on his body: it tells the story of his refusal to *be* a hand" (225) in the sense that Stephen Blackpool is a hand, is an insightful one.

15.   The phrase is Magwitch's (*Great* 314). For Jaggers's account of rescuing Estella, see 408–9.

16.   Frances Armstrong 134. For dissenting views, see Calder 26; Phelan 179–84; Raphael 410; and Tambling 133.

17.   I am indebted to Damon Marcel DeCoste for this articulation of the grounds for the barrenness of Wemmick's Castle.

Conclusion
Household Reasons and Political Subjects

> University teaching and scholarship too finally only make sense in terms of freedom and citizenship. Scholarly life is a vocation: it is a response to the Western call to freedom. Scholars act on that call when they take free inquiry and its wide-spread enculturation as their practice. This they do not just through their research and publication, but equally through their teaching. University teachers are called professors for a reason, at least in the liberal view of the matter. They are professors — and not merely trainers or instructors — because they profess something; and what they profess, through their practices of teaching and their scholarship, is their commitment to freedom, to free and open inquiry in a free and open cultural space called the university.
>
> — Frederick C. DeCoste, "The Academic and the Political"

I suggested in my Introduction that political fiction addresses the instability, contingency, or particularity of social arrangements; underlying this claim is the assumption that a writer may be an agent in a political and ethical domain. In this sense the writer of political fiction is "engaged," as Sartre says; "[h]e knows that to reveal is to change and that one can reveal only by planning to change" (*What is Literature?* 14). And this project of revealing involves, for Sartre, a certain kind of practice, which I take to be *praxis* in that the free inquiry and reason necessary to this project are "action in history and on history" (*What is Literature?* 165). I showed in chapter 1 that the liberal notion of reason lies at the heart of early feminist demands for changes in the education of women. Mary Astell and Lady, Mary Chudleigh were political writers, by my account, because they engaged the condition of women through inquiry and reason; more than this, they were professors in that they were responding to what DeCoste terms "the Western call to freedom" (362) by insisting on free inquiry for women and by demanding a free and open space for the cultivation of such practice. It need hardly be added that this call to freedom, properly understood, is not the negative liberty Rousseau espoused for women, but positive freedom: It involves the cultivation and the realization, for women, of the liberal self.

I went on to contend that the liberal self is construed as a juridical person — a bearer of rights, a citizen — through the attribution of mental qualities. Mary Wollstonecraft understood this when she laid claim to such qualities on behalf of women, vindicating their rights in precisely this way. This is not to claim that Wollstonecraft predicated her argument on the actual equality of men and women. Rather, like Descartes and Locke, she called for those rights on the basis of common capacity, and laid claim likewise to education, which for Wollstonecraft as for DeCoste is the enculturation of a praxis of free and reasoned inquiry. Education in this sense is a crucial part of Wollstonecraft's political theory, because the reason so cultivated is the ground of private virtue and of citizenship, which, again, and like Rousseau, she construes in terms of mental qualities. For Wollstonecraft, the health of political space depends on the existence of a coincident space in which the self may become a citizen.

My emphasis on the concept of liberal self-fulfillment is not intended as an atomistic individualism, and indeed my readings of Opie's *Adeline Mowbray* and Edgeworth's *Belinda* arise in part from my conviction that such atomism misunderstands the liberal project. Opie and Edgeworth have both authored political-domestic fictions, but far differently than Wollstonecraft in either *Mary* or her *Wrongs of Woman*. By their accounts the social arrangements regarding the status of women are contingent and local, but while I read these books likewise in terms of a call to freedom, they are in no way a call to revolution. Indeed, the tenor of *Adeline Mowbray* and *Belinda* is mediatory rather than revolutionary. This is so because both Opie and Edgeworth recognize that the self, if it is a self at all, is so and comes to be so in a community. And membership in a community confers on it, for these thinkers, significant obligations.[1] One of these obligations involves a commitment to the shared goods of the community; another requires the practice and extension of individual virtue, on which, for them as for Wollstonecraft, the social good depends. I take this social good to be freedom, and I take the virtue on which it depends to be the praxis of free and reasoned inquiry. More, I share with Maria Edgeworth and Elizabeth Gaskell a conviction that the health of the liberal polity depends on this relationship.

What does this mean? I said in chapter 4 that domestic fiction inquires into the conditions of freedom. Because freedom includes the pursuit of the noble ends of life, it has as its conditions the means to life (self-sufficiency) as well as the praxis of free inquiry that must refuse tyranny everywhere and all the time, even the tyranny of means. Indeed, as *Wives and Daughters* makes clear, while the means to life are a necessary condition of freedom, they are in no way sufficient, and among the dangers to our freedom is a confusion of our ends with our means. Freedom, conceived in this way, is the property of the liberal self, the rights-bearer. But the rights-bearer in this philosophy is so only as figured in a certain way, and that is as a self possessed of interiority, capable not only of reason and evaluation but of emotion. Thus, the cultivation of these qualities in the self is the practice by which liberalism fulfills and extends itself. And the project of domestic fiction is to trace this cultivation, which is liberal praxis; the domestic plot is driven by the movement of the young from their unfree state to freedom in the community (*Bildung*) through this cultivation. This is why the intimate space of the household is the province of such fiction. Because the household is the site of the self-cultivation through which we become bearers of rights, it is also the ground on which the liberal polity is founded. Because such space is governed by affective relations, it is also the space of liberal fulfillment, of ends rather than market means.

My term "intimate space" is intended to capture the ways in which the so-called private sphere is not, in fact, withdrawn or separate from the public, political domain. This means, as I showed in my treatment of *North and South*, that even avowedly political fiction likewise depends on the originary and intimate space of the household in order to make its revolutionary claims. Sartre tells us that this claim is always that "'we too are men'" ("Materialism" 217); I maintain that it is made through the revelation of self that an account of intimate space allows. This revelation is a demand for recognition; more, it is a demand for that recognition that is a species of assent.   This is the recognition that, according to Alasdair MacIntyre, is incompatible with reason, as I note in chapter 6. I show there that MacIntyre's starved and utilitarian conception of the Enlightenment emphasis on the reasoning subject is, finally, a misunderstanding of the liberal project, turning to Charles Dickens and John Stuart Mill to argue that, insofar as the idea of reason is used to refuse the recognition of the other as end, it is allied with feudal despotism and not with liberal freedom. For Dickens, this was the error of utilitarian "liberalism"; in both *Hard Times* and *Great Expectations*, he charts the consequences of the failure of recognition, a failure he sees as the inevitable result of the failure of sympathy. Both Dickens and Mill, then, argue for the necessity of private affections, and thus the intimate and affective domain, not only to our notions of the good, but to the expansion of the just and free life to all. In other words, that recognition of the other as citizen, as end and not means, which is the central condition of the extension of rights, is impossible without the affective dimension of reason, which can only be forged in intimate space.

Frances Power Cobbe, in 1868, insisted on such recognition. "We wish," she wrote, "that we could persuade men more often to try and realise for themselves what is actually the life of a woman" (127). She was contending that better education would fit women to adopt the responsibilities of citizenship. I have argued that it is in the household that this recognition, for women and for men, must occur, and that this is so because the very structure of the liberal self depends upon the intimate space of that household. Cobbe believed, I think, that if once this realization, this recognition was achieved, women would gain the civil and political rights to which she laid claim. Recognition, not some inarticulable idea of equality, was the point: "'Granted,' [a woman] answers to all rebuffs; 'let me be physically, intellectually, and morally your inferior. So long as you allow I possess moral responsibility and sufficient intelligence to know right from wrong (a point I conclude you will concede, else why hang me for murder?) I am quite content. It is *only* as a Moral and Intelligent Being I claim my civil rights. Can you deny them to me on that ground?'" (128). Crucially, Cobbe here joins moral life, which I have been claiming is forged in the intimate space of the household, to reason; both, she contends, are necessary to the ethical stance of the citizen, just as both are necessary to the recognition of the self *as* citizen.

This conjoining of the just and moral life with reason is the substance of the Western call to freedom. It is only in the context of a conception of the ends of life that the Cartesian injunction to rationality can do other than bode a return to tyranny; it is only through the education of *affective* reason that we can lay claim to the determination of our own ends. Freedom in this sense is both commitment and capacity. If, in this millenarian moment, we dread that the despotism of the past may any day return, and not without cause, it is because in our busy grasping at the future we have forgotten the lessons of the past. The nineteenth century ought to have taught us that the liberal freedom we seek, and that is still coming into being, is possible only when the language of ends, a language that both constitutes and is constituted in household space, informs our means, and not the other way around. We ought to have learned that unless the intimate space of ends stands as the originary space of the liberal polity, the very freedom that we seek, the freedom to determine our own ends in our own way, will be bankrupted by the tyranny of means, which is to say, the ends of despotic others.

Once, the household stood as the embattled space of ends. But even as I have been contending that it was not, for the Victorians, withdrawn from the polity and the public good, I am contending that it is now, the reactionary rhetoric of family values notwithstanding, so withdrawn. In its place the academy has sought to preserve that active freedom, both commitment and capacity, that depends on a notion of ends. This is what DeCoste, in my epigraph, means when he says that "[u]niversity teaching and scholarship too finally only make sense in terms of freedom and citizenship" (362). But as has been becoming clear for some time, the university, too, is under seige; everywhere the language of the market, of means rather than of ends, is threatening the education of the self as citizen, the profession of freedom without which the university will indeed be irrelevant. Let us not, in our haste to choose Nietzsche or Aristotle, forget the lessons of John Stuart Mill; let us not, in our haste to fulfill and extend the liberal marketplace, permit the self-determination of a liberal citizenry to become another lost cause or forsaken belief, without even the university in which to take refuge.

NOTE

Charles Taylor clarifies this point:

I am arguing that the free individual of the West is only what he is by virtue of the whole society and civilization which brought him to be and which nourishes him; that our families can only form us up to this capacity and these aspirations because they are set in this civilization; and that a family alone outside of this context — the real old patriarchal family — was a quite different animal which never tended these horizons. And I want to claim finally that all this creates a significant obligation to belong for whoever would affirm the value of this freedom; this includes all those who want to assert rights either to this freedom or for its sake. (*Papers* 2: 206)

References

I. PRIMARY SOURCES

Dickens, Charles. *Great Expectations* 1860–61. Ed. Margaret Cardwell. Intro. Kate Flint. Oxford and New York: Oxford UP, 1994.

———. *Hard Times; For These Times* 1854. Ed. Graham Law. Broadview Literary Texts Ser. Peterborough: Broadview P, 1996.

Edgeworth, Maria. *Belinda* 1801. Vols. 11–12 of *Tales and Novels by Maria Edgeworth*. New York: J. & J. Harper, 1834. 18 vols bound in 9.

Gaskell, Elizabeth. *North and South* 1854–55. Ed. Dorothy Collin. Intro. Martin Dodsworth. Harmondsworth: Penguin, 1970, rpt. 1972.

———. *Wives and Daughters* 1864–66. Ed. and intro. Angus Easson. Oxford and New York: OUP, 1987.

Opie, Amelia. *Adeline Mowbray; or, The Mother and Daughter* 1804. Vol. 1 of *The Works of Mrs. Amelia Opie* 1843. Women of Letters Reprint Ser. New York: AMS Press, 1974. 3 vols. 111–227.

Wollstonecraft, Mary. *Collected Letters of Mary Wollstonecraft*. Ed. Ralph M. Wardle. Ithaca and London: Cornell UP, l979.

———. *The Wrongs of Woman, or Maria; A Fragment* 1798. Vols. 1–2 of *Posthumous Works of the Author of* A Vindication of the Rights of Woman. Ed. William Godwin. The Feminist Controversy in England 1788–1810 Ser. Pref. Gina Luria. New York and London: Garland, 1974. 4 vols.

———. *Mary, A Fiction* 1788. The Feminist Controversy in England 1788–1810 Ser. Pref. Gina Luria. New York and London: Garland, 1974.

———. "On Poetry." Vol. 7 of *The Works of Mary Wollstonecraft*. Ed. Janet Todd and Marilyn Butler. London: William Pickering, 1989. 7 vols. 7–11.

———. *Original Stories from Real Life; With Conversations, Calculated to Regulate the Affections, and Form the Mind to Truth and Goodness* 1788. Pref. Miriam Brody Kramnick. The History of Little Jack *and* Original Stories from Real Life. New York: Garland, 1977. Var. pag.

————. *Thoughts on the Education of Daughters with Reflections on Female Conduct, in the More Important Duties of Life* 1787. The Feminist Controversy in England 1788–1810 Ser. Pref. Gina Luria. New York and London: Garland, 1974.

————. *A Vindication of the Rights of Men, in a Letter to the Right Honourable Edmund Burke* 1790. Vol. 5 of *The Works of Mary Wollstonecraft*. Ed. Janet Todd and Marilyn Butler. London: William Pickering, 1989. 7 vols. 1–60.

————. *A Vindication of the Rights of Woman: With Strictures on Political and Moral Subjects* 1792. Vol. 5 of *The Works of Mary Wollstonecraft*. Ed. Janet Todd and Marilyn Butler. London: William Pickering, 1989. 7 vols. 61–266.

II. SECONDARY SOURCES

Addison, Joseph. *Guardian* 55 (September 8, 1713). Rpt. in Vol. 11 of Lynam, ed. 211–24.

————. *Spectator* 10 (March 12, 1710). Rpt. in Vol. 4 of Lynam, ed. 47-49.

Adorno, Theodor. *Minima Moralia: Reflections from a Damaged Life*. Trans. EFN. Jephcott. London: New Left Books, 1974.

Ahearn, Edward J. *Marx and Modern Fiction*. New Haven: Yale UP, 1989.

[Allestree, Richard]. *The Ladies Calling in Two Parts, By the Author of the Whole Duty of Man*. Oxford: 1705.

Allott, Miriam. *Elizabeth Gaskell*. Writers and Their Work Ser. 124. London: Longmans, Green, 1960.

Althusser, Louis. "Ideology and Ideological State Apparatuses (Notes Towards and Investigation)" 1971. *Essays on Ideology*. London: Verso, 1984. 1–60.

Altman, Rick. "An Introduction to the Theory of Genre Analysis." *The American Film Musical*. Bloomington: Indiana UP, 1987. 1–15.

Arato, Andrew and Gebhardt Eike, eds. *The Essential Frankfurt School Reader*. New York: Continuum, 1982.

Aristotle. *Nicomachean Ethics*. Trans. Terence Irwin. Indianapolis: Hackett, 1985.

————. *The Politics*. Trans. T.A. Sinclair. Rev. ed. Trevor J. Saunders. Harmondsworth: Penguin, 1981.

Armstrong, Frances. *Dickens and the Concept of Home*. Nineteenth-Century Studies Ser. Ann Arbor and London: UMI Research P, 1990.

Armstrong, Meg. "'The Effects of Blackness': Gender, Race, and the Sublime in Aesthetic Theories of Burke and Kant." *The Journal of Aesthetics and Art Criticism* 54 (1996): 213–36.

Armstrong, Nancy. *Desire and Domestic Fiction: A Political History of the Novel*. Oxford and New York: Oxford UP, 1987.

Astell, Mary. *A Serious Proposal to the Ladies* 1692. New York: Source Book P, 1970. Rpt. of 1701 edition.

Atkinson, Colin B., and Jo Atkinson. "Maria Edgeworth, *Belinda*, and Women's Rights." *Eire-Ireland: A Journal of Irish Studies* 19 (1984): 94–118.

Auerbach, Nina. *Woman and the Demon*. Cambridge and London: Harvard UP, 1982.

Bakhtin, Mikhail. *The Dialogic Imagination: Four Essays*. Ed. Michael Holquist. Trans. Caryl Emerson and Michael Holquist. University of Texas Press Slavic Ser. 1. Austin: U of Texas P, 1981.

Barnes, Annette. *On Interpretation: A Critical Analysis*. Oxford: Basil Blackwell, 1988.

Basch, Françoise. *Relative Creatures: Victorian Women in Society and the Novel*. Trans. Anthony Rudolf. Studies in the Life of Women Ser. New York: Schocken, 1974.

de Beauvoir, Simone. *The Second Sex*. Trans. and ed. H.M. Parshley. London: Bantam, 1952.

Belenky, Mary Field, Blythe McVicker Clinchy, Nancy Rule Goldberger, and Jill Mattuck Tarule. *Women's Ways of Knowing: The Development of Self, Voice and Mind*. New York: Basic Books, 1986.

Benhabib, Seyla. *Situating the Self: Community and Postmodernism in Contemporary Ethics*. New York: Routledge, 1992.

Bergmann, Helena. *Between Obedience and Freedom: Woman's Role in the Mid-Nineteenth Century Industrial Novel*. Gothenberg Studies in English 45. Goteborg: Acta Universitatis Gothoburgensis, 1979.

Bermingham, Ann. *Landscape and Ideology: The English Rustic Tradition, 1740–1860*. Berkeley, L.A., London: U of California P, 1986.

Blackstone, Sir William. *Commentaries on the Laws of England*. 12th edn. 4 vols. London: T. Cadell, 1793.

Blake, William. "Visions of the Daughters of Albion" 1793. *The Complete Writings of William Blake with Variant Readings*. Ed. Geoffrey Keynes. London: OUP, 1966. 189–95.

Blakemore, Steven. "Rebellious Reading: The Doubleness of Wollstonecraft's Subversion of *Paradise Lost*." *Texas Studies in Literature and Language* 34 (1992): 451–80.

Blease, W. Lyon. *The Emancipation of English Women*. London: Constable and Co., 1910.

Blom, J.M. "The English 'Social-Problem' Novel: Fruitful Concept or Critical Evasion?" *English Studies: A Journal of English Language and Literature* 62 (1981): 120–27.

Blotner, Joseph Leo. *The Modern American Political Novel, 1900–1960*. Austin and London: U of Texas P, 1966.

Bodenheimer, Rosemarie. *The Politics of Story in Victorian Social Fiction*. Ithaca and London: Cornell UP, 1988.

Boone, Joseph Allen. "Wedlock as Deadlock and Beyond: Closure and the Victorian Marriage Ideal." *Mosaic* 17 (1984): 65–81.

Booth, William James. *Households: On the Moral Architecture of the Economy*. Ithaca and London: Cornell UP, 1993.

Bourdieu, Pierre, and Jean-Claude Passeron. *Reproduction in Education, Society and Culture*. Trans. Richard Nice. Theory, Culture, and Society Ser. London, Newbury Park, New Delhi: Sage, 1990.

Brantlinger, Patrick. *The Spirit of Reform: British Literature and Politics, 1832–1867*. Cambridge, MA: Harvard UP, 1977.

Brodetsky, Tessa. *Elizabeth Gaskell*. Berg Women's Ser. Leamington Spa: Berg, 1986.

Browne, Alice. *The Eighteenth Century Feminist Mind*. Brighton: Harvester, 1987.

Buchanan, Laurie. "Mothers and Daughters in Elizabeth Gaskell's *Wives and Daughters*: In a Woman's World." *The Midwest Quarterly* 31 (1990): 499–513.

Burke, Edmund. *A Philosophical Enquiry into the Origin of Our Ideas of the Sublime and the Beautiful* 1757. Ed. James T. Boulton. London: Routledge and Paul, 1958.

Butler, Judith. "Contingent Foundations: Feminism and the Question of 'Postmodernism.'" *Feminist Contentions: A Philosophical Exchange*. Ed. Linda Nicholson. Thinking Gender Ser. Routledge: New York and London, 1995. 35–57.

———. *Gender Trouble: Feminism and the Subversion of Identity*. Thinking Gender Ser. New York and London: Routledge, 1990.

Butler, Marilyn. *Jane Austen and the War of Ideas*. Oxford: Clarendon, 1975.

———. *Maria Edgeworth: A Literary Biography*. Oxford: Clarendon, 1972.

———. *Romantics, Rebels and Reactionaries: English Literature and its Background, 1760–1830*. Oxford: Oxford UP, 1981.

Cahn, Susan. *The Industry of Devotion: The Transformation of Women's Work in England, 1500–1600*. New York: Columbia UP, 1987.

Calder, Angus. "Introduction." *Great Expectations*. Charles Dickens. Harmondsworth: Penguin, 1965. 11–29.

Carlyle, Thomas. "Chartism" 1839. Vol. 4 of *Critical and Miscellaneous Essays.* . . . New York: AMS, 1969. 5 vols. 118–204.

———. "Signs of the Times." Vol. 2 of *Critical and Miscellaneous Essays.* . . . New York: AMS, 1969. 5 vols. 56–82.

Carpenter, Mary. "The Education of Pauper Girls" 1862. *The Education Papers: Women's Quest for Equality in Britain, 1850–1912*. Ed. Dale Spender. Women's Source Library Ser. New York and London: Routledge and Kegan Paul, 1987. 50–57.

Cazamian, Louis. *The Social Novel in England, 1830–1850: Dickens, Disraeli, Mrs. Gaskell, Kingsley* 1903. Trans. Martin Fido. London and Boston: Routledge and Kegan Paul, 1973.

[Chamberlayne, Edward]. *An Academy or Colledge: Wherein Young Ladies and Gentlewomen May at a Very Moderate Expence be duly Instructed in the True Protestant Religion, and in all Vertuous Qualities that may Adorn that Sex: Also be Carefully Preserved, and Secured, till the Day of their Marriage, under the Tuition of a Lady Governess, and Grave Society of Widdows and Virgins, Who Have Resolved to Lead the Rest of Their Lives in a Single Retir'd Religious Way, According to the Pattern of some Protestant Colledges in Germany*. London: 1671.

Chekhov, Anton. "The Cherry Orchard." Trans. Constance Garnett. *Great Russian Plays*. Ed. Norris Houghton. Laurel Drama Ser. New York: Dell, 1960. 303–61.

Chudleigh, Mary, Lady. "Essays Upon Several Subjects in Prose and Verse" 1710. *The Poems and Prose of Mary, Lady Chudleigh*. Women Writers in English 1350–1850 Ser. Ed. Margaret J.M. Ezell. Oxford: OUP, 1993. 244–390.

———. "The Ladies Defence: Or, The Bride-Woman's Counsellor Answer'd" 1701. *The Poems and Prose of Mary, Lady Chudleigh*. Women Writers in English 1350–1850 Ser. Ed. Margaret J.M. Ezell. Oxford and New York: OUP, 1993. 3–40.

Cobbe, Frances Power. "'Criminals, Idiots, Women and Minors.'" *Fraser's Magazine* (December 1868). Rpt. in *"Criminals, Idiots, Women, and Minors": Victorian Writing By Women on Women*. Ed. Susan Hamilton. Peterborough: Broadview P, 1995. 108–31.

Cocks, Joan Elizabeth. *The Oppositional Imagination: Feminism, Critique, and Political Theory*. London and New York: Routledge, 1989.

Cohen, William A. "Manual Conduct in *Great Expectations*." *ELH* 60 (1993): 217–59.

Corbett, Mary Jean. "Public Affections and Familial Politics: Burke, Edgeworth, and the 'Common Naturalization' of Great Britain." *ELH* 61 (1994): 877–97.

Cottom, Daniel. "Taste and the Civilized Imagination." *Journal of Aesthetics and Art Criticism* 39 (1980–81): 367–80.

Cressy, David. *Literacy and the Social Order: Reading and Writing in Tudor and Stuart England*. London and New York: Cambridge UP, 1980.

David, Deirdre. *Fictions of Resolution in Three Victorian Novels:* North and South, Our Mutual Friend, Daniel Deronda. New York: Columbia UP, 1981.

Davidoff, Leonore. *Worlds Between: Historical Perspectives on Gender and Class*. New York: Routledge, 1995.

Davidoff, Leonore, and Catherine Hall. *Family Fortunes: Men and Women of the English Middle Class, 1780–1850*. Women in Culture and Society Ser. Chicago: U of Chicago P, 1987.

DeCoste, Frederick C. "The Academic and the Political: A Review of *Freedom and Tenure in the Academy*." *Review of Constitutional Studies/Revue d'études constitutionelles* 1 (1994): 356–90.

Descartes, René. Discourse on Method *and* Meditations 1637 and 1641. Trans. Laurence J. Lafleur. Library of Liberal Arts Ser. London: Collier; New York: Macmillan, 1960.

DuPlessis, Rachel Blau. *Writing Beyond the Ending: Narrative Strategies of Twentieth-century Women Writers*. Bloomington: Indiana UP, 1985.

Dworkin, Andrea. *Intercourse*. London: Secker and Warburg, 1987.

Dworkin, Ronald. *Taking Rights Seriously*. London: Duckworth, 1977.

'E.T.M.' "An Interior View of Girton College, Cambridge" 1876. *The Education Papers: Women's Quest for Equality in Britain, 1850–1912*. Ed. Dale Spender. Women's Source Library Ser. New York and London: Routledge and Kegan Paul, 1987. 277–83.

Eagleton, Terry. *Literary Theory: An Introduction*. Minneapolis: U of Minnesota P, 1983.

Easson, Angus. *Elizabeth Gaskell*. London: Routledge and Kegan Paul, 1979.

Eberle, Roxanne. "Amelia Opie's *Adeline Mowbray*: Diverting the Libertine Gaze; or, The Vindication of a Fallen Woman." *Studies in the Novel* 26 (1994): 121–52.

Edgeworth, Maria, and Richard Lovell Edgeworth. *Practical Education* 1798. The Feminist Controversy in England 1788–1810 Ser. Pref. Gina Luria. New York and London: Garland, 1974. 2 vols.

Elam, Diane, and Robyn Wiegman, eds. *Feminism Beside Itself*. New York and London: Routledge, 1995.

Elliott, Dorice Williams. "The Female Visitor and the Marriage of Classes in Gaskell's *North and South*." *Nineteenth-Century Literature* 49:1 (1994): 21–49.

Ellis, [Mrs.] Sarah. *The Daughters of England: Their Position in Society, Character, and Responsibilities*. London, 1845.

———. *The Mothers of England: Their Influence and Responsibility*. London, 1843.

———. *The Wives of England*. London: 1843.

———. *The Women of England: Their Social Duties, and Domestic Habits*. London, 1839.

Elster, John. "Conventions, Creativity, Originality." *Rules and Conventions: Literature, Philosophy, Social Theory*. Ed. Mette Hjort. Parallax Re-visions of Culture and Society Ser. Baltimore and London: Johns Hopkins UP, 1992. 32–44.

An Essay in Defence of the Female Sex. London: 1696.

Fabricant, Carole. "The Aesthetics and Politics of Landscape in the Eighteenth-Century." *Studies in Eighteenth-Century British Art and Aesthetics*. Ed. Ralph Cohen. Clark Library Professorship Ser. Berkeley, Los Angeles, London: U of California P, 1985. 49–81.

Filmer, [Sir] Robert. *Patriarcha, or, The Natural Power of Kings*. London: Chiswell, Gillyflower, Henchman, 1680.

Flax, Jane. "Postmodernism and Gender Relations in Feminist Theory." *Feminist Theory in Practice and Process*. Ed. Micheline R. Malson, Jean F. O'Barr, Sarah Westphal-Wihl, and Mary Wyer. Chicago: U of Chicago Press, 1989. 51–73.

Flint, Kate. "Introduction." *Great Expectations*. Charles Dickens. Oxford and New York: OUP, 1994. vii–xxi.

Foster, Shirley. *Victorian Women's Fiction: Marriage, Freedom and the Individual*. London and Sydney: Croom Helm, 1985.

Foucault, Michel. *The History of Sexuality*. Trans. Robert Hurley. Vol. 1. New York: Random House, 1980.

Fox-Genovese, Elizabeth. *Feminism Without Illusions: A Critique of Individualism*. Chapel Hill and London: U of North Carolina P, 1991.

———. "Placing Women's History in History." *New Left Review* (1982): 5–29.

Fraser, Antonia. *The Weaker Vessel: Women's Lot in Seventeenth-century England.* London: Weidenfeld and Nicolson, 1984.

Gadamer, Hans-Georg. *Truth and Method.* New York: Seabury- Continuum, 1975.

Gallagher, Catherine. *The Industrial Reformation of English Fiction: Social Discourse and Narrative Form, 1832–1867.* Chicago and London: U of Chicago P, 1985.

Ganz, Margaret. *Elizabeth Gaskell: The Artist in Conflict.* New York: Twayne, 1969.

Gérin, Winifred. *Elizabeth Gaskell: A Biography.* Oxford: OUP, 1976.

Gilbert, Sandra M., and Susan Gubar. *The Madwoman in the Attic: The Woman Writer and the Nineteenth-century Literary Imagination.* New Haven: Yale UP, 1979.

Gilligan, Carol. *In a Different Voice: Psychological Theory and Women's Development.* Cambridge, MA: Harvard UP, 1982.

———. "In a Different Voice: Women's Conceptions of Self and of Morality." *Harvard Educational Review* 47.4 (1977): 481–507.

Gilmour, Robin. *The Idea of the Gentleman in the Victorian Novel.* London: George Allen & Unwin, 1981.

Giltrow, Janet. "'Painful Experience in a Distant Land': Mrs. Moodie in Canada and Mrs. Trollope in America." *Mosaic* 14:2 (1981): 131–44.

Godwin, William. *Memoirs of the Author of* A Vindication of the Rights of Woman 1798. Feminist Controversy in Britain 1788–1810 Ser. Pref. Gina Luria. New York and London: Garland, 1974.

Gonda, Caroline. *Reading Daughters' Fictions, 1709–1834: Novels and Society from Manley to Edgeworth.* Cambridge Studies in Romanticism 19. Cambridge: Cambridge UP, 1996.

Greene, Gayle, and Coppélia Kahn. "Feminist Scholarship and the Social Construction of Woman." *Making a Difference: Feminist Literary Criticism.* Ed. Gayle Greene and Coppélia Kahn. New Accents Ser. London and New York: Routledge, 1985. 1–36.

Guy, Josephine. *The Victorian Social-Problem Novel: The Market, the Individual and Communal Life.* Houndsmills and London: Macmillan, 1996.

Habermas, Jürgen. *Communication and the Evolution of Society.* Trans. Thomas McCarthy. Boston: Beacon, 1979.

Halperin, David M. "Is There a History of Sexuality?" *History and Theory* 28.3 (1989): 257–74.

Hannerz, Ulf. *Cultural Complexity: Studies in the Social Organization of Meaning.* New York: Columbia UP, 1992.

Harden, O. Elizabeth. *Maria Edgeworth's Art of Prose Fiction.* The Hague: Mouton, 1971.

Harman, Barbara Leah. *The Feminine Political Novel in Victorian England.* Victorian Literature and Culture Ser. Charlottesville and London: UP of Virginia, 1998.

———. "In Promiscuous Company: Female Public Appearance in Gaskell's *North and South*." *Victorian Studies* 31 (1998): 351–74.

Harsh, Constance D. *Subversive Heroines: Feminist Resolutions of Social Crisis in the Condition-of-England Novel.* Ann Arbor: U of Michigan P, 1994.

Hawkesworth, Mary. "Knowers, Knowing, Known: Feminist Theory and Claims of Truth." *Signs* 14 (1989): 533–57.

Hawthorne, Mark D. *Doubt and Dogma in Maria Edgeworth.* Gainesville: U of Florida P, 1967.

Hilton, Nelson. "An Original Story." *Unnam'd Forms: Blake and Textuality.* Ed. Nelson Hilton and Thomas A. Vogler. Berkeley: University of California Press, 1986. 69–104.

Hirsch, E.D., Jr. *Validity in Interpretation.* New Haven: Yale UP, 1967.

Hjort, Mette, ed. *Rules and Conventions: Literature, Philosophy, Social Theory.* Parallax Re-visions of Culture and Society Ser. Baltimore and London: Johns Hopkins UP, 1992.

Hobbes, Thomas. *Leviathan*. Ed. C.B. MacPherson. Harmondsworth: Penguin, 1981.

Holcombe, Lee. "Victorian Wives and Property: Reform of the Married Woman's Property Law, 1857–1870." *A Widening Sphere: Changing Roles of Victorian Women*. Ed. Martha Vicinus. Bloomington and London: Indiana UP, 1977.

Hopkins, A.B. *Elizabeth Gaskell: Her Life and Work*. London: John Lehman, 1952.

Houston, Gail Turley. "'Pip' and 'Property': The (Re)Production of the Self in *Great Expectations*." *Studies in the Novel* 24 (1992): 13–25.

Huet, Marie-Hélène. "The Revolutionary Sublime." *Eighteenth-Century Studies* 28 (1994): 51–64.

Hussey, Christopher. *The Picturesque: Studies in a Point of View*. 2nd ed. London: Frank Cass, 1967.

James, H.R. *Mary Wollstonecraft: A Sketch*. Oxford: OUP; London: Humphrey Milford, 1932.

Jameson, Frederic. *The Political Unconscious: Narrative as a Socially Symbolic Act*. London: Methuen, 1981.

Johnson, Mary Lynn, and John E. Grant, eds. *Blake's Poetry and Designs*. Norton Critical Editions Ser. New York: W.W. Norton, 1979.

Johnson, Patricia E. "*Hard Times* and the Structure of Industrialism: The Novel as Factory." *Studies in the Novel* 21.2 (1989): 128–37.

Johnston, Susan. "Reconstructing the Wilderness: Margaret Atwood's Reading of Susanna Moodie." *Canadian Poetry: Studies/Documents/Reviews* 31 (1992): 28–54.

Juhl, P.D. *Interpretation: An Essay in the Philosophy of Literature*. Princeton: Princeton UP, 1980.

Kant, Immanuel. *The Critique of Judgement* 1790. Trans. Werner S. Pluhar. Indianapolis: Hackett, 1987.

———. *Observations on the Feeling of the Beautiful and the Sublime* 1764. Trans. John T. Goldthwait. Berkeley: U of California P, 1981.

Kelly, Gary. "Amelia Opie, Lady Caroline Lamb, and Maria Edgeworth: Official and Unofficial Ideology." *Ariel* 12.4 (1981): 3–24.

———. *English Fiction of the Romantic Period, 1789–1830*. Longman Literature in English Ser. London and New York: Longman, 1989.

Kettle, Arnold. "The Early Victorian Social-Problem Novel." *From Dickens to Hardy*. Rev. ed. Vol. 6 of *The Pelican Guide to English Literature*. Ed. Boris Ford. Harmondsworth: Penguin, 1960. 7 vols. 169–87.

King, James. *William Blake: His Life*. New York: St. Martin's, 1991.

Knight, Richard Payne. *An Analytical Inquiry into the Principles of Taste* (1805). Excerpted in *The Genius of the Place: The English Landscape Garden 1620–1820*. Ed. John Dixon Hunt and Peter Willis. London: Paul Elek, 1975. 348–50.

———. *The Landscape, A Didactic Poem* (1794). Excerpted in *The Genius of the Place: The English Landscape Garden 1620-1820*. Ed. John Dixon Hunt and Peter Willis. London: Paul Elek, 1975. 342–48.

Kowaleski-Wallace, Elizabeth. *Their Fathers' Daughters: Hannah More, Maria Edgeworth, and Patriarchal Complicity*. Oxford: OUP, 1991.

The Ladies Library. *Written by a Lady*. London: Richard Steele, 1714.

Langland, Elizabeth. *Nobody's Angels: Middle-Class Women and Domestic Ideology in Victorian Culture*. Reading Women Writing Ser. Ithaca and London: Cornell UP, 1995.

Lansbury, Coral. *Elizabeth Gaskell and the Novel of Social Crisis*. Novelists and Their World Ser. London: Paulelek, 1975.

Lister, Raymond. *William Blake: An Introduction to the Man and to His Work*. London: G. Bell and Sons, 1968.

Locke, John. *The Correspondence of John Locke*, Vol. 2. Ed. E. S. de Beer. Clarendon Edition of the Works of John Locke. Oxford: Clarendon, 1976. 8 vols.

———. *An Essay Concerning Human Understanding* 1690. Ed. Peter H. Nidditch. Clarendon Edition of the Works of John Locke. Oxford: Clarendon, 1975.

———. *Some Thoughts Concerning Education* 1693. *The Educational Writings of John Locke: A Critical Edition with Introduction and Notes*. Ed. James L. Axtell. Cambridge: Cambridge UP, 1968. 110–325.

———. *Two Treatises of Government*. Ed. Peter Laslett. Cambridge: Cambridge UP, 1960.

Lovell, Terry. *Consuming Fiction*. London: Verso, 1987.

Lynam, Rev. Robert, ed. *The British Essayists, with Prefaces Biographical, Historical, and Critical*. London: J. F. Dove, 1827. 30 vols.

MacFadyen, Heather. "Lady Delacour's Library: Maria Edgeworth's *Belinda* and Fashionable Reading." *Nineteenth-Century Literature* 48 (1994): 423–39.

MacIntyre, Alasdair. *After Virtue: A Study in Moral Theory*. 2nd edn. Notre Dame: University of Notre Dame P, 1984.

MacKinnon, Catherine. *Toward a Feminist Theory of the State*. Cambridge, MA: Harvard UP, 1989.

Marx, Karl. "Theses on Feuerbach." Vol. 5 of *Karl Marx and Frederick Engels: Collected Works*. New York: International Publishers, 1976. 30 vols. 3–5.

Mazzaro, Jerome. "At the Start of the Eighties." *The Hudson Review* 33 (1980): 455–68.

Michals, Teresa. "Commerce and Character in Maria Edgeworth." *Nineteenth-Century Literature* 49 (1994): 1–20.

Middleton, Victoria. *Elektra in Exile: Women Writers and Political Fiction*. New York: Garland, 1988.

Mill, John Stuart. *On Liberty* 1859. *Essays on Politics and Society*. Vol. 18 of *Collected Works of John Stuart Mill*. Ed. J. M. Robson. Intro. Alexander Brady. Toronto and Buffalo: U of Toronto P; London: Routledge and Kegan Paul, 1977. 213–310.

———. *The Subjection of Women* 1869. *Essays on Equality, Law, and Education*. Vol. 21 of *Collected Works of John Stuart Mill*. Ed. J. M. Robson. Intro. Stefan Collini. Toronto and Buffalo: University of Toronto P; London: Routledge and Kegan Paul, 1984. 259–340.

———. *Utilitarianism* 1861. *Essays on Ethics, Religion and Society*. Vol. 10 of *Collected Works of John Stuart Mill*. Ed. J. M. Robson. Intro. F. E. L. Priestley. Toronto: U of Toronto P; London: Routledge and Kegan Paul, 1969. 203–59.

Milton, John. *Paradise Lost. A Poem in Twelve Books* 1674. *Complete Poems and Major Prose*. Ed. Merritt Y. Hughes. New York: Macmillan, 1957. 207–469.

Moodie, Susanna Strickland. *Roughing It In the Bush; or Life in Canada* 1852. Ed. Carl Ballstadt. Centre For Editing Early Canadian Texts Ser. 5. Ottawa: Carleton UP, 1990.

More, Hannah. *Strictures on the Modern System of Female Education* 1799. The Feminist Controversy in England 1788–1810 Ser. Pref. Gina Luria. New York and London: Garland, 1974. 2 vols.

Myers, Mitzi. "Politics from the Outside: Mary Wollstonecraft's First *Vindication*." *Studies in Eighteenth-century Culture* 6 (1977): 113–32.

[Neville, Henry]. *Newes from the New-Exchange, or The Commonwealth of Ladies, Drawn to the Life, in Their Severall Characters and Concernments*. London: 1650.

Newcomer, James. *Maria Edgeworth the Novelist, 1767–1849: A Bicentennial Study*. Fort Worth: Texas Christian UP, 1967.

Norton, Caroline. *English Laws for Women in the Nineteenth Century* 1854. *Selected Writings of Caroline Norton.* Intro. and notes, James O. Hoge and Jane Marcus. Delmar, NY: Scholars' Facsimiles and Reprints, 1978.

———. *Lost and Saved* 1863. Intro. S. Bailey Shurbutt. Delmar, NY: Scholars' Facsimiles and Reprints, 1988.

Nussbaum, Martha C. *Love's Knowledge: Essays on Philosophy and Literature.* Oxford and New York: OUP, 1990.

———. *Poetic Justice: The Literary Imagination and Public Life.* Boston: Beacon P, l995.

Orwell, George. "Charles Dickens" 1939. *An Age Like This: 1920–1940.* Vol. 1 of *The Collected Essays, Journalism and Letters of George Orwell.* Ed. Sonia Orwell and Ian Angus. New York: Harcourt Brace & World, 1968. 413–60.

Patmore, Coventry. *The Angel in the House.* In *The Broadview Anthology of Victorian Poetry and Poetic Theory.* Ed. Thomas J. Collins and Vivienne J. Rundle. Peterborough: Broadview P, 1999. 739–60.

Paulson, Ronald. *Representations of Revolution (1789–1820).* New Haven: Yale UP, 1983.

Perry, Ruth. *The Celebrated Mary Astell: An Early English Feminist.* Women in Culture and Society Ser. Chicago and London: U of Chicago P, 1986.

———. "Mary Astell and the Feminist Critique of Possessive Individualism." *Eighteenth-Century Studies* 23 (1989–90): 444–57.

Phelan, James. "Reading for the Character and Reading for the Progression: John Wemmick and *Great Expectations*." *Journal of Narrative Technique* 19 (1989): 70–84. Rpt. in *Great Expectations*, ed. Roger D. Sell. New Casebooks Ser. NY; St. Martin's P, l994. 177–86.

Piercy, Marge. *Circles on the Water: Selected Poems of Marge Piercy.* New York: Knopf, 1986.

Poovey, Mary. *Uneven Developments: The Ideological Work of Gender in Mid-Victorian England.* Women in Culture and Society Ser. Chicago and London: U of Chicago P, 1988.

Price, Uvedale. *An Essay on the Picturesque* (1794). Excerpted in *The Genius of the Place: The English Landscape Garden 1620–1820.* Ed. John Dixon Hunt and Peter Willis. London: Paul Elek, 1975. 351–57.

Raphael, Linda. "A Re-vision of Miss Havisham: Her Expectations and Our Responses." *Studies in the Novel* 21 (1989). Rpt. in *Great Expectations*, ed. Roger D. Sell. New Casebooks Ser. NY; St. Martin's P, l994. 400–412.

Rawlins, Jack P. "Great Expiations: Dickens and the Betrayal of the Child." *Studies in English Literature* 23 (1983): 667–83. Rpt. in *Critical Essays on Charles Dickens's Great Expectations*, ed. Michael Cotsell. Boston: G. K. Hall, l990. 168–82.

Ross, Stephanie. "The Picturesque: An Eighteenth-Century Debate." *Journal of Aesthetics and Art Criticism* 46 (1987): 271–79.

Rousseau, Jean-Jacques. *Emile, or On Education* 1762. Trans. Allan Bloom. New York: Basic Books, 1979.

———. *The First and Second Discourses* 1750 and 1755. Ed. and intro. Roger D. Masters. Trans. Roger D. Masters and Judith R. Masters. New York: St. Martin's P, 1964.

———. *On the Social Contract* ca. 1756. On the Social Contract *with* Geneva Manuscript *and* Political Economy. Ed. Roger D. Masters. Trans. Judith R. Masters. New York: St. Martin's P, 1978.

Rule, Jane. *Desert of the Heart* 1964. Tallahassee: Naiad P, 1992.

Ruskin, John. *Sesame and Lilies* 1865. Vol. 11–12 of *The Complete Works of John Ruskin.* New York : Kelmscott Society, 1900. 30 vols. Var. pag.

Sanders, Gerald DeWitt. *Elizabeth Gaskell*. New Haven: Yale UP; London: Humphrey Milford; Oxford: OUP, 1929.

Sandford, [Mrs.] J. *Woman in Her Social and Domestic Character*. London: 1839.

Sapiro, Virginia. *A Vindication of Political Virtue: The Political Theory of Mary Wollstonecraft*. Chicago: U of Chicago P, 1992.

Sartre, Jean-Paul. "Materialism and Revolution." In *Literary and Philosophical Essays*. Trans. Annette Michelson. London: Rider and Co., 1955. 185–239.

———. *Truth and Existence*. Text and notes, Arlette Elkaim-Sartre. Trans. Adrian van den Hoven. Ed. Ronald Aronson. Chicago: U of Chicago P, 1992.

———. *What Is Literature?* Trans. Bernard Frechtman. New York: Washington Square P, 1966.

Schurman, Anna Maria. *The Learned Maid; or, Whether a Maid May be a Scholar? A Logick Exercise*. London: 1659.

Shaffer, Julie. "Not Subordinate: Empowering Women in the Marriage-Plot — The Novels of Frances Burney, Maria Edgeworth, and Jane Austen." *Criticism* 34 (1992): 51–73.

Shapiro, Gary. "From the Sublime to the Political: Some Historical Notes." *New Literary History* 16 (1985): 213–35.

Sharps, John Geoffrey. *Mrs. Gaskell's Observation and Invention: A Study of her Non-Biographic Works*. Fontwell, Sussex: Linden Press; London: Centaur Press, 1970.

Shurbutt, S. Bailey. "Introduction." *Lost and Saved*. Caroline Norton. Delmar, NY: Scholars' Facsimiles and Reprints, 1978. 3–28.

Siskin, Clifford. "Gender, Sublimity, Culture: Retheorizing Disciplinary Desire." *Eighteenth-Century Studies* 28 (1994): 37–50.

Smith, Hilda L. *Reason's Disciples: Seventeenth-Century English Feminists*. Urbana, Chicago, Illinois: U of Illinois P, 1982.

Smith, Sheila. *The Other Nation: The Poor in English Novels of the Eighteen-Forties and Eighteen-Fifties*. Oxford: Clarendon; New York: OUP, 1980.

Sophia (pseud.). *Woman's Superior Excellence Over Man: In Answer to Man Superior to Woman*. London: 1740.

Speare, Morris Edmund. *The Political Novel: Its Development in England and in America*. New York: Russell and Russell, 1966.

Spector, Stephen J. "Monsters of Metonymy: *Hard Times* and Knowing the Working Class." *ELH* 51 (1984): 365–84.

Sprint, Sir John. *The Bride-Woman's Counsellor, Being a Sermon Preach'd at a Wedding, May the 11th, 1699, at Sherborsin, in Dorsetshire*. London: Hills, n.d.

Steele, Richard. *Tatler* 32 (June 23, 1709). Rpt. in Vol. 1 of Lynam, ed. 188–93.

———. *Tatler* 61 (August 30, 1709). Rpt. in Vol. 1 of Lynam, ed. 340–46.

———. *Tatler* 248 (November 9, 1710). Rpt. in Vol. 3 of Lynam, ed. 321–24.

Stone, Lawrence. *Road to Divorce: England 1530–1987*. Oxford: OUP, 1990.

Stoneman, Patsy. *Elizabeth Gaskell*. Key Women Writers Ser. Brighton: Harvester, 1987.

Sturrock, Jane. "Something To Do: Charlotte Yonge, Tractarianism, and the Question of Women's Work." *Victorian Review* 18.2 (1992): 28–48.

Tambling, Jeremy. "Prison-Bound: Dickens and Foucault." *Essays in Criticism* 36 (1986): 11–31. Rpt. in *Great Expectations*, ed. Roger D. Sell. New Casebooks Ser. NY; St. Martin's P, 1994. 123–42.

Taylor, Charles. *Philosophical Papers*. Cambridge: Cambridge UP, 1985. 2 vols.

———. "The Politics of Recognition." *Multiculturalism and "The Politics of Recognition."* Ed. Amy Gutmann. Princeton: Princeton UP, 1992. 25–73.

———. *Sources of the Self: The Making of the Modern Identity*. Cambridge, MA: Harvard UP, 1989.

Trilling, Lionel. "Manners, Morals, and the Novel." *The Liberal Imagination: Essays on Literature and Society*. New York: Viking, 1951. 205–22.

Trollope, Anthony. *Can You Forgive Her?* 1864 Intro. Simon Raven. St. Albans, Herts.: Panther-Granada, 1973.

———. *The Duke's Children* 1879-1880. St. Albans, Herts.: Panther-Granada, 1973.

———. *The Eustace Diamonds* 1873. Ed. Stephen Gill and John Sutherland. Harmondsworth: Penguin, 1969.

———. *Phineas Finn, The Irish Member* 1869. Ed. and intro. John Sutherland. Harmondsworth: Penguin, 1972.

———. *Phineas Redux* 1874. Pref. R. W. Chapman. Illus. T. L. B. Huskinson. Oxford: OUP, 1973.

———. *The Prime Minister* 1876. Pref. Rt. Hon. L. S. Amery. Illus. Hector Whistler. Oxford: OUP, 1973.

Vanbrugh, Sir John. *The Provoked Wife* 1697. Ed. Anthony Coleman. Manchester: Manchester UP, 1982.

Wainwright, Valerie. "Discovering Autonomy and Authenticity in *North and South*: Elizabeth Gaskell, John Stuart Mill, and the Liberal Ethic." *Clio* 23.2 (1993): 149–65.

Wardle, Ralph M., ed. *Collected Letters of Mary Wollstonecraft*. Ithaca: Cornell UP, 1979.

Weiskel, Thomas. *The Romantic Sublime: Studies in the Structure and Psychology of Transcendence*. Baltimore: Johns Hopkins UP, 1976.

Wheatley, Kim. "Death and Domestication in Charlotte M. Yonge's *The Clever Woman of the Family*." *Studies in English Literature 1500–1900* 36 (1996): 895–915.

The Whole Duty of a Woman: Or a Guide to the Female Sex from the Age of Sixteen to Sixty, &c. Being Directions How Women of all Qualities and Conditions Ought to Behave Themselves in the Various Circumstances of this Life, for their Obtaining, Not Only Present but Future Happiness. Written by a Lady. London: 1707.

Williams, Raymond. *Culture and Society, 1780–1950*. New York: Harper & Row, 1966.

Wittgenstein, Ludwig. *Philosophical Investigations*. Trans. G. E. M. Anscombe. Oxford: Basil Blackwell, 1953.

Woolley, Hannah. *A Guide to Ladies, Gentlewomen and Maids: Containing Directions of Behaviour, in All Places, Companies, Relations, and Conditions From Their Childhood Down to Old Age: viz. as Children to Parents, Scholars to Governours, Single to Servants, Virgins to Suiters, Married to Husbands, Housewifes to the House, Mistresses to Servants, Mothers to Children, Widows to the World, and as Prudent to all: With Letters Upon all Occasions, With Several Tales, and the Ladies Farewell: Whereunto is Added, a Guide for Cook-maids, Dairy-maids, Chambermaids, and all Others that Go To Service: The Whole Being Exact Rules for the Female Sex in Generall*. London: 1668.

Yeatman, Anna. *Postmodern Revisionings of the Political*. Thinking Gender Ser. New York and London: Routledge, 1994.

Yeazell, Ruth Bernard. "Why Political Novels Have Heroines: *Sybil, Mary Barton*, and *Felix Holt*." *Novel* 18 (1985): 126–44.

Yonge, Charlotte Mary. *The Clever Woman of the Family* 1865. Afterword Georgina Battiscombe. Virago Modern Classics Ser. Harmondsworth: Penguin-Virago, 1985.

———. *The Daisy Chain* 1856. Pref. Susan M. Kenney. New York: Garland, 1977. Rpt. of 1868 edition.

Young, Iris Marion. "The Ideal of Community and the Politics of Difference." *Feminism/Post/modernism*. Ed. Linda Nicholson. Thinking Gender Ser. New York: Routledge, 1990. 300–323.

————. "Impartiality and the Civic Public: Some Implications of Feminist Critiques of Moral and Political Theory." *Feminism as Critique: On the Politics of Gender.* Ed. Seyla Benhabib and Drucilla Cornell. Feminist Perspectives Ser. Minneapolis: U of Minnesota P, 1987. 57–76.

Index

Mowbray, 72–77; Editha Mowbray, 72–73, 76; Glenmurray, 72, 73–77; Sir Patrick O'Carroll, 73–76, 81n.22; Mrs. Pemberton, 77

Opinions: how formed, 28; public, 29–30, 47, 65–67, 71, 74–77, 142

Orwell, George, 138–39, 142, 144

Other, the: construction of, 3, 86, 110, 125, 137; knowledge of, 94, 110, 123, 128–29, 130, 151; recognition of, 110, 128, 132, 137, 141, 145–46, 150–53, 159. *See also* Class; Labour; Woman

Passeron, Jean-Claude, 14–15, 32, 35, 36n.2–3, 40.

Passion(s), 44–48, 52, 70–71, 94

Patmore, Coventry, 2, 84

Patriarchy, 16–18, 53, 60n.25, 138, 149. *See also* Divine right

Perry, Anne, 38n.24

Person: as bearer of rights, 4, 10, 50–51, 92–93, 100, 128, 153, 158; female, as bearer of rights, 40, 50–51, 87; as object, 40, 54–57, 107, 110–11, 125, 134n.9, 152; as self-owner, 136, 151. *See also* Wollstonecraft, Mary

Picturesque, the, 105–7, 117, 134n.9

Political, the: definition of, 5, 6–7, 13–14; contained by, 4–7, 103; in fiction, 103

Political economy, 40, 92, 127

Political fiction, 10, 63, 81n.15; characteristics of, 1, 4–11, 12n.9, 14, 143, 158–59; critics on, 5, 7, 11–12n.7–8, n.10; definition of, 7, 11–12n.7–1, 157; and domestic fiction, 4–8, 143; function of, 4–5, 55, 100; theories of, 5, 6–8, 11–12n.7–11

Polity, English, 140

Polity, liberal, 57–58, 94, 99–100, 127, 140, 142–43, 151, 158–60; definition of, 5–6, 55, 64, 79, 87, 92, 143; transformation of, 114, 132, 145

Poovey, Mary, 2–3

Private sphere: characteristics of, 100; definitions of, 1; as intimate space, 129, 142, 148, 150, 158; relation to polity, 5–6, 78–79, 87, 100, 143, 150, 158–59; and sexuality, 85, 105; theories of, 103; virtue in, 57, 71–72, 148, 150. *See also* Armstrong, Nancy; Auerbach, Nina;

Domestic ideology; Domesticity; Gilbert, Sandra; Gubar, Susan; Household; Intimate space; Public sphere; Separate spheres

Psychological depth, 32, 40, 44, 86–87, 95, 128, 132, 137; and self, 142, 153; as claim to rights, 50, 55, 64, 137, 153, 158. *See also* Citizenship, grounds of; Emotion(s)

Public sphere, 10; characteristics of, 1–3, 100, 124; exclusion from, 138; relation to private sphere, 2, 72, 100, 105, 129, 158–59; theories of, 2, 103. *See also* Citizenship; Marketplace; Political, the; Polity, liberal

Qualitative distinctions, 41; vs. Quantitative, 2, 141

Rape, 33, 76–77, 81–82n.22, 81–82n.22

Rationality, 160; definitions of, 93, 94, 101n.16; MacIntyre on, 136, 140–41, 147, 154n.1; Mill on, 140–41, 147; theories compared, 136–37, 140, 147; utilitarian, 137–39, 142; of women, 17, 19

Reason: and authority, 14, 23, 68, 74, 138, 158–60; as capacity, 21–22, 56, 138, 158; and citizenship, 58, 93, 132, 157–60; and education, 19, 52–53, 56, 58, 157; and emotion, 33, 54, 72, 86, 132, 147; exercise of, 9, 124, 147; and freedom, 33, 147, 157–60; impartial, 86; instrumental, 136; and morals, 141; and passions, 4, 46–48, 52, 121; and virtue, 46–47, 52–54, 71, 74, 94, 113; and women, 19, 23–27, 46, 93. *See also* Wollstonecraft, Mary

Reputation, of women, 97

Responsibility. *See* Duty

Revolution: American, 53; Glorious, (English Civil War), 18; Industrial, 1, 6, 92, 129, 131. *See also* French Revolution

Rights: 5–6, 87, 135; of children, 147; claims to, 21–22, 53–55, 87, 129, 130, 135, 150–52, 159; discourse of, 135–37, 147; equality of, 64, 92–93, 128; inalienability of, 57, 146; of men, 21, 53, 94, 128; of women, 8, 21, 41,

About the Author

SUSAN JOHNSTON is Visiting Assistant Professor of English at Concordia University and Assistant Professor of English at the University of Regina.